A THOREAU HANDBOOK

WALTER HARDING

NEW YORK UNIVERSITY PRESS 1961

FOR MARJORIE

cB1

MAR 4

TABLE OF CONTENTS

PREFACE

Although Henry David Thoreau was once one of America's most neglected authors, modern students have more than made up for the neglect. The scholarly work on Thoreau is prodigious—so prodigious, in fact, that only the extreme specialist can hope to assimilate more than a small part of it. Thoreau's collected works, though not complete, fill twenty large volumes. *Walden* has been issued in more than 130 different editions. There have been twenty-four book-length biographies published, plus seventeen book-length studies of special phases of his life or works. The periodical articles on Thoreau run into the thousands. James Woodress' recent check list enumerates thirty-two doctoral dissertations on Thoreau; the masters' theses on the subject have never been counted. Little wonder then that the student is easily lost in a seeming morass. As secretary of the Thoreau Society, I receive a constant stream of inquiries asking where particular information on Thoreau can be found, or whether some specific phase of Thoreau's life has yet been studied. I have therefore compiled this handbook in the hope that it may serve as a guide through the welter of Thoreau scholarship, pointing out just what scholarly work has been done, what still needs doing. It is not intended as a substitute for the Thoreau scholarship but as a guide to it.

I have divided this handbook into five sections. Chapter One summarizes Thoreau's life and evaluates the various biographies. Chapter Two discusses each of his individual works. Chapter Three points out the sources of his ideas and attitudes. Chapter Four summarizes his ideas. Chapter Five charts the course of his fame. For quick reference a brief chronology of Thoreau's life and publications has been placed at the beginning. A short check list of the leading bibliographies has been placed at the end. These divisions are necessarily arbitrary, and inevitably there is some repetition. But I have tried through cross references and the index to eliminate as much duplication as possible.

Each chapter is divided into two sections. The first and longer attempts to summarize and evaluate all the significant scholarship on the subject. Particular emphasis has been placed on unpublished doctoral dissertations, both because they are not easily available and because they contain a wealth of important material of which most students are not aware. Bibliographical references have been cut down to a minimum in order not to distract the general reader. The second section of each chapter concentrates entirely on the bibliography, citing where further information is available.

A large portion of any handbook such as this is necessarily devoted to evaluation. Objectivity is of course the ideal in any such case, but unfortunately it is not a human characteristic. ("There is no such thing as pure *objective* observation. Your observation, to be interesting, i.e. to be significant, must be subjective," said Thoreau [J, VI, 236].) I have tried to be as fair and honest as possible in my judgments. But I have purposely used the first person frequently in the text to emphasize that the judgments are mine. My hope is that they do not too frequently display my personal prejudices.

With the vast amount of material to be covered, it is inevitable that I have made omissions. When, as is often the fact, two or more studies have appeared that to a large extent duplicate each other, I have tried to select the most competent for full discussion, although I have usually at least mentioned the other studies in my source notes. I was able to obtain none of the German doctoral dissertations on Thoreau and only a small number of the American masters' theses. A few periodical articles proved too elusive to be caught in a seining of a goodly number of public and university libraries and private collections. But I think it would not be an unfair estimate to say that I have read 95 per cent of the material written on Thoreau in the preparation of this handbook. I hope that none of the remaining 5 per cent was omitted through oversight.

It is impossible to make adequate acknowledgment of all the assistance I have received. I have tried to indicate through the use of quotation marks and bibliographical notes the sources of all borrowed ideas, but it is inevitable that I have unconsciously missed some. Thoreau scholars and collectors have been most generous in coming to my aid. They have searched their files and their attics to find copies of elusive articles. They have sent me manuscripts, photostats, microfilms, and even galleyproofs of forthcoming books and articles. They have answered my queries with utmost patience. To each and all of them, even though I cannot list them individually, I extend my thanks.

I do wish however to make special acknowledgment to Carl Bode, of the University of Maryland, who some years ago announced his intention of compiling a Thoreau handbook, but who graciously turned the project over to me when I mentioned an interest in it; to Gay Wilson Allen, of New York University, both for giving me valuable suggestions in the initial stages of the project and for setting me a high goal to aim at in his own *Walt Whitman Handbook;* to the Research Council of the University of Virginia for granting me funds to obtain microfilms of all the American doctoral dissertations on Thoreau; and to the staffs of the libraries of the University of Virginia, Princeton University, and State University Teachers College at Geneseo, New York, for aid in tracking down many rare pieces of Thoreauviana.

For permission to quote from and summarize their unpublished doctoral dissertations, I am indebted to Raymond Adams of the University of North Carolina; John C. Broderick of Wake Forest College; John A. Christie of Vassar College; Robert Cobb of the University of Kansas; Mary Cochnower of the State University College for Teachers in Buffalo, New York; George D. Craig of Northern Montana College; Wendell Glick of the University of Minnesota, Duluth Branch; Raymong D. Gozzi of the University of Massachusetts; Christian P. Gruber of Harpur College; Harold Guthrie of Winona [Minnesota] State College; George Hendrick of the University of Colorado; Carl F. Hovde of The Ohio State University; Anton M. Huffert of Adelphi College; William H. Kirchner of Ohio University; Fred W. Lorch of Iowa State College in Ames; Charles R. Metzger, Lake Grove, Oregon; Dean John Sylvester Smith of Dillard University; Leo Stoller of Wayne State University; Anne Whaling of Arlington [Texas] State College; and Lawrence Willson of the University of California at Santa Barbara. For permission to summarize and quote from their unpublished masters' theses, I am indebted to Harry H. Crosby of Boston University; William Drake, Canyon, California; Edwin Moser, Hicksville, New York; and Lee M. Nash of the University of Oregon.

I am also indebted to Belknap Press of Harvard University Press for permission to quote from Robert Henry Welker's *Birds and Men;* to Houghton Mifflin Company for permission to quote from *The Writings of Thoreau,* Henry Seidel Canby's *Thoreau,* Edward Emerson's *Henry Thoreau as Remembered by a Young Friend,* and F. B. Sanborn's *The Life of Henry David Thoreau;* to William Sloane Associates, Inc. for permission to quote from Joseph Wood Krutch's *Henry David Thoreau;* and to Yale University Press for permission to quote from Ethel Seybold's *Thoreau: The Quest and the Classics.* Further, I am indebted to the editors of the *Boston Public Library Quarterly,*

Colorado Quarterly, and the *Humanist* for permission to use in revised and abbreviated form articles of my own which appeared in their pages.

And finally I am indebted to my wife who far more than she has ever realized has helped in the preparation of this and my other writings.

WALTER HARDING

A NOTE ON

BIBLIOGRAPHICAL ABBREVIATIONS

All quotations, unless otherwise indicated, taken from Thoreau's writings are from the Manuscript Edition of his works published by Houghton Mifflin of Boston in 1906. This edition consists of twenty volumes: the first six, his regularly published works; the last fourteen, his *Journal.* All references to this edition have been indicated by a parenthetical note immediately after the quotation: "W," volume number, and page number referring to the first six volumes; "J," volume number, and page number, to the last fourteen volumes. (The pagination of the Walden Edition and of the 1949 edition of the *Journal* coincides with that of this edition.)

For all other bibliographical notations I have used the standard form, with the following exceptions. (1) I have adopted the abbreviations of the Modern Language Association for references to periodicals. (2) Where an author has written one major work on Thoreau, for example, Henry Seidel Canby or Joseph Wood Krutch, I have often referred to it only by the author's name, without the full title. (3) I have distinguished between the *Thoreau Society Booklets* and the *Thoreau Society Bulletin* by referring to the former with roman numerals (i.e., *TSB* IV) and the latter by arabic (i.e., *TSB* 42). For unpublished masters' theses and doctoral dissertations I cite only the university and date of completion (i.e., Harvard University, Ph.D., 1937).

Articles that have been reprinted in S. A. Jones, *Pertaining to Thoreau* (Detroit, 1901), I have marked *PT*; those that I reprinted in *Thoreau: A Century of Criticism* (Dallas, 1954), I have marked *TCC*.

A THOREAU CHRONOLOGY

1817   Born in Concord, Massachusetts, July 12.

1818   Family moved to Chelmsford, Massachusetts.

1821   Family moved to Boston, Massachusetts.

1823   Family returned to Concord, Massachusetts.

1827   Earliest known essay, "The Seasons."

1833   Entered Harvard University.

1835   Taught school in Canton, Massachusetts, between terms. Studied German with Orestes Brownson.

1836   Visited New York City with father peddling pencils.

1837   Graduated from Harvard. Began *Journal*. Taught for a few days in public schools in Concord.

1838   Opened private school with brother John. Delivered first lecture at Concord Lyceum. Made first trip to Maine.

1839   Made excursion on the Concord and Merrimack Rivers with brother John. Ellen Sewell visited Concord.

1840   Published his first essay, "Aulus Persius Flaccus," and his first poem, "Sympathy," in the *Dial*. Wrote *The Service*.

1841   Went to live with Ralph Waldo Emerson for two years. Published numerous pieces in the *Dial*.

1842   Contributed many more pieces to the *Dial*. Brother John died, January 12.

1843   From this point on, lectured almost annually before the Concord Lyceum. Helped Emerson edit the *Dial* and contributed further articles and poems to it and to the *Boston Miscellany* and the *Democratic Review*. From May to December tutored William Emerson's children on Staten Island.

1844   Contributed further pieces to the final volume of the *Dial*. Accidentally set fire to Concord woods.

1845 Began work on his Walden cabin in March. Moved in on July 4. Published "Wendell Phillips Before the Concord Lyceum" in the *Liberator*.

1846 Was arrested and put in jail overnight in midsummer for nonpayment of taxes. Made trip to Maine woods.

1847 Left Walden Pond in September to spend a year in Emerson's house while the latter was lecturing abroad. Published essay on Carlyle in *Graham's Magazine*. Began submitting natural history specimens to Agassiz at Harvard.

1848 Delivered lecture on "The Rights and Duties of the Individual in Relation to Government" ("Civil Disobedience") before the Concord Lyceum, January 26. Delivered first lecture outside Concord, in Salem, at invitation of Hawthorne, November 22. Published "Ktaadn and the Maine Woods" in the *Union Magazine*. Returned to live at his father's house.

1849 Published *A Week on the Concord and Merrimack Rivers*, May. Published "Resistance to Civil Government" ("Civil Disobedience") in *Aesthetic Papers*. Made first trip to Cape Cod. Sister Helen died, May 2.

1850 Made second trip to Cape Cod. Visited Fire Island, searching for the body of Margaret Fuller Ossoli. Made excursion to Canada with Ellery Channing.

1853 Made second trip to Maine woods. Published "A Yankee in Canada" in *Putnam's Magazine*.

1854 Published *Walden*, August. Lectured on "Slavery in Massachusetts" in Framingham, published in *Liberator*.

1855 Received gift of Oriental books from Thomas Cholmondeley. Visited Cape Cod. Published portions of *Cape Cod* in *Putnam's Magazine*.

1856 Did surveying at "Eagleswood," Perth Amboy, New Jersey. Met Walt Whitman in Brooklyn.

1857 Visited Cape Cod and the Maine woods. Met Captain John Brown.

1858 Published "Chesuncook" in the *Atlantic Monthly*. Visited the White Mountains and Mount Monadnock.

1859 Lectured on "A Plea for Captain John Brown" and "After the Death of John Brown." Father died, February 3.

1860   Camped out on Mount Monadnock with Ellery Channing. Published "A Plea for Captain John Brown" in *Echoes of Harper's Ferry;* "The Last Days of John Brown," in the *Liberator;* and delivered "The Succession of Forest Trees" as a lecture at the Middlesex Cattle Show, later published in *Transactions of the Middlesex Agricultural Society.* Contracted the cold that led to his fatal illness.

1861   Visited Minnesota with Horace Mann, Jr., May 11 to July 10. Revised many of his manuscripts.

1862   Died, May 6. "Walking," "Autumnal Tints," "Wild Apples" appeared posthumously in the *Atlantic Monthly. Walden* and *A Week on the Concord and Merrimack Rivers* appeared in second editions.

1863   *Excursions,* edited by Sophia Thoreau and R. W. Emerson, published.

1864   *The Maine Woods,* edited by Sophia Thoreau and Ellery Channing, published.

1865   *Cape Cod,* edited by Sophia Thoreau and Ellery Channing, and *Letters to Various Persons,* edited by R. W. Emerson, published.

1866   *A Yankee in Canada, with Anti-Slavery and Reform Papers,* edited by Ellery Channing and Sophia Thoreau, published.

1873   *Thoreau: The Poet-Naturalist,* by Ellery Channing, first book-length biography of Thoreau, published.

1881   *Early Spring in Massachusetts,* edited by H. G. O. Blake, published.

1884   *Summer,* edited by H. G. O. Blake, published.

1888   *Winter,* edited by H. G. O. Blake, published.

1892   *Autumn,* edited by H. G. O. Blake, published.

1894   *Familiar Letters,* edited by F. B. Sanborn, included in the eleven-volume Riverside Edition, edited by Horace E. Scudder, first collected edition of Thoreau, published.

1902   *The Service,* edited by F. B. Sanborn, published.

1905   *First and Last Journeys of Thoreau* and *Sir Walter Raleigh,* edited by F. B. Sanborn, published.

1906   Twenty-volume Walden Edition, including fourteen volumes of the *Journal,* edited by Bradford Torrey and Francis H. Allen, published.

1927 *The Moon,* edited by Francis H. Allen, published.

1932 *The Transmigration of the Seven Brahmans,* edited by Arthur Christy, published.

1943 *Collected Poems,* edited by Carl Bode, published.

1958 *The Correspondence of Henry David Thoreau,* edited by Walter Harding and Carl Bode, published.

A more detailed chronology, including contemporary events, may be found in Leonard Kleinfeld, *Henry David Thoreau Chronology* (Forest Hills, N. Y., 1950). Thoreau himself includes a brief chronology of his life in his *Journal* (VIII, 64–67).

CHAPTER ONE

Thoreau's Life

I

Henry David Thoreau was the only member of the famed "Concord Group" of the mid-nineteenth century who was a native of the town of Concord. Born on July 12, 1817, in his grandmother's farmhouse on Virginia Road, on the outskirts of the village, he was the product of a heterogeneous ancestry—Scotch, English, and French. His paternal grandfather, John, an immigrant from the Isle of Jersey just before the Revolution, had accumulated a considerable estate as a Boston merchant. But Thoreau's father, John, had quickly lost his share in a series of unfortunate shopkeeping experiments. Thoreau's maternal grandfather, Asa Dunbar, a Harvard graduate, had abandoned a career in the ministry for one in law in Keene, New Hampshire. Thoreau's mother, Cynthia, was an energetic woman with a gift for talking and a keen interest in the world of nature around her. In nearly every respect she contrasted with her quiet-spoken husband, a fact that in no respect seemed to flaw their harmony. An older sister, Helen, and a brother, John, were five and two years older respectively. A second sister, Sophia, was born in 1819. Helen was so quiet and self-effacing that little record of her remains. A teacher by profession, she apparently helped pay Henry's way through college. Her death from tuberculosis in 1849 is not even noted in her brother's *Journal*. John was the sparkling, vibrant member of the household. In the opinion of many of his fellow townsmen he was the genius of the family, and unquestionably he was the object of his younger brother's wholehearted worship. Although John never attended college, he joined with Henry in operating a private school for several years. His tragic death from lockjaw in 1842 had a traumatic effect on Henry, who developed a serious, indeed nearly fatal, case of sympathetic lockjaw. Had John lived longer, Brooks Atkinson suggests, "there might have been a warmer glow in the social thoughts of Henry Thoreau" (*Cosmic Yankee,* p. 54). Sophia, like Helen, was quiet and self-effacing. During Henry's final illness she devoted herself to his care, and after his death to the defense and enhancement of his reputation. In later years the Thoreau household was filled with a goodly company of maiden aunts, an eccentric bachelor uncle, and an assortment of spinster and widowed boarders.

Thoreau's father's financial misfortunes continued for some years after Henry's birth. The family moved from Concord to nearby Chelmsford, to Boston, and, in 1823, back to Concord again. Finally the father hit upon the manufacturing of pencils, a trade already successfully practiced in Concord, and managed to earn a small but steady income.

Comparatively little is known of Thoreau's youth. Apparently it was the typical childhood of any small-town, early-nineteenth-century American youth, except that the family's penchant for natural history and reading gave him an unusually strong background in those fields. His home was a center of religious discussion, and the various members vacillated back and forth between the Trinitarian and Unitarian churches in the town. Thoreau himself never joined any church and when, upon achieving legal maturity, he received a tax bill from the Unitarian church, he made haste to sign off from its rolls. Yet when he died, his sister, much to the dismay of some of his friends, insisted that he be buried from the Unitarian church.

At a comparatively early date it was decided that Henry, unlike his brother, should receive a college education. The basis for this decision, particularly in the light of John's apparent abilities, is not known. Henry was enrolled in Concord Academy, one of the better college preparatory schools of its day, where, under the direction of Phineas Allen, he received a sound education directed primarily at the entrance requirements for Harvard College. Thoreau probably joined the Concord Lyceum in his early teens (it was founded in 1829), and he continued an interest in its activities throughout his life. His earliest extant essay, "The Seasons," written in 1827 at the age of ten, is not a particularly remarkable work, but it displays his already awakened interest in nature.

He entered Harvard College in 1833 at the then not unusually early age of sixteen. Our conception of his life at college has changed considerably in recent years, thanks to the efforts of scholars in uncovering various hitherto unknown documents. The old picture, based primarily on the memoirs of his classmate the Rev. John Weiss, depicted him as a shy, retiring, and somewhat eccentric student, almost completely ignored by his classmates, who later astonished them when he became the best-known member of the class. The fact that his grades were not always among the highest has often been cited as evidence that his genius did not mature early. But now we have a clearer and quite different picture. We see a college lad who joined in friendly "bull sessions" with his classmates, wrote facetious letters to them, and attempted to come to the rescue of one of the pranksters impaled on the horns of faculty discipline. When he attended classes regularly, his grades were actually well above average. It was only his long illness in his junior year that lowered his final standing. And even then he stood high enough in his class to take part in a disquisition at the graduation ceremonies.

It was also in his junior year that Thoreau took advantage of a college ruling that permitted him to drop out for several months to teach and thus add to his income. He had the good fortune of going to Canton, Massachusetts, where he met Orestes Brownson, then the pastor of the local Universalist church. The two immediately struck up a friendship and embarked on a study of German together.

One of the most frequently repeated legends about Thoreau is that he refused to pay five dollars and so never received his college diploma. His diploma is extant today. But there is a basis for the legend. Harvard granted a master of arts degree to all, as Edward Emerson once commented, "who proved their physical worth by being alive three years after graduating, and their saving, earning or inheriting quality or condition by having Five Dollars to give the college" (Raymond Adams, "Thoreau's Di-

ploma," p. 175). It was probably this semifraudulent degree, not
his B.A., that Thoreau rejected.

On graduation from Harvard Thoreau applied for a position
in the Concord schools and was accepted. But his teaching experience there lasted only a few weeks. A member of the school committee insisted that he must not "spare the rod" in disciplining
his pupils. Thoreau, in reply, called six children at random from
his class, feruled them, and handed in his resignation, telling the
committee he could not accept its interference.

For some months thereafter both Thoreau and his brother
searched for new teaching positions, but the depression of 1837
was at its height and no jobs were available. As an alternative,
the next summer Thoreau opened a private school in his home.
It immediately prospered. In a few months his brother joined him
and they moved the school into the then vacant Concord Academy.
The school continued until March, 1841, when, because of John's
rapidly failing health, they were forced to close. They had no
difficulty in recruiting pupils. Children of the leading families
of the town were among their students, and out-of-towners
boarded with the Thoreau household. The teaching techniques
used were those of twentieth-century progressive education. The
ferule was abandoned. Many classes were held out of doors. Wherever possible the class situations were related to real life. John
was apparently the favorite of the pupils, but Henry's abilities
were also recognized.

It was in these years that Thoreau's one romance occurred.
Ellen Sewall was the daughter of the Unitarian minister in Scituate, Massachusetts. Her aunt, Prudence Ward, had long boarded
with the Thoreau family. In the summer of 1839 Ellen visited in
the Thoreau household for several weeks, and both John and
Henry fell in love with her. In July, 1840, John visited her in
Scituate and proposed. In her surprise she first accepted him, only
later to reject him when she realized that it was Henry she loved.
In November, Henry, apparently ignorant of John's proposal and
rejection, proposed himself in a letter to Ellen, then visiting in
Watertown, New York. Unfortunately the battle between the
conservative Unitarians and the Transcendentalists was at its
height, and Ellen's father, shocked at the thought of having a
"radical" in his family, directed her to write a letter of refusal.

"I never felt so badly at sending a letter in my life," she later wrote (T. M. Raysor, "The Love Story of Thoreau," p. 459). But in 1844 she married Joseph Osgood, a Unitarian minister in Cohasset, Massachusetts, and spent nearly fifty years of happily wedded life with him. Henry Seidel Canby probably evaluated the romance accurately when he said, "I doubt whether he [Thoreau] wanted to marry her; for after the idyllic opening of this relationship she became more and more for him an experiment in the philosophy of love" (*Thoreau,* pp. 121–22).

Her younger brother, Edmund, was for some time a pupil in the Thoreau school. Edmund, too, captured Thoreau's heart, and Thoreau wrote his poem "The Gentle Boy" about him.

It is not known exactly when Thoreau and Ralph Waldo Emerson became acquainted. The evidence is so contradictory that we can assert only that sometime within a year or two after Emerson settled in Concord in 1835, the two met and that their friendship ripened rapidly after Thoreau had returned to Concord from Harvard in 1837. It is obvious that in later years a rift developed. Each complained in his journal of a lack of understanding on the part of the other. Some of the misunderstanding may be blamed on Thoreau's sensitiveness to the frequent accusations that he was an imitator of Emerson and some on his desire to be completely independent. Some of it too may be blamed on Emerson's growing conservatism. But the break was never complete. Emerson delivered Thoreau's funeral sermon in 1862 and aided in the posthumous publication of a number of his works.

Thoreau developed a warm affection for Emerson's second wife, Lidian, an affection that Canby greatly exaggerated in his biography of Thoreau. Brooks Atkinson, in a letter to me, evaluated the situation much more objectively when he said: "Thoreau had—I suppose unconsciously—a tender, romantic attachment to her. I think he was longing for affection. Since she was older than he and also married, I think he found her a safe and no doubt worthy object of adoration."

In 1841 Emerson invited Thoreau to join his household as a handy man about the yard. Thoreau, unlike Emerson, could wield a hammer and a saw. In return for his services he was to receive free room and board. The *Dial* had been founded in 1840, and gradually Emerson shouldered its responsibility as Margaret

Fuller, the nominal editor, became more and more discouraged with its progress. Thoreau was asked frequently to contribute. Despite the fact that Miss Fuller often blue-penciled his writings, he saw thirty-one of his contributions in print in its pages in the four years of its publication. Emerson gradually turned many of the editorial duties over to Thoreau and asked him to edit the entire April, 1843, issue.

In January, 1842, Thoreau's brother John died suddenly of lockjaw, and fifteen days later Emerson's son Waldo died as suddenly of scarlatina. The double tragedy undoubtedly served to weld even more firm the friendship of Emerson and Thoreau.

Later that year Nathaniel Hawthorne brought his bride to the Old Manse to live. Thoreau soon paid a call and the two became friends. Whereas Hawthorne always felt a little ill at ease in Emerson's presence, he delighted in Thoreau's independence and individuality. In later years Hawthorne did much to spread Thoreau's fame in England.

Another influential friend was Bronson Alcott, who, attracted by Emerson, had moved to Concord in 1840. With the exception of occasional brief residences elsewhere, he remained in Concord the rest of his life. He was quickly drawn to Thoreau and was among the earliest to recognize his genius. Although Alcott could rarely be enticed out into the woods and Thoreau was more than a little amused at Alcott's impracticality, the two spent many hours in congenial conversation. Thoreau never succumbed to Alcott's invitations to join the ill-fated Fruitlands experiment, although he did pay it some visits. Alcott's refusal to pay his poll taxes in 1843 probably encouraged Thoreau to do the same three years later.

In 1843 Emerson decided it was time for Thoreau to see more of the world and obtained a position for him as tutor for his brother William Emerson's sons on Staten Island. Thoreau accepted, thinking it would give him an entree into the publishing world in New York City. But the experiment was a failure. Thoreau was homesick from the moment he left Concord in early May. A visit home at Thanksgiving time was too much for him, and he returned to Staten Island for only long enough to pack up his belongings.

Thoreau found one new friend in New York, Horace Greeley,

editor of the influential *New York Tribune,* who was to be a benefactor for years to come. Greeley offered his services gratis as Thoreau's literary agent and for the remaining years of Thoreau's life spent many hours annually in placing Thoreau's essays in magazines and touting his two books in the pages of the *Tribune.*

Just before Thoreau left Concord for Staten Island, Ellery Channing, Margaret Fuller's brother-in-law and nephew of the great Unitarian divine, William Ellery Channing, moved to Concord. Apparently he was already acquainted with Thoreau, for he had asked him to supervise the preparation of his new Concord residence. But it was after Thoreau's return from Staten Island that their friendship ripened. Channing became Thoreau's closest companion for the rest of his life. They were an oddly assorted pair. Channing was as irresponsible to his obligations as Thoreau was meticulous. Channing was of the earth earthy and shocked Thoreau with his off-color stories. But the two had in common an unbounded love for the out of doors, and they spent most of their time together roaming the woods and fields and rivers of Concord.

It was in 1844 that an incident occurred that blackened Thoreau's reputation among his fellow townsmen for generations to come. In April he and Edward Hoar, son of the town's most prominent family, went fishing on the Sudbury River. They built a fire on the banks of Fairhaven Bay to cook their catch, but the fire got away from them and was soon roaring through the dry woods. Thoreau ran to town for help, but then, instead of returning, climbed a nearby hill to watch. The townspeople were enraged, and it has been suggested that had not young Hoar been his companion, he might have been prosecuted. Even today he is known to some Concordians as "the man who burned the woods."

It was also in 1844, that, after moving from house to house for many years, Thoreau's father, with Henry's aid, built a house out beyond the Concord railroad station in the section known as Texas. The house was destroyed by fire and hurricane in the late 1930's, but the well-laid foundation still attests to the sturdiness of its construction.

For some years Thoreau had been mulling over the advantages of living a simple life in comparative solitude. Maintaining himself in town was taking more of his time than he wished. Ever since John's death he had been wishing to memorialize an excursion they had taken together on the Concord and Merrimack Rivers in 1839, and yet he never seemed to find the time. Once he was on the verge of buying the Hallowell Farm on the outskirts of Concord. Another time he considered building a cabin on Flint's Pond in nearby Lincoln, but the owner of the land was unwilling. Then, in October, 1844, Emerson purchased some woods on the north shore of Walden Pond, a mile and a half south of Concord, to prevent their destruction. Soon afterward Thoreau entered into an agreement with him that he might build a cabin there and in return clear part of the land for a garden.

In March, 1845, Thoreau started construction of the cabin with a borrowed ax, and on Independence Day he moved in. There he succeeded in his endeavor to simplify his life, to reduce his expenses, and to write not only *A Week on the Concord and Merrimack Rivers,* but also the major part of his masterpiece, *Walden.* He lived there two years, two months, and a few days.

In late July, 1846, Thoreau spent a night in Concord jail for nonpayment of his poll tax. Like Alcott's earlier experience, it was primarily a protest against a government that supported slavery. Sam Staples, the Concord constable and a long-time friend, misunderstanding Thoreau's intentions, offered to pay the tax for him. But when Thoreau refused, Staples arrested him. That night, under cover of darkness, someone (probably Thoreau's maiden Aunt Maria, shocked to see her nephew in the local jail) paid his tax, and the next morning he was released. It has been recorded that he was angry when released and implied that his wrath was directed at the fact of arrest. It is more logical to assume that he was angry because the payment of his tax forestalled effective protest.

There is a legend that Emerson visited Thoreau in the jail and asked, "Why are you here?" and that Thoreau replied, "Why are you not here?" The story has been discounted because there is no record of Emerson's visit. But the tale has been handed down in the Emerson family as true, and the incident could just as well have taken place outside the jail after Thoreau's release.

The arrest inspired Thoreau to write his most famous essay, known variously as "On Resistance to Civil Government," "On the Duty of Civil Disobedience," and more commonly as "Civil Disobedience." Thoreau first delivered it as a lecture to his fellow townsmen at the Concord Lyceum on January 26, 1848, and again in February. It was first printed in Elizabeth Peabody's short-lived experimental magazine, *Aesthetic Papers,* in 1849.

Meanwhile Thoreau's interest in the lyceum had not been dormant. He delivered his first lecture, "Society," on April 11, 1838, and continued to lecture there regularly the rest of his life. At various periods he also served as secretary and as curator of the lyceum. In 1848 he was invited by Hawthorne to lecture in Salem, and in later years he lectured as far afield as Portland, Maine, and Philadelphia. Several attempts to arrange a Western lecture tour did not materialize. It has been frequently remarked that Thoreau was not a success as a lecturer. The fact is that he was unpopular only when he was too Transcendental for his audience. His humorous lectures, particularly those on his excursions, were always well received.

It was while Thoreau was at Walden that he made his first excursion to the Maine woods, to be followed by later excursions in 1853 and 1857. These expeditions were the basis for various magazine articles later combined into his posthumous book, *The Maine Woods.* He made similar excursions to Cape Cod in 1849, 1850, 1855, and 1857; an excursion to Canada in 1850; one to Vermont in 1856; and various trips to the White Mountains and Monadnock.

When in the fall of 1847 Emerson went to England on a lecture tour, he persuaded Thoreau to look after his house and family. It was in this period that Thoreau became best acquainted with the Emerson children, and the warmth of that friendship is reflected in the letters he wrote Emerson in England.

An amusing episode of this period was Thoreau's "romance" with Sophia Foord (or Ford, as it was sometimes spelled). A friend of the Alcotts and tutor of the Emerson children, Miss Foord thought Thoreau to be her "soul's twin," and proposed marriage. Thoreau fired back "as distinct a *no* as I have learned to pronounce after considerable practice." Rumors spread that she had committed suicide in her dejection, but she lived on to be eighty-two, carrying with her to the end an interest in Thoreau.

Sometime about this period Thoreau took up the profession of surveying, to add to his income while enjoying the woods and fields of his native town. At times it undoubtedly irked him to be tied to so routine an occupation, but most of the time he found it congenial. In later years he was often called upon by the town to walk its boundaries and to make official surveys.

In the summer of 1848, on Emerson's return from England, Thoreau returned to live with his family at the Texas House. In 1850, with their pencil business prospering, the family purchased a more pretentious house on Main Street, and he lived there with them for the rest of his life.

Thoreau had always been a willing aid in the pencil business. Using knowledge he had gained from his college courses, he experimented with methods of preparing the graphite ("lead") and perfected a pencil superior to any other then manufactured in the country. But he refused to capitalize on the invention and was satisfied to see his father's business quietly prosper as a result of his ingenuity. Later the family found it more profitable to abandon pencil making and concentrate on selling the graphite mixture wholesale to other manufacturers. At his father's death in 1859, Thoreau took over most of the responsibility for the business. Just how much effect working with the fine pencil and graphite dust had on his tendency toward tuberculosis is problematical. Unquestionably it did not help matters any.

Thoreau's first disciple was Harrison Gray Otis Blake, a Worcester schoolteacher who, like Emerson, had abandoned the Unitarian ministry. A frequent visitor to Emerson's home, he happened to reread Thoreau's paper on Persius in the *Dial* and was so impressed that he sent Thoreau a long letter in March, 1848. It was the beginning of Thoreau's longest and largest correspondence. Blake arranged almost annual lectures in Worcester for Thoreau and surrounded him there with a coterie of admirers. Years later Sophia Thoreau willed her brother's manuscripts to Blake, and from them he edited the four seasonal volumes of excerpts from the *Journal, Early Spring in Massachusetts* (1881), *Summer* (1884), *Winter* (1887), and *Autumn* (1892).

A Week had been virtually completed before Thoreau left Walden in 1847, but it was two years before it was published. It wandered from one publishing house to another, always returning with a rejection slip, despite Emerson's forceful influence. After each rejection Thoreau revised it (the essay on "Friendship" in the "Wednesday" chapter, for example, was one of the late additions). Finally, in desperation, he paid James Munroe and Company of Boston to publish it in an edition of 1,000 copies in the spring of 1849. It was one of the most complete failures in literary history. Only three reviews of any length appeared, and two of these were largely unfavorable. In 1853 the publishers wrote Thoreau complaining that only 219 copies had been sold and 75 given away. They asked him to take the remainder off their hands. The upshot of the failure was that the publication of *Walden,* which had been promised "soon" in the back pages of *A Week,* was postponed for five years.

In the late 1840's Thoreau's interest in natural history per se had been rapidly growing. He had collected specimens of various fish, reptiles, and small mammals for Louis Agassiz and his assistant James Elliot Cabot at Harvard. In 1850 Thoreau was elected a corresponding member of the Boston Society of Natural History, for contributing an American goshawk to their museum. In 1853 he was offered membership in the Association for the Advancement of Science, but rejected it on the ground that his science was too Transcendental for them to appreciate. But to any careful reader of his journals it is obvious that he was becoming more and more preoccupied with scientific data. It was a fact that did not please him; he often bewailed in his journals that he was taking a narrower view of the world of nature.

In July, 1850, Margaret Fuller was drowned in the wreck of the ship *Elizabeth* off the coast of Long Island. Thoreau was dispatched to the scene by her Concord friends to find her body and rescue her unpublished history of the Italian revolution of 1848. He was not successful in either endeavor. But he did recover the body of Charles Sumner's brother, lost in the same wreck, and thus established a friendship with Sumner that continued throughout the remaining years of Thoreau's life.

Thoreau and Margaret Fuller had long been acquainted through their common friendship with Emerson and through Ellery Channing's marriage to Margaret's sister. But there was little warm feeling lost between them. Miss Fuller was outspoken in her criticism of the articles he submitted to the *Dial,* and he found little charming in her personality. There have been from time to time rumors that the two were once engaged and a tale that when he was told of the gossip he replied, "In the first place, Margaret Fuller is not fool enough to marry me; and second, I am not fool enough to marry her." But there is no evidence for either the rumor or his comment on it.

Walden was finally published in August, 1854, thanks this time apparently to Emerson's good offices with the rising firm of Ticknor and Fields. Greeley gave the book a good send-off with the preliminary publication of large excerpts in his *New York Tribune*. The reviewers could not all agree as to its virtues, but it received enough praise to guarantee a comparatively good sale. It took nearly until 1862 to sell off the first edition of 2,000 copies, but that was a marked improvement over the sale of *A Week*.

The fame of *Walden* attracted a number of disciples. The most notable was the New Bedford Quaker, Daniel Ricketson. He read *Walden* as soon as it was published and wrote to Thoreau on August 12, 1854. Thoreau took nearly two months to reply, but the delay did not dismay Ricketson. They met the following Christmas Day, when Thoreau visited New Bedford on his way to lecture at Nantucket. (Ricketson made an amusing little caricature of Thoreau at the time, our only full-length drawing from life.) They visited back and forth and corresponded frequently (for Thoreau, that is) until Thoreau's death. Ricketson at one point even considered moving to Concord to be near him. Unlike some of the other disciples, Ricketson had a sense of humor that brought out the best in Thoreau.

B. B. Wiley, a young Providence businessman, was another admirer attracted by *Walden*. He later moved to Chicago, but continued to correspond at length, often asking Thoreau for guidance in planning his life.

Thomas Cholmondeley, a young Englishman, came to Concord in the fall of 1854 to visit Emerson. Meeting Thoreau, however, he neglected Emerson. When he returned to England he sent Thoreau a gift of forty-four rare Oriental works. Thoreau's interest in the Orient, at its height in the early 1840's when he had first had access to Emerson's library, had now largely subsided, but he nonetheless received the treasure with great joy. Cholmondeley frequently invited Thoreau to visit him in England and, when Thoreau failed to do so, came back to Concord to see him again in 1858. Their correspondence continued until Thoreau's death.

Thoreau's interest in the abolition movement has been much debated. In 1844 he wrote a commendatory notice of the antislavery *Herald of Freedom* for the *Dial;* in 1845 he defended Wendell Phillips' right to speak on the movement before the Concord Lyceum; his antislavery opinions were a major motive in his refusal to pay his taxes; he aided at least one runaway slave on his way to Canada, and from 1854 on he spoke out frequently against slavery. But Canby was quite right when he said Thoreau was not an Abolitionist, for he never officially joined any formal organization.

It is unfortunate that Thoreau's medical records—if they were ever written down by the family physician—are not extant. Tuberculosis, or "consumption" as it was termed at the time, carried off a number of members of Thoreau's family. Concord town records indicate that it was by far the leading cause of death in the town, as it was elsewhere. Thoreau was ill enough in his late teens to withdraw from college for several months. He was ill again at the time of his brother's death, again just before he went to Staten Island, and also in 1851. In 1855 he was ill most of the spring, and his legs felt weak for many months. We cannot be certain that all these illnesses were caused by lesions of the lung, but it is not unlikely. Had Thoreau not spent so many hours of each day in the out of doors, it is quite possible that tuberculosis would have carried him off earlier than it did. Raymond Adams has suggested that Thoreau's "increasing ill health will account about as much for the absence of creative work during Thoreau's latter years as will the usual explanation, that his duties as a naturalist crowded out his duties as an author" (*Thoreau's Literary Theories and Criticism*, p. 73).

In the fall of 1856 Marcus Spring, a well-known abolitionist, invited Thoreau to survey the land for his experimental community, "Eagleswood," near Perth Amboy, New Jersey. Although Thoreau had visited both Brook Farm and Fruitlands, this was his only extensive association with any of those utopian experiments that dotted the landscape in the mid-nineteenth century. And it is obvious that he was not particularly impressed.

It was during this visit that Bronson Alcott led him to Brooklyn to meet Walt Whitman. The two were ill at ease in the presence of others, but they were mutually impressed, and Whitman gave Thoreau *Leaves of Grass*. Shortly thereafter Thoreau wrote two letters to H. G. O. Blake, evaluating both Whitman and his work, displaying a keen insight into Whitman's accomplishments and refusing to join the mob in condemning Whitman's "indecency." He later sent a copy of *Leaves of Grass* to his friend Thomas Cholmondeley in partial recompense for the "nest of Oriental books."

In 1855 Franklin Benjamin Sanborn, a recent graduate of Harvard, moved to Concord and established a private school. A bachelor, he took meals daily with the Thoreau family for some years. He became involved in supporting John Brown's activities and in 1857 and again in 1859 introduced Brown to Thoreau. Thoreau knew nothing of Brown's Harpers Ferry plans in advance. But no sooner did news of the attack and its failure reach Concord than Thoreau came to Brown's defense.

In 1857 the long-projected *Atlantic Monthly* was started under the editorial guidance of James Russell Lowell. Thoreau was asked to contribute and submitted some chapters on his excursion to Maine. Lowell accepted them but without permission deleted a sentence that seemed sacrilegious. Thoreau wrote an angry letter denying Lowell's right of censorship and refused to submit any further work to the magazine.

In the late 1850's Thoreau's growing interest in scientific data led him to a study of tree growth. Although almost simultaneously several other scientists reached the same conclusions, he independently discovered the principle of "The Succession of Forest Trees" and read a paper on that subject before the Middlesex Agricultural Society in 1860. It was perhaps his major contribution to natural science.

Thoreau acquired a severe cold while examining tree stumps on Smith's Hill on December 3, 1860. He had promised to deliver a lecture in Waterbury, Connecticut, on December 11. His friends attempted to persuade him to cancel the lecture, but he insisted on keeping the engagement. The strain was too much; the cold developed into bronchitis and eventually into acute tuberculosis. His illness gradually worsened. By late spring his doctors told him his only chance was to try another climate. He decided upon Minnesota and asked first Channing and then Blake to accompany him. When they declined, he turned to the young botanist, Horace Mann Jr. On May 11 they set out, stopping at Niagara Falls and Chicago on the way. But it was soon obvious that Thoreau was deriving no benefit from the excursion and by July he was back in Concord.

Thoreau acknowledged his fate and faced it calmly. He began to assemble his manuscripts and to prepare them for publication, telling his friends that a man must leave some estate to his heirs. As he gradually weakened, he was forced to resort to dictating his papers and correspondence to his sister Sophia. Ironically, he was on the verge of the fame that had so long eluded him. Lowell had resigned as editor of the *Atlantic Monthly* and had been succeeded by James T. Fields, who eagerly requested essays. *Walden* had gone out of print and Fields assured him that a new edition was demanded and on the way. Not only that, but Ticknor and Fields would purchase the remainder of the first edition of *A Week* and reissue it. Bronson Alcott wrote a tribute entitled "The Forester," which appeared in the April *Atlantic*.

But it was too late. As Thoreau lay on his deathbed in the living room of the Main Street house, friends, neighbors, fellow townsmen, and children, streamed in to visit him. He greeted them all cheerfully. When asked if he had thought of the other world, he replied, "One world at a time." When asked if he had made his peace with God, he replied, "I did not know that we had ever quarreled." At nine on the morning of May 6, 1862, he died so quietly that the moment of passing was not apparent. Ironically, he died of tuberculosis, the scourge of civilized life.

He was buried from the First Parish Church with a eulogy by Ralph Waldo Emerson. Concord schools were dismissed and children strewed wild flowers on his coffin. He was buried in the Dunbar family lot in the New Burying Ground. Some years later his body was transferred to nearby Sleepy Hollow Cemetery, where it lies under a small stone marked simply "Henry," only a few steps from the graves of his friends Alcott, Hawthorne, and Emerson.

II

The first book-length biography of Thoreau appeared in 1873, eleven years after his death. *Thoreau: The Poet-Naturalist* was written by his most intimate friend and companion on many of his excursions, Ellery Channing. It has a curious bibliographical history. Channing wrote it immediately after Thoreau's death and in 1863 made arrangements with F. B. Sanborn for it to appear in his Boston *Commonwealth* serially. Publication began on December 25, 1863 and continued weekly until February 19, 1864. But Sanborn then omitted an installment to give space to other literary matters, and Channing, taking offense, withdrew the rest of the manuscript, leaving the book incomplete. However, in 1873 Roberts Brothers, the Boston publishers, offered to issue it. Channing completely rewrote it. But the text was not long enough to suit the publishers and Channing used a unique device to enlarge it. In 1853 Emerson had hired Channing to compose a volume to be known as *Walks and Talks in Concord,* or *Country Walking,* to be made up of selections, arranged in conversational form, from the unpublished *Journals* of Thoreau, Emerson, and Channing. Although Channing completed the task, the book was never published. He now lifted two chapters from that volume and inserted them into the middle of the new volume, not bothering to assign the selections to the individual authors, but instead merely prefacing them with the comment, "To furnish a more familiar idea of Thoreau's walks and talks with his friends and their locality, some reports of them are furnished for convenience in the interlocutory form." These inserted chapters have little relation to the rest of the book and serve only to confuse the reader. He appended to the volume eight poems which he had written about Thoreau and which he entitled "Memorial Verses."

The volume without these two curious additions is unusual enough in itself. In large part it is made up of direct (but carelessly quoted) excerpts from Thoreau's published and unpublished writings. Channing had a keen ear for Thoreau at his best as a nature writer, but he made no attempt to identify the source of his quotations. There is very little biographical detail, the

Walden experiment and the jail experience, for example, being hardly more than mentioned. Chronological order is almost completely abandoned. Most of the space is devoted to Thoreau as a naturalist or nature writer. But Channing does insert into the text many anecdotes that have become a standard part of the Thoreau legend, and his critical comments on Thoreau's writing are sharp and to the point. Thoreau once said that Channing's poetry was written in the sublime-slipshod style, and much the same could be said about the prose in this volume. It is a curious mélange of irrelevant material and very worth-while information. The book is a gold mine to the biographer (and every biographer since Channing has used it), but it is otherwise of little value to the modern reader.

In 1902, after Channing's death, Sanborn reissued the volume. "In my new edition," states Sanborn (p. xii), "based upon a copy with the author's revision and notes, I have inserted here and there passages of no great length which I find in the original sketch, and which make the meaning plainer and the story more consecutive. At the end of this volume will be found some additions to the 'Memorial Poems' which evidently belong there." This later edition contains some material not in the earlier. But anyone familiar with Sanborn's methods of editing will approach it warily. The table of contents indicates that Sanborn felt free both to retitle some of Channing's chapters and to divide some. No one can say how much more he meddled with the text, and how much of the editing was actually based on Channing's annotated copy, since its present location is unknown.

The second book-length study of Thoreau, entitled *Thoreau: His Life and Aims*, appeared five years later, in 1878. It was by A. H. Japp, a professional biographer writing under the pseudonym H. A. Page and was the first study of Thoreau written by an Englishman. Japp states explicitly in his preface (p. xi) that the book "professes to be a Study only: an effort to gain a consistent view of the man's character, rather than an exhaustive record of the facts of his life." He originally wrote a magazine article on Thoreau and it was so favorably received that he expanded it into the book. It is ostensibly a thesis book: "I see a kind of real likeness between this so-called 'Stoic' of America, with his unaffected love for the slave, his wonderful sympathies and attractions for the lower creatures, his simplicities, and his liking for the labour of the hand, and . . . St. Francis" (pp. ix–x).

The book is divided into two lengthy chapters, the first developing the St. Francis theme, and the second making a broader study of the implications of Thoreau's philosophy. Unfortunately, in the few biographical details given, there are many factual errors (such as misdating his trip to the West by a year, and his death by 363 days). But Japp, unlike Channing, does not confine himself to Thoreau the naturalist. He places special emphasis on the social implications of Thoreau's philosophy (something British biographers of Thoreau were to emphasize more than American biographers) and is quick to clear Thoreau of any implications of escapism. He devotes much more space to the Walden, "Civil Disobedience," and John Brown episodes than did Channing. His book, although it gives little new biographical detail, is important in tracing the gradual evolution of interest from Thoreau as a nature writer to Thoreau as a social philosopher.

The third biography of Thoreau was *Henry D. Thoreau*, by F. B. Sanborn, issued in the "American Men of Letters" series in 1882. Sanborn lived in Concord the last years of Thoreau's life, boarded in the Thoreau house, and knew all the members of the Concord group well. In later years he considered himself the official historian and biographer of the group. This firsthand acquaintance with Thoreau and his friends lends an authority to Sanborn's writings, and like Channing, he was able to put into print many details of Thoreau's life that would otherwise have been lost. Unlike the Channing and Japp volumes, this biography records many factual details. Sanborn includes the texts of many otherwise unpublished letters (notably the correspondence between Thoreau and Greeley), essays (Thoreau's college writings in particular), and other important manuscripts. Unfortunately, Sanborn apparently considered himself a better writer than Thoreau and did not hesitate to take liberties with his manuscript materials. Thus, his text can never be completely trusted.

Sanborn, in speaking of Channing's biography, terms it "a mine of curious information on a thousand topics, relevant and irrelevant" (p. 11). No more appropriate description could be made of Sanborn's own book. He drags into it any material he happens to have on hand; for example, there are pages and pages on Daniel

Webster which by no stretch of the imagination could be said to pertain to Thoreau. But the book is important because it does contain primary source material unobtainable elsewhere. It is indispensable to the biographer of Thoreau, even though he may frequently curse Sanborn's arbitrary editing and his careless handling of facts.

In 1910 Houghton Mifflin reissued the biography in its "Riverside Popular Biographies" series. Sanborn, in the preface (p. xv), states that "its few errors [were] corrected." But since the new edition is obviously printed from the same plates, no major changes were made. However, Sanborn's new preface does shed some light on some of his techniques. He states, for example, that Sophia Thoreau had provided him with the manuscripts of some of Thoreau's letters that had been withheld by Emerson in editing his edition of Thoreau's letters and some of his unpublished college essays. But, he adds, "I withheld them [the letters] from full publication, foreseeing that I should probably have occasion to edit the letters in full at some later time; and I made but sparing use of the early essays" (p. xii), and says later, "I held back for the 'Familiar Letters' the more intimate details of Thoreau's self-devoted life, and did not draw heavily on the thirty-odd volumes of the Journals, to which, at Worcester, Mr. Blake gave me free access" (p. xiii). He also adds, to justify the inclusion of so much extraneous material, "I perceived that the character and genius of Thoreau could not be well understood unless some knowledge was had of the Concord farmers, scholars, and citizens, among whom he had spent his days" (p. xii)—an admirable aim, it must be admitted, but hardly ample justification for some of the completely irrelevant material included.

The fourth biography, issued in 1890, was *The Life of Henry David Thoreau*, by the British biographer and critic H. S. Salt. Salt was a pacifist, a vegetarian, and a socialist. He delighted in calling himself "a compendium of cranks." Offhand, a biography of Thoreau by such a man would not seem promising. But Salt kept his personal propaganda out of the volume and wrote what still is, in the minds of most scholars, the best biography of Thoreau. His aim, which he adequately fulfills, is stated briefly in his "Prefatory Note": "To combine the various records and reminiscences of Thoreau, many of which are inaccessible to the majority of readers, and so to present what may supply a real want—a comprehensive account of his life, and a clear estimate of his ethical teaching."

In writing this volume Salt was handicapped by the fact that he had never visited the United States. But one would never suspect it from the book. He writes with a clear and steady hand, basing his work on virtually all the material on Thoreau in print at the time and on extended correspondence with most of Thoreau's friends then still living. More recent students have been able to add biographical details, but little Salt says can be contradicted and one does not feel that any of his omissions are of major significance.

The first two-thirds of the book are straightforward biography, displaying a sense of organization and insight lacking in all the earlier works. Salt has a sense of proportion in handling the details of Thoreau's life that all other biographers before and since might well have emulated. The concluding chapters are an evaluation of Thoreau's writings and philosophy. Salt approaches the problem objectively. He does not hesitate to point out Thoreau's weaknesses, but he is also effective in emphasizing and evaluating Thoreau's major contributions to both literature and ethics. It is a sad comment on the state of Thoreau scholarship that the best biography of Thoreau is now more than sixty-five years old. But it will not be superseded until another scholar with the perception and carefulness of Salt approaches the problem.

In 1896 Salt's biography was reissued in abbreviated form (omitting, in particular, lengthy quotations from Thoreau's writings) with some revision and correction of minor errors.

Annie Russell Marble, *Thoreau: His Home, Friends, and Books* (1902), is a difficult book to evaluate, and critics have generally been prone to dismiss it as insignificant. True, it is a highly sentimentalized approach to Thoreau, almost completely ignoring his salient, sturdier characteristics in favor of the sentimental nature lover. But as she says in her foreword: "Through the kindness of relatives and friends of the Thoreau family, there have been loaned for this volume some letters and diaries hitherto guarded from the public. Interviews have also been granted by a few surviving friends of Henry and Sophia Thoreau, who have now first given utterance to certain anecdotes and impressions"

(p. viii). It is unfortunate that since many of these documents have disappeared, she did not quote from them more fully or identify them more particularly, but the important fact is that she did get many of these anecdotes and documents into print.

Her book is, in a strict sense, not a biography, even though it contains some new biographical information. Neither is it particularly successful in carrying out her aim "to estimate his rank and services as a naturalist and author" (p. viii). But because of the source material she alone had available and because of the background information she presents in such chapters as "Thoreau's Concord and Its Environs," "The Thoreau Family," and "Thoreau and His Friends," her book cannot be ignored by any conscientious student of Thoreau's biography.

Mark Van Doren's *Henry David Thoreau: A Critical Study* appeared in 1916. In its original form it had been an undergraduate honors thesis at the University of Illinois, but it displays a gift both for writing and criticism beyond the usual collegiate level. It was the first full-length critical study of Thoreau to appear after the publication of the complete journal, and Van Doren took advantage of it. He was able to correct many of the earlier misunderstandings. But unfortunately he was not basically sympathetic with his subject. He looked upon Thoreau as a bitterly disappointed man (p. 62, *et passim*), although how he reconciled that belief with the serenity of Thoreau's last days is not explained. He also stressed the loneliness and imbalance of Thoreau's personal life. Van Doren was at his best in analyzing Thoreau's writing style, and his chapter on "The Specific" effectively emphasized Thoreau's avoidance of the abstruseness of his fellow Transcendentalists.

In 1917 a number of books and articles commemorating the centennial of Thoreau's birth appeared. One of the most delightful was Dr. Edward Emerson's little book, *Henry Thoreau as Remembered by a Young Friend*. Dr. Emerson, Ralph Waldo Emerson's son and for many years a Concord physician, had, as a boy, known Thoreau intimately as neighbor, friend, and housemate. "Troubled at the want of understanding, both in Concord and among his [Thoreau's] readers at large, not only of his character, but of the events of his life—which he did not tell to everybody—and by the false impressions given by accredited writers," Dr. Emerson "undertook to defend my friend" (pp. v–vi). Ironically, though it is on James Russell Lowell's shoulders that Dr. Emerson places most of the blame for the prevalent false conception of Thoreau, in actuality the blame can be placed as justly on Dr. Emerson's father. For it was Ralph Waldo Emerson's funeral sermon for Thoreau and his editing of Thoreau's letters that perhaps more than anything else created the concept of Thoreau as a cold, almost inhuman, stoic. But Dr. Emerson, through this little book, did more than anyone else to correct the false impression.

Henry Thoreau as Remembered by a Young Friend, as its title implies, is not a formal biography. It is instead a brief memoir, supplemented by reminiscences Dr. Emerson solicited from other surviving acquaintances of Thoreau:

I saw that I must at once improve my advantage of being acquainted, as a country doctor, with many persons who would never
put pen to a line, but knew much about him—humble persons
whom the literary men would never find out, like those who
helped in the pencil mill, or in a survey, or families whom he
came to know well and value in his walking over every square rod
of Concord, or one of the brave and humane managers of the
Underground Railroad, of which Thoreau was an operative. Also
I had the good fortune to meet or correspond with six of the
pupils of Thoreau and his brother John, all of whom bore witness
to the very remarkable and interesting character of the teachers
and their school (pp. vi–vii).

As a portrait of Thoreau the human being, this little volume has not been excelled. It is, and should be, the final answer to those who would dismiss Thoreau as a misanthrope, for the man who emerges from these pages is a warm, friendly, kindly, and genial man, appreciated by his neighbors and beloved by the children of his town.

It was also in 1917 that Sanborn published his final biography of Thoreau. This was a completely new and different book from his earlier biographies. Unquestionably it is a great improvement. It is less discursive, more straightforward, and contains another invaluable hoard of otherwise unpublished Thoreau manuscripts, most notably a long series of Thoreau's college essays. Its appendix contains a catalogue of Thoreau's library, a partial list of his read-

ing, and several documents pertaining to his ancestors. But Sanborn nonetheless remained Sanborn to the end. Francis H. Allen
(*Thoreau's Editors,* pp. 15–16) tells us:

As an editor for Houghton Mifflin Company I had the not un-
mixed pleasure of seeing this book through the press, and, finding
that the author had followed his custom of using great freedom
in the treatment of quoted matter, I asked him if he would not
make some statement in his preface which would explain why his
versions of matter already printed differed from the previous
forms. To this he consented, apparently without reluctance and
in writing, but the statement never came, and he died on the very
day when the proof of his preface was mailed to him—the preface,
always the last of a book that the author sees in proof and now his
last chance of keeping his promise.

The first full-length biography of Thoreau in a foreign language was Leon Bazalgette, *Henry Thoreau, Sauvage* (1924). Bazalgette produced what is primarily a "fictionized" biography, pur-
porting to give the actual words of Thoreau's conversations with
his friends and often the thoughts in Thoreau's mind. It is true
that the author bases these conversations and thoughts on ideas
expressed in Thoreau's own writings. But he is treading on thin
ice when he assigns a particular quotation to a particular conversation. It is appropriate that on the title page appears a quotation
from Thoreau's *Journal,* "My friend will be bold to *conjecture.*
He will *guess* bravely at the significance of my words." [My italics.]
Since Bazalgette worked under the handicap of a distance of several thousand miles from his subject, most of his information is
derived from secondary sources, and he thus offers little or nothing
new except interpretation. Gay Wilson Allen, in evaluating Bazalgette's biography of Whitman, could also be evaluating the
Thoreau biography when he says: "He is a critic rather than a
biographer, for he is interested less in discovering facts and establishing new evidences for his interpretations than in reading the
text sympathetically; and at times his reading is so sympathetic
that he too becomes a mythmaker" (*Walt Whitman Handbook,*
p. 49).
      It is only fair to Bazalgette to point out that when Madeleine
Stern made a study of the leading biographies of Thoreau, she
came to the conclusion that his was the outstanding one. But

then it must also be remembered that she was primarily writing a defense of the fictionalized (or, as she terms it, "chronological") technique which she has used in her own biographies of Margaret Fuller and Louisa May Alcott.

In 1927 Brooks Atkinson published his *Henry Thoreau: The Cosmic Yankee.* Although in one of his opening remarks Atkinson complains that "in a generation of critics and biographers who were first of all placid gentlemen, reassured by their own formalism and sentimentality, the evanescent dreams of Thoreau were patronizingly set down as charming" (p. 4), Atkinson's own approach is somewhat patronizing. He tends to dismiss Thoreau the critic of society as betokening "nothing more admirable than want of sympathy, and arid understanding" (p. 49). The opening chapter of *Walden* he dismisses as "pure truculence" (p. 112). Yet in Thoreau's nature writings he finds "the essence of nature, the whole gamut of sights, movements, odors, sounds, and the all-pervading mystery" (p. 35). It is in discussing Thoreau as a nature writer and an excursionist that Atkinson is at his best. And it is not surprising, with such an approach, that in conclusion he was not sure whether Thoreau's "philosophy succeeded; *i.e.,* whether he won happiness in the life scheme he devised" (p. 153). Despite its faults, Atkinson's book is beautifully written and effectively demonstrates Thoreau's felicity of style.

It is only fair to add that in a conversation with me a few years ago, Atkinson said that he did not wish to have this book considered his final word on Thoreau. His preface to the Modern Library edition of Thoreau's writings, written ten years later, although much briefer, presents a better-rounded and more understanding portrait. In fact, it is one of the best brief introductions to Thoreau in print.

Henry Seidel Canby's biography, *Thoreau* (1939), is an exceedingly difficult book to evaluate fairly; it has many good points, and yet at the same time is disappointing in many respects. Those of us who were interested in Thoreau at the time and had read Canby's many penetrating essays on Thoreau, looked forward to the publication of the book with the greatest of interest. Yet the book cannot be described, as we had hoped it might be, as *the* definitive biography.

On the positive side it gathers into one volume more factual information about the life of Thoreau than any previous biography, and since it is well indexed, it proves an invaluable reference book. Canby was the first to make extensive use of the large and hitherto chiefly unpublished correspondence of the Ward family. Two members of the Ward family boarded with the Thoreaus for many years. It was they who introduced the Thoreaus to the Sewall family and they kept up a voluminous, gossipy correspondence filled with intimate details of the Thoreau family life. Canby made extensive and judicious use of this material, printing much of it verbatim. He was also the first biographer of Thoreau to have available such invaluable tools as Rusk's edition of Emerson's letters and Odell Shepard's edition of Alcott's journals, making wise use of both.

Canby studied the materials at hand with an almost Transcendental insight and thus produced many thoughtful and enlightening comments that help us to understand the life of Thoreau. A careful reader will discover that a large proportion of the book is based on such intuitive thought. Canby, himself a professional writer and editor, was primarily interested in this facet of Thoreau's life—"A life of Thoreau must chiefly emphasize the creative thinker" (p. xx)—and so included a more detailed discussion of Thoreau as a writer than had theretofore appeared. Finally, with his knowledge of modern psychology, Canby created a very human portrait by placing greater emphasis on the emotional factors that made Thoreau the man he was.

However, the book appears to have been written too hastily. It is filled with factual errors (some of which were corrected in later impressions), and the vitally important Harvard period in Thoreau's life is very inadequately covered (granted that much new information has come to light *since* Canby wrote his book). But the major weakness, and one for which most of the scholarly reviewers of the book assailed Canby, was his handling of the relationship between Thoreau and Emerson's wife. It is Canby's thesis that "Thoreau was what the common man would call in love with Emerson's wife" (p. 163). I think that any objective student will agree that he was emotionally involved with her. And Canby digs up a great deal of evidence in an attempt to support his thesis. But unfortunately most of the evidence is weak, even though taken from Thoreau's own *Journal* and various unpub-

lished writings, for Thoreau masked his identifications in pronoun references or such vague terms as "my sister." And we have
only Canby's word that it was Mrs. Emerson of whom he was
speaking. Indeed, to back up his statements, Canby at times is
forced to change the sex of Thoreau's pronoun references from
"he" to "she." There he is indeed treading on thin ice. Raymond
Adams, in a review of the book, gives us a careful discussion of
this phase, and comes to the conclusion, "I think Mr. Canby shows
that there was a slight mother-fixation about the Thoreau-Lidian
Emerson relationship, but nothing more." To sum it up: Canby
made many notable contributions to our knowledge of Thoreau,
but his book must be read with care.

Joseph Wood Krutch, *Henry David Thoreau* appeared in 1948.
It is primarily critical rather than biographical, although the
criticism is hung on a slight biographical frame. Nothing new is
added to our knowledge of the facts of Thoreau's life, but Krutch
does present the most rounded and balanced interpretation of
Thoreau's ideas yet to appear. He approaches his subject objectively and has few axes to grind. As a nature writer himself, he has
much to say on Thoreau as a nature writer, but he does not neglect
Thoreau the social critic. He sees the contradictions in Thoreau's
philosophy between the individualist and the social reformer not
as weaknesses but as sources of strength, because they kept Thoreau
always on the alert for a solution to his dilemma. Krutch dis-
tinguishes clearly between Emerson's philosophy and that of Thoreau, and feels that the break between the two men came when
Thoreau realized that his own ideas went far beyond Emerson's.
Perhaps most important is Krutch's emphasis on the essential
happiness of Thoreau's life.

The most recent biography of Thoreau (available only on micro-
film) is Raymond Gozzi, "Tropes and Figures: A Psychological
Study of David Henry Thoreau" (1957). Since Gozzi's work is
based on a Freudian analysis of all Thoreau's writings and his conclusions have been reached only after a huge marshaling of evidence, it is unfair to summarize his findings without presenting
his evidence. But that unfortunately is what must be done here.
He believes that Thoreau had an insecure childhood because of
his father's continued financial failures (pp. 3–4); that Thoreau
had an unresolved Oedipus complex (p. 32); that his prevailing

attitude was that sex was evil (p. 43); that he was colossally egotistic (p. 99); that his personality never matured (p. 102); that he had a compulsive, obsessional personality (p. 113); that his physical breakdown of 1855–1857 was the response of his unconscious to the success of *Walden* (p. 141); that arrowheads, trees, and fungi were unconscious phallic symbols to him (pp. 175–90); that his love of nature was an unconscious expression of his fixation on his mother (p. 228); that he consciously expressed toward the state unconscious emotions of hatred toward his family (p. 263); that the unconscious feelings of love and hate he had toward his father became controlling by the process of transference in his relation to Emerson (p. 330); and that his death was brought about subconsciously through a feeling of remorse and guilt after his father's death. Gozzi has come to some startling conclusions. Although they will undoubtedly disturb many a Thoreau devotee, they should not be condemned or ignored without a careful study of Gozzi's entire thesis. He has raised problems that all serious future biographers of Thoreau must at least consider, if only to refute. While I do not agree with all his findings, I have emerged from a reading of his dissertation with a feeling that I know Thoreau better than I ever had before.

There are a number of lesser studies, all brief, and they can be evaluated in a few words:

The Personality of Thoreau is another of F. B. Sanborn's many volumes on Thoreau. In large part it repeats what he has already said in other volumes. But it does have the one advantage, as its title implies, of concentrating more on Thoreau as an individual, and so records a number of revealing anecdotes and insights into his character.

Elbert Hubbard, *Thoreau* is a garrulous anecdotal account of Thoreau's life, notable chiefly for its high percentage of misinformation.

A good biography that is little known because it appeared only serialized in the pages of a magazine of small circulation and never in book form is "Thoreau, the Rebel Idealist," by David Boyd. While Boyd obviously depended on secondary sources for his information, his interpretations of Thoreau's philosophy are wisely and concisely expressed.

In 1940 Nathaniel Hawthorne's granddaughter, Hildegarde

Hawthorne, brought out a life of Thoreau entitled *Concord's Happy Rebel*. It is primarily a children's biography and adds little or nothing to our knowledge. It follows Canby so closely that it even repeats one of his misprints and many of his interpretations of fact.

Reginald Lansing Cook, *The Concord Saunterer* is a brief but thoughtful study. "Focussing on Thoreau as an adventurer on the plane of beauty, on which he searched intently, observed shrewdly, and articulated expressively the multiple forms of natural phenomena in their compositional harmony and design" (p. viii), it concentrates primarily on Thoreau's attitude of mind. Cook concludes that Thoreau is most aptly described as a poet-naturalist rather than as a scientist, and demonstrates that "his goal was that of a nature mystic in that he aimed to wrest significance from the natural phenomenon by perceiving wherein both he and it were related as on a plane of intense consciousness" (p. 25).

Harry Lee, *More Day to Dawn: The Story of Thoreau of Concord* is a biography of Thoreau in verse. Its primary importance is that by setting up many prose passages from *Walden* as free verse, Lee convincingly demonstrates the musical quality of Thoreau's prose.

George Whicher's brief tribute to Thoreau on the centennial of the Walden experiment, *Walden Revisited*, adds little new to our understanding or knowledge of Thoreau; it was intended primarily as an introductory essay. But it does manage to present a well-rounded criticism, and like most of the more recent studies, tends to concentrate on Thoreau the philosopher rather than the nature writer.

Joseph Ishill and others, in *Thoreau: The Cosmic Yankee,* present a series of essays on Thoreau from the libertarian point of view.

In 1949 Reginald Lansing Cook published a longer and more detailed study, *Passage to Walden*. Like his earlier work, it is a collection of essays rather than a unified study, and it omits many aspects of Thoreau's work. It demonstrates convincingly that Thoreau's interest in nature was a means toward a better understanding of life, not an end in itself. As I have frequently pointed out, there has been a tendency to approach Thoreau either as a nature writer or as a social critic. Cook is one of the few who have been able to bridge the gap.

Biancamaria Tedeschini Lalli, *Henry David Thoreau* (1954) is a critical study published in Rome. Biographical material is quite understandably based on secondary sources. But she does have some worth-while comments to make on Thoreau's word choice and prose style, emphasizing the rhythm of his sentences and his sensitivity to sound, color, and space.

William Condry, *Thoreau* is perhaps the best short biography of Thoreau. Condry is nature warden for a sanctuary in Wales and his volume is one of the "Great Naturalist" series. Quite understandably, he emphasizes Thoreau as a nature writer at the expense of the political, economic, or philosophical thinker. But Condry does not avoid these other facets. He handles them forthrightly and succinctly. Above all, he, like his fellow countrymen Salt and Japp, seems to achieve a clear-sightedness and objectivity toward his subject that the biographers on this side of the Atlantic lack.

Charles Norman, *To a Different Drum* is a children's biography. It is chiefly a rehash of the earlier biographies, unfortunately filled with errors of fact, and not particularly adapted to a young person's interests.

A recent biography, *Thoreau of Walden,* is by the well-known newspaper editor, Henry Beetle Hough. It is manifestly a "popular" biography, a sympathetic account filled both with appropriate quotations from Thoreau's own writings and many delightful anecdotes. But unfortunately it too is marred by many errors of fact and fails to take advantage of recent discoveries presented in scholarly articles.

To sum up, we do not yet have a really satisfactory biography of Thoreau. For sympathetic understanding and interpretation, Salt's life is the best, but it is sixty-five years old and thus out of date. For factual details, Canby's has become the standard reference, but it must be used with care. There are several scholars in the field who have expressed interest or intentions of producing a new biography of Thoreau. Perhaps one of these will fulfill our need.

III

The problems of the biographer in handling Thoreau's life are many. Since he was not particularly famous in his own lifetime, there is a comparative dearth of reminiscences (however, none of his biographers has yet taken full advantage of what there are).

Neither has there been an adequate study of the development of Thoreau's mind. Many of his biographers and critics have been satisfied to accept opinions he expressed in one period of his life as definitive of his ideas for his entire lifetime, forgetting that his viewpoints often developed and changed. As just one brief example, compare the opinions on war expressed in *The Service*, in "Yankee in Canada," in his letters to Cholmondeley, and in his letter to F. B. Sanborn written just after the outbreak of the Civil War.

Another difficulty is the wideness of the range of Thoreau's interests. Canby (p. xvi) did not overstate the case in the least when he said: "The truth is that there are a half-dozen possible biographies of Thoreau, depending upon the view the biographer takes of his subject. This is true of all complex characters, but seems to be particularly the case with this reserved researcher into the values of living" (p. xvi).

Still another difficulty lies in the fact that because of the popularity of Emerson's funeral essay on Thoreau and James Russell Lowell's and Robert Louis Stevenson's essays, there is a widespread belief that Thoreau's philosophy was primarily negative. While most twentieth-century biographers disagree with this interpretation, they are almost automatically forced to assume a negative approach and state over and over again, "Thoreau was not this, but that." The result is that altogether too often his biographers have appeared to have a chip on their shoulders.

Worse yet, if the biographer has not had a chip on his shoulder, he has had a thesis on his mind. As Mark Van Doren has said:

Among the critics, the personality of Thoreau has never been presented in full, mainly because it has been treated in no case by any one who was not interested in proving a point—that Thoreau was a hermit, that Thoreau was not a hermit, that Thoreau had pity and humor, that Thoreau was cold and in-

human, that Thoreau was a perfect stoic, that Thoreau was a
sentimentalist, that Thoreau was a skulker (pp. 4–5).

Closely related to this problem is the very fundamental question of the success of Thoreau's life. Yet fundamental as it is,
there has been anything but a basic unanimity among his biographers and critics. Mark Van Doren obviously considers Thoreau's
life to have been a failure and Thoreau an embittered man in his
last years (pp. 62 ff.). Brooks Atkinson, in *Thoreau: The Cosmic
Yankee,* was not sure if Thoreau won happiness in the life scheme
he devised (p. 153). Ethel Seybold detected a bitterness in his life
in the early 1850's but concluded that he later overcame it. Yet
Canby looked upon Thoreau as the happiest of the whole Concord group. It is my opinion that Canby is closest to the truth on
this point, but the whole question needs further study.

Finally, we need as a foundation for all the other approaches,
a detailed, factual account of his day-by-day life. Until such a
biography is published, we cannot hope for adequate interpreta-
tive biographies.

SOURCES FOR CHAPTER ONE

The major biographical studies of Thoreau are listed below in the notes for the second portion of this chapter. More specialized studies giving detailed information on particular phases of his life are listed in an order approximating that of the text of the first part of the chapter.

The standard history of Concord is Townsend Scudder, *Concord: American Town* (Boston, 1947). Mrs. Caleb Wheeler, "The Thoreau Houses" (*TSB* 31), identifies the many homes Thoreau dwelt in. An excellent map of the Concord of Thoreau's day, with his favorite haunts carefully identified, is Herbert Gleason, "Map of Concord, Mass." (*J*, XIV, 347; *TSB* 10.) Robert Stowell, *A Thoreau Gazetteer* (Calais, Vt., 1948) includes not only the Gleason map but also detailed maps of Thoreau's excursions. For Thoreau's ancestry, see E. Harlow Russell, "Thoreau's Maternal Grandfather, Asa Dunbar" (*Amer. Antiquarian Soc. Proc.*, XIX, 1909, 66–76); Raymond Adams, "A Thoreau Family Tree" (*TSB* 17), and Cephas Guillet, "The Thoreau Family" (*TSB* 19). There is no biographical study of Thoreau's father. Before accepting the traditional harsh picture of Thoreau's mother, one should be careful to read Jean Munro Lebrun, "Henry Thoreau's Mother" (*Boston Advertiser*, February 14, 1883, reprinted in pamphlet form by Edwin B. Hill, Lakeland, Mich., 1908; and Ysleta, Tex., 1940). A vivid picture of the Thoreau family household can be found in Mabel Loomis Todd, *The Thoreau Family Two Generations Ago* (*TSB* XIII). The relationship between Thoreau and his brother John is discussed in R. C. Francis, "Two Brothers" (*Dalhousie Rev.*, IX, 1929, 48). For details of John's death, see Max Cosman, "Apropos of John Thoreau" (*AL*, XII, 1940, 241–

43). For Sophia Thoreau, see S. G. Pomeroy, *Little-Known Sisters of Well-Known Men* (Boston, 1912) and Walter Harding, "The Correspondence of Sophia Thoreau and Marianne Dunbar" (*TSB* 33); see also George Hendrick, "Pages from Sophia Thoreau's Journal" (*TSB* 61), and Christopher McKee, "Thoreau's Sister in the White Mountains" (*Appalachia,* XXIII, 1957, 551–56). For the Thoreau family's religious vacillations, see H. H. Hoeltje, "Thoreau in Concord Church and Town Records" (*NEQ,* XII, 1939, 349–59). See also Kenneth Cameron, "The Thoreau Family in Probate Records" (*ESQ,* XI, 1958, 17–24).

For Thoreau's early schooling, see Hoeltje, "Thoreau and the Concord Academy" (*NEQ,* XXI, 1948, 103–9) and Kenneth Cameron, "Young Henry Thoreau in the Annals of the Concord Academy" (*ESQ,* IX, 1957, 1–42). For Thoreau's interest in the Concord Lyceum, see Hoeltje, "Thoreau as Lecturer" (*NEQ,* XIX, 1946, 485–94), Anton Huffert, "Thoreau as a Teacher, Lecturer, and Educational Thinker" (New York University, Ph.D., 1951), and Walter Harding, "Thoreau and the Concord Lyceum" (*TSB* 30). An accurate version of Thoreau's childhood essay, *The Seasons,* was published by E. B. Hill (Ysleta, Tex., n.d.).

Thoreau's Harvard years are presented in [John Weiss] "Thoreau" (*Christ. Exam.,* LXXIX, 1865, 96–117, *PT*), but more accurately in Raymond Adams, "Thoreau at Harvard: Some Unpublished Records" (*NEQ,* XIII, 1940, 24–33) and F. T. McGill, "Thoreau and College Discipline" (*NEQ,* XV, 1942, 349–53). John O. Eidson, *Charles Stearns Wheeler: Friend of Emerson* (Athens, Ga., 1951) adds important details, as do Kenneth Cameron, "Thoreau Discovers Emerson: A College Reading Record" (*BYNPL,* LVII, 1953, 319–34) and H. W. L. Dana, "Longfellow and Thoreau" (*TSB* I, 14–16). A facsimile of Thoreau's college diploma is included in *TSB* V; further details are given in Raymond Adams, "Thoreau's Diploma" (*AL,* XVII, 1945, 174–75). See also Kenneth Cameron, "Freshman Thoreau Opposes Harvard's Marking System" (*ESQ,* VIII, 1957, 17–18) and Cameron, "Jones Very and Thoreau—The 'Greek Myth' " (*ESQ,* VII, 1957, 39–40). For Thoreau's participation in graduation and alumni activities, see Kenneth Cameron, "The Solitary Thoreau of the Alumni Notes" (*ESQ,* VII, 1957, 2–37). "Harvard and Thoreau Battle over Books" in Kenneth Cameron, *The Transcendentalists and Minerva* (Hartford, Conn., 1958, pp. 474–89) documents Thoreau's relationship with his college library after graduation.

Kenneth Cameron, "Thoreau's Three Months Out of Harvard and His First Publication" (*ESQ*, V, 1956, 2–12) adds many details to our knowledge of Thoreau's life in 1837. The most detailed study of Thoreau's teaching experience is Anton Huffert, "Thoreau as a Teacher" (cited above), but see also Cameron, "Thoreau Bills His Pupils at Concord Academy" (*ESQ*, VII, 1957, 47–50). Thoreau's romance with Ellen Sewall is discussed in T. M. Raysor, "The Love Story of Thoreau" (*SP*, XXIII, 1926, 457–63), with added details in Florence Lennon, "The Voice of the Turtle" (*TSB* 15); light on her father's attitude is found implicitly in C. H. Faust, "The Background of the Unitarian Opposition to Transcendentalism" (*MP*, XXV, 1938, 297–324). Edmund Sewall's experiences in the Thoreau school are presented in Clayton Hoagland, "The Diary of Thoreau's 'Gentle Boy' " (*NEQ*, XXVIII, 1955, 473–89). Edwin Way Teale retraces Thoreau's route on his "Week on the Concord and Merrimack" in *The Lost Woods* (New York, 1945, pp. 81–91). Christopher McKee, "Thoreau's First Visit to the White Mountains" (*Appalachia*, XXXI, 1956, 199–209) fills in many details of the one-week interlude in the "Week" when Thoreau and his brother wandered through the White Mountains.

For the Thoreau-Emerson relationship, see J. B. Moore, "Thoreau Rejects Emerson" (*AL*, IV, 1932, 241–56) and Andrée Bruel, *Emerson et Thoreau* (Paris, 1929). Miss Bruel's findings are summarized in Charles Cestre, "Thoreau et Emerson" (*Rev. Anglo-Américaine*, VII, 1930, 215–30). See also F. B. Sanborn, "Thoreau and Emerson" (*Forum*, XXIII, 1897, 218–27). For Thoreau's work on the *Dial*, see Clarence Gohdes, *The Periodicals of American Transcendentalism* (Durham, N. C., 1931) and G. W. Cooke, *An Historical and Biographical Introduction to Accompany the Dial* (Cleveland, 1902). For Thoreau's friendship with Hawthorne, see Hawthorne, *American Notebooks,* edited by Randall Stewart (New Haven, 1932), and Frank Davidson, "Thoreau's Contributions to Hawthorne's *Mosses*" (*NEQ*, XX, 1947, 535–42). For Thoreau's friendship with Alcott, see Alcott, *Journals,* edited by Odell Shepard (Boston, 1938) and Frances Henry, "Henry David Thoreau and Bronson Alcott: A Study of Relationships" (*Teach-*

ers College Journal, July 1942, pp. 126–28 ff.). See also Kenneth W. Cameron, "Emerson, Thoreau, and the Town and Country Club" (*ESQ,* VIII, 1957, 2–17). The fullest account of Thoreau's Staten Island venture is Max Cosman, "Thoreau and Staten Island" (*Staten Island Historian,* VI, 1943, 1–7). For a brief account of Thoreau's friendship with Greeley, see Walter Harding, "Thoreau and Horace Greeley" (*TSB* 11). There is no separate study of Thoreau's friendship with Ellery Channing, although F. T. McGill has a biography of Channing under way. Channing himself wrote a satire on the Concord group, and the Thoreau portion of it has been published in F. B. Dedmond, "William Ellery Channing on Thoreau" (*MLN,* LXVII, 1952, 50–52). The original newspaper account of Thoreau's fire is reprinted in *TSB* 32. For a study of the reaction of Concordians to Thoreau, see Raymond Adams, "Thoreau and His Neighbors" (*TSB* 44). Thoreau's friendship with Father Isaac Hecker, who later founded the Paulists, is recounted in E. H. Russell, "A Bit of Unpublished Correspondence between Henry Thoreau and Isaac Hecker" (*Atlantic,* XC, 1902, 370–76).

The best account of Thoreau's arrest is S. A. Jones, "Thoreau's Incarceration" (*Inlander,* IX, 1898, 96–103, reprinted in *TSB* IV); but for the reasons for his "civil disobedience," see John Broderick, "Thoreau, Alcott, and the Poll Tax" (*SP,* LIII, 1956, 612–26). For Thoreau as a lecturer, see the material cited above under Concord Lyceum; Walter Harding, "A Check List of Thoreau's Lectures" (*BNYPL,* LII, 1948, 78–87); Harding, "Thoreau on the Lecture Platform" (*NEQ,* XXIV, 1951, 365–74); and Carl Bode, *The American Lyceum* (New York, 1956). For Thoreau's visit to Vermont, see Elliott S. Allison, "Thoreau in Vermont" (*Vermont Life,* IX, 1954, 11–13). Details of Thoreau's climb to the top of Red Hill in New Hampshire in the summer of 1858 are given in Allison, "A Thoreauvian on Red Hill" (*Yankee,* XIV, 1950, 36). For the week he spent on Mt. Washington on the same journey, see Christopher McKee, "Thoreau: A Week on Mt. Washington and in Tuckerman Ravine" (*Appalachia,* XXX, 1954, 169–83), which in its careful authentication of details and in its exposé of the accumulated errors of the various biographers in their accounts of this trip sets a model for further studies of the details of Thoreau's life; but see also Jeannette Graustein, "Thoreau's Packer on Mt. Washington" (*Appalachia*, XXXI, 1957, 414–17) for a correction of McKee's article. F. W. Kilbourne, "Thoreau and the White Mountains" (*Appalachia*, XIV, 1919, 356–67) is largely superseded by the above. For Thoreau's trips to Mount Monadnock, see Allen Chamberlain, "Thoreau's Camps" in *The Annals of the Grand Monadnock* (Concord, N. H., 1936, 70–80).

Thoreau's misadventures with Sophia Foord are recounted in Walter Harding, "Thoreau's Feminine Foe" (*PMLA*, LXIX, 1954, 110–16). For Thoreau as a surveyor, see Leo Stoller, "Thoreau and the Economic Order" (Columbia, Ph.D., 1956, pp. 57–89) and John D. Gordan, "A Thoreau Handbill" (*BNYPL*, LIX, 1955, 253–58), although I believe that the handbill should have been dated several years earlier than Gordan has dated it. For facsimiles of Thoreau surveys, see Benton Hatch, "Thoreau's Plan of a Farm" in *Papers in Honor of Andrew Keogh, Librarian of Yale University* (New Haven, Conn., 1938, pp. 317–24), and *TSB* 20. The fullest details on Thoreau's pencil manufacturing will be found in Kurt Steel, "Prophet of the Independent Man" (*Progressive*, September 24, 1945). Ruth Frost has contributed a series of articles on Blake and Thoreau's other Worcester friends to *Nature Outlook* (III–V, 1944–1947), but see also Daniel G. Mason, "Harrison G. O. Blake, '35, and Thoreau" (*Harvard Monthly*, XXVI, 1898, 87–95). For Thoreau's membership in the Boston organization, see Walter Harding, "The Boston Society of Natural History" (*TSB* 17). For his rejection of membership in the Association for the Advancement of Science, see Harding, *Mr. Thoreau Declines an Invitation* (Richmond, Va., 1956). For the rumor that Thoreau was engaged to Margaret Fuller, see Elbert Hubbard, *Thoreau* (East Aurora, N. Y., 1904, p. 168). For a similar preposterous rumor that Louisa May Alcott was in love with Thoreau, see Anna B. Comstock, "Henry David Thoreau" (*Nature and Science Education Rev.*, II, 1930, 54).

Thoreau's friendship with Daniel Ricketson is fully detailed in Anna and Walton Ricketson, *Daniel Ricketson and His Friends* (Boston, 1902) and summarized in Earl J. Dias, "Daniel Ricketson and Henry Thoreau" (*NEQ*, XXVI, 1953, 388–96). Thoreau's visit to Nantucket is recounted in James Monaghan, "Thoreau in Nantucket" (*Proc. of Nantucket Hist. Assoc.*, July 27, 1942, pp.

24–30). The friendship with Cholmondeley is detailed in F. B. Sanborn, "Thoreau and His English Friend Thomas Cholmondeley" (*Atlantic*, LXXII, 1893, 741–56) and a comparison of the philosophies of the two men in Joseph Jones, "Walden and Ultima Thule: A Twin Centennial" (*LCUT*, V, 1954, 12–22). The fullest account of Thoreau's abolitionist activity is Wendell Glick, "Thoreau and Radical Abolitionism" (Northwestern University, Ph.D., 1950). There are briefer accounts in N. A. Ford, "Henry David Thoreau, Abolitionist" (*NEQ*, XIX, 1946, 359–71) and in Walter Harding, "Thoreau and the Negro" (*Negro Hist. Bul.*, October, 1946). For Thoreau's visit to Eagleswood, see Maud Honeyman Greene, "Raritan Bay Union, Eagleswood, New Jersey" (*NJHSP*, LXVIII, 1950, 1–19). For Thoreau's visit to Walt Whitman, see Andrew Schiller, "Thoreau and Whitman" (*NEQ*, XXVIII, 1955, 186–97), Viola White, "Thoreau's Opinion of Whitman" (*NEQ*, VIII, 1935, 262–64), and Harold Blodgett, "Thoreau and Whitman" (*Concord Journal*, July 21, 1955). The fullest account of Thoreau's relationship with John Brown is in the Glick dissertation cited above.

For Thoreau's study of tree growth, see Kathryn Whitford, "Thoreau and the Woodlots of Concord" (*NEQ*, XXIII, 1950, 291–306), but see also the Stoller dissertation cited above. For Thoreau's trip to Minnesota, see John T. Flanagan, "Thoreau in Minnesota" (*Minn. Hist.*, XVI, 1935, 35–46), R. L. Straker, "Thoreau's Journey to Minnesota" (*NEQ*, XIV, 1941, 549–55), and *TSB* 57. For Thoreau's editing of his essays in his final illness, see James Austin, *Fields of the Atlantic Monthly* (San Marino, Calif., 1953, pp. 302–5). For the correct details on Thoreau's interment, see Raymond Adams, "Thoreau's Burials" (*AL*, XII, 1940, 105–7).

William Ellery Channing's biography first appeared serially as "Henry D. Thoreau" (*Commonwealth*, December 25, 1863–February 19, 1864), then in book form as *Thoreau: The Poet-Naturalist* (Boston, 1873), and finally in an enlarged and revised version edited by F. B. Sanborn (Boston, 1902). Sanborn gives a detailed history of the vagaries of Channing's biography in "A Concord Note-Book: Ellery Channing and His Table-Talk" (*Critic*, XLVII, 1905, 268–70).

A. H. Japp published his *Thoreau: His Life and Aims* (London, 1878) under the pseudonym of H. A. Page.

F. B. Sanborn's first biography was *Henry D. Thoreau* (Boston, 1882). It was later slightly revised and issued under the same title (Boston, 1910). *The Life of Henry David Thoreau* (Boston, 1917) is a completely rewritten book. Francis H. Allen has discussed Sanborn's editorial techniques in *Thoreau's Editors* (*TSB* VII), and Walter Harding has added further details in "Franklin B. Sanborn and Thoreau's Letters" (*BPLQ*, III, 1951, 288–93).

Henry Salt's first biography was *The Life of Henry D. Thoreau* (London, 1890). It was later abridged and revised as *Life of Henry D. Thoreau* (London, 1896). Details of the publication of the Salt biographies are given in J. T. Flanagan, "Henry Salt and His Life of Thoreau" (*NEQ*, XXVIII, 1955, 237–46).

Annie Russell Marble, *Thoreau: His Home, Friends, and Books* (New York) appeared in 1902; Mark Van Doren, *Henry David Thoreau: A Critical Study* (Boston) in 1916; and Edward Emerson, *Henry Thoreau as Remembered by a Young Friend* (Boston) in 1917.

Leon Bazalgette, *Henry Thoreau, Sauvage* (Paris, 1924) was the first book-length biography to appear in a foreign language. It was translated into English by Van Wyck Brooks as *Henry Thoreau: Bachelor of Nature* (New York, 1924). Madeleine B. Stern, "Approaches to Biography" (*SAQ*, XLV, 1946, 362–71) includes evaluations of most of the other biographies of Thoreau as well as of Bazalgette's.

J. Brooks Atkinson, *Henry Thoreau: The Cosmic Yankee* (New York, 1927), in its author's opinion, is now superseded by his introduction to Thoreau, *Walden and Other Writings* (New York, 1937).

Henry Seidel Canby, *Thoreau* (Boston) was published in 1939. Raymond Adams' review appeared in *AL*, XII, 1940, 113–14. Two other challenges of Canby's views on the Thoreau–Lidian Emerson relationship are Mary Culhane, "Thoreau, Melville, Poe and the Romantic Quest" (University of Minnesota, Ph.D., 1945, pp. 79 ff.) and Ralph Rusk, *The Life of Ralph Waldo Emerson* (New York, 1949, p. 533).

Joseph Wood Krutch, *Henry David Thoreau* (New York, 1948) is a volume in the "American Men of Letters" series.

Raymond Gozzi, "Tropes and Figures: A Psychological Study of David Henry Thoreau" (New York University, Ph.D., 1957) is unfortunately at the moment still unpublished, although a summary is included in *TSB* 58. The only other psychological studies of Thoreau that have as yet appeared in print are Joseph Collins, *The Doctor Looks at Biography* (New York, 1925, pp. 79–88) and David Kalman, "A Study of Thoreau" (*TSB* 22).

The lesser biographies include F. B. Sanborn, *The Personality of Thoreau* (Boston, 1901), Elbert Hubbard, *Thoreau* (East Aurora, N. Y., 1904), David Boyd, "Thoreau, the Rebel Idealist" (*Americana*, XXX, 1936, 89–118, 286–323), Hildegarde Hawthorne, *Concord's Happy Rebel* (New York, 1940), Reginald L. Cook, *The Concord Saunterer* (Middlebury, Vt., 1940), Harry Lee, *More Day to Dawn* (New York, 1941), George Whicher, *Walden Revisited* (Chicago, 1945), Joseph Ishill *et al., Thoreau: The Cosmic Yankee* (Los Angeles, 1946), R. L. Cook, *Passage to Walden* (Boston, 1949), B. T. Lalli, *Henry David Thoreau* (Rome, 1954; I am indebted to William Condit for summarizing the contents of this book for me), William Condry, *Thoreau* (New York, 1954), Charles Norman, *To a Different Drum* (New York, 1954), and Henry Beetle Hough, *Thoreau of Walden* (New York, 1956). There is a good evaluation of the early biographies in S. A. Jones, "Thoreau and His Biographers" (*Lippincott's Monthly Magazine*, XLVIII, 1891, 224–28).

Sherman Paul, *The Shores of America: Thoreau's Inward Exploration* (Urbana, Ill., University of Illinois Press, 1958), was published just too late to be discussed in this book. I wish here, however, to call it to the attention of Thoreau scholars as the first really significant study of the development of Thoreau's mind—in fact, just the type of book I call for earlier in this chapter.

CHAPTER TWO

Thoreau's Works

I

Although an ideal way to study an author's works is the chronological approach, this causes many problems in Thoreau's case. A few of his works present no difficulty—"A Plea for Captain John Brown," for example, must obviously have been written between October 17, 1859, the date of Brown's raid on Harpers Ferry, and October 30, 1859, when Thoreau delivered the essay as a lecture in Concord Town Hall. But unfortunately very few of his works can be dated so precisely. "Autumnal Tints" for example, contains excerpts from his *Journal* as early as 1851 and as late as 1858. It was apparently first used as a lecture in February, 1859, but he repeated it as late as December, 1860, and he apparently revised it for publication in the last months before his death. It did not reach print until October, 1862. Which of these is the date of composition? *A Week* was published in May, 1849, but he had completed a version of it as early as 1846. It tells the tale of a journey he had taken in 1839. And it includes excerpts from his *Journal* as early as 1837. What then is its date of composition?

It should by now be obvious that no final order of composition of Thoreau's works can be established. I have therefore had to compromise and place the works in the order in which I think he last revised them. In many instances there is concrete evidence for this type of dating. But in many others, for example, those essays which he revised just before his death, I have had to rely on my own judgment. In this particular case I have placed most of the "posthumous" essays in the order in which they were finally published. Another problem arises with those essays later incorporated into books, such as the individual chapters of *The Maine Woods* and *Cape Cod*. Here again I have been quite arbitrary and assigned the date of book publication rather than of periodical publication, since most of these essays were revised before incorporation into book form. The letters, the poems, and the *Journal* present still another problem, since they were worked on throughout Thoreau's adult life. These I have placed, again quite arbitrarily, at the end of the chapter. But despite all these compromises, I believe that the order in which I have discussed Thoreau's works offers for the first time an opportunity to see the growth and development of his mind and thought.

II

"The Seasons" is the earliest extant essay by Thoreau and is not included in his collected works. Apparently a schoolboy essay, it was written when Thoreau was approximately ten years old. Although it is by no means great literature, it does display remarkable facility for a child of that age and reflects his already keen interest in, and perception of, the world of nature.

The most important of the uncollected works of Thoreau are his college essays and book reviews. There are at least twenty-nine of the former and four of the latter extant. Twenty-eight of the essays were apparently written as assignments for Edward Tyrrel Channing's classes; the twenty-ninth ("The Commercial Spirit"), as part of a graduation "conference" with his classmate Henry Vose. It is not known why he wrote the book reviews, but Bode suggests (p. 312) that they were possibly for one of the undergraduate literary societies at Harvard.

What Glick (p. 60) says of the book reviews—"Had Thoreau written nothing after 1837, these pieces would long ago have suffered a merited extinction, for they are not the stuff of which fame is made"—might be said of the essays too, for they "are as empty of first-hand contact as a stale sermon" (Canby, p. 50). Even Professor Channing rated most of them "C" themes (Glick, p. 59).

Nonetheless, they are important to those who wish to study the development of Thoreau's thoughts and style. Joseph J. Kwiat says they may "be thought of as first attempts to integrate his formal Harvard studies, with their emphasis upon the Scottish philosophy, his efforts at self-culture, and the many contemporary influences, especially Emerson's, into some sort of personal expression, a major preoccupation with Thoreau during his entire mature life" (pp. 54–55). Moser adds: "Many a young Harvardite had been brought to a Transcendental position through the curriculum. The 'common sense' school had brought them to a rejection of the materialism of Locke, and by rejecting the Scottish school itself . . . budding Transcendentalists emerged" (pp. 18–19). All this is readily evident in these essays.

In examining the essays themselves, we find such typically Thoreauvian statements as: "So far as my experience goes, man *never* seriously maintained an objectionable principle, doctrine or theory. Error *never* had a sincere defender" (Moser, p. 148). "The fear of displeasing the world ought not, in the least, to influence my actions" (p. 152). "The majority of mankind are too easily induced to follow any course which accords with the opinion of the world" (p. 167). "The civilized man is the slave of matter" (p. 172). "The order of things should be somewhat reversed,— the seventh should be man's day of toil, wherein to earn his living by the sweat of his brow, and the other six his sabbath of the affections and the soul, in which to range this wide-spread garden and drink in the soft influences and sublime revelations of Nature" (p. 184). "He who is dependent upon himself alone for his enjoyments,—who finds all he wants within himself, is really independent" (p. 70).

Surely, in the light of these remarks it is difficult to understand Adams' assertion: "At the time he [Thoreau] walked out of Harvard Yard in the summer of 1837 he seems to have created for himself very little that might be called transcendental" (*Henry Thoreau's Literary Theories and Criticism*, pp. 15–16). For "all of Thoreau's basic ideas are in the college essays, the seeds are all present, awaiting maturation" (Moser, p. 62). He needed but to develop his style to express them in the memorable phrasing of his later writing.

"Died," the brief obituary for Anna Jones, which Thoreau published in the Concord *Freeman's Gazette* for November 25, 1837
(p. 3) was his first writing to reach print. It adds little to our
knowledge of Thoreau except to indicate his early interest in
writing.

The Service, apparently originally written for the *Dial* but rejected by Margaret Fuller, was not published until 1902. (The
version included in the collected works [W, IV, 277–79] is only
a fragment.) It was derived chiefly from his *Journal* for the years
from 1837 to 1840. Stylistically it is the young Thoreau in his
most pompous and aphoristic vein, obviously influenced by the
most vapid of his Transcendentalist contemporaries. While I do
not agree with Mark Van Doren (p. 46) that "perhaps more of the
essential Thoreau can be seen in 'The Service' than in any other
twenty-five pages of him," I do agree that Thoreau's thoughts on
the well-rounded or "spherical" man are important to an understanding of Thoreau's broader aims in life. But most of the ideas
in this brief essay he expressed more succinctly in his later works.

The "Natural History of Massachusetts" (W, V, 103–31) was
first published in the *Dial* for July, 1842. It was derived from the
Journal for the years from 1837 to 1842. Nominally a review of
*Reports—On the Fishes, Reptiles, and Birds; The Herbaceous
Plants and Quadrupeds; The Insects Injurious to Vegetation; and
the Invertebrate Animals of Massachusetts,* "published agreeably
to an Order of the Legislature, by the Commissioners on the
Zoological and Botanical Survey of the State" of Massachusetts, it
is actually a nature essay drawn chiefly from the pages of Thoreau's own *Journal,* interspersed with much of his own poetry, and
only in the last five brief paragraphs deals to any marked degree
with the books reviewed. Although Thoreau chides the authors
for their prosaic approach and points out a few errors in their
texts, he welcomes their pioneer contributions to a systematic
study of American flora and fauna. Thoreau continued to use the
volumes for reference throughout his career.

But the modern reader will ignore those last few paragraphs
and concentrate on the central theme: Thoreau's joy in the world

of nature around him. It is his first published essay in the genre that was to make him famous. "The observations are correct but unremarkable; the diction is facile but not distinguished . . . nor had he achieved the insights which later so distinguished his writing" (Welker, p. 107). Best are the few brief paragraphs on muskrats (pp. 114–17) and on fishing (pp. 119–23), which are almost worthy of a place in *Walden*.

"A Walk to Wachusett" (W, V, 133–52) was first published in the *Boston Miscellany* for January, 1843, and Thoreau apparently never succeeded in obtaining payment for it. The essay is an account of a walking excursion with Richard Fuller, brother of Margaret Fuller, in July, 1842, to the solitary mountain just north of Worcester, Massachusetts. (He derived material, however, from his *Journal* for 1837, 1838, and 1841 in particular.) In quality it seems a slight retrogression from the "Natural History of Massachusetts." It is marred with the abstruseness characteristic of some of his earlier writings. But it improves in quality as he approaches and ascends the mountain, its literary peak coinciding with the mountain peak. The poem with which the essay opens was apparently written somewhat earlier and submitted to the *Dial*, but was rejected by Margaret Fuller in her long, analytical letter of October 18, 1841.

Thoreau's translation of "The Prometheus Bound" by Aeschylus (W, V, 337–75) first appeared in the *Dial* for January, 1843. Little more than a literary exercise, it "is very literally and exactly and unimaginatively rendered; word order is sometimes painfully preserved" (Seybold, p. 18). Leo Kaiser, however, points out that it does include a few "unnecessarily free translations." And C. C. Felton, Thoreau's professor of Greek at Harvard, spoke of its having been "executed with ability." There have been long-standing rumors that in the late nineteenth century it was reprinted and circulated among students at Harvard as a pony, but I have never seen any such edition. Thoreau also did a translation of the "Seven Against Thebes," which has not yet been printed.

Sir Walter Raleigh is not one of Thoreau's masterpieces. It is of interest only as an apprentice piece. Apparently first written as a lecture and delivered before the Concord Lyceum on February 8, 1843, it was later revised for publication—note the reference to "our readers" on p. 72—possibly for the *Dial*, which suspended publication before it could be included.

The essay adds little or nothing to our knowledge of Raleigh. It is more concerned with his character and his literary ability than with his life. In fact, it sheds more light on Thoreau's own youthful hero worship than on anything else. It is comparatively dull reading; none of Thoreau's later wit shows through.

Most interesting is the long passage (pp. 76–80) on "the necessity of labor . . . to the scholar," reflecting the ideas of Emerson's "American Scholar," and Thoreau's closing statement: "We have considered a fair specimen of an Englishman in the sixteenth century; but it behoves us to be fairer specimens of American men in the nineteenth" (pp. 89–90).

"The Landlord" (W, V, 153–62), first published in the *Democratic Review* for October, 1843, was an attempt at the familiar essay in the style of Lamb and Hazlitt. It is poor Thoreau. It discusses the virtues of innkeepers, and obviously Thoreau's heart is not in the matter. He would rather be outdoors than in a tavern. In all probability, since it was written at Staten Island when Thoreau was making his first serious attempt to become a professional writer, it was an effort to please the general public. Thoreau himself described it as "a short piece that I wrote to sell" (W, VI, 111). Thoreau is at his best only when he is trying to be himself, not someone else.

"A Winter Walk" (W, V, 163–83), derived chiefly from the *Journal* for 1841 (although there are a few excerpts from the 1838 *Journal*), first appeared in the *Dial* for October, 1843, but only after Emerson had edited it severely. He not only cut from it an entire poem (which Sanborn later printed in *First and Last Journeys*, I, 142–46), but also apparently edited many sentences, objecting to their *mannerism:* "for example, to call a cold place sultry, a solitude public, a wilderness *domestic* (a favorite word), and in the woods to insult over cities, armies, etc." Yet for the

modern reader the essay is one of Thoreau's best. Welker terms
it

> perhaps the most evocative and lyrical short prose work Thoreau
> ever wrote. . . . Thoreau was beginning to transcend common-
> place observations . . . and to look more deeply and react more
> subtly. . . . Here is the type of intimate and empathetic look
> into nature for which Thoreau is famous. He does not condescend,
> he does not go too far in personalizing his creatures, he does not
> moralize; instead he finds his way into their lives as far as his
> knowledge and understanding will permit. . . . Certainly Tho-
> reau was saying nothing new; but he was foreshadowing . . .
> both the alienation from his time, and the compensating rapport
> with things of the wild, which would make *Walden* at once so
> somber and so heartening a book" (pp. 107–8).

Indeed the spirit of the whole essay is close to some of the best
pages of nature description in *Walden*. The later book at times
even echoes words and phrases from it. And I suspect the wood-
man's hut here so vividly described (pp. 172–73) is that of Hugh
Quoil, described again in *Walden* (W, II, 289–90). Despite the
fact that "The Landlord" and "A Winter Walk" were first published in the same month, it is hard to believe they were written
by the same hand. The former is jejune, almost puerile; the latter,
Thoreau at his best.

"Paradise (to be) Regained" (W, IV, 280–305) is a review of
J. A. Etzler, *The Paradise within the Reach of All Men, without
Labor, by Powers of Nature and Machinery. An Address to All
Intelligent Men* (Part First, Second English Edition, published in
London in 1842), written while Thoreau was on Staten Island
and published in the *Democratic Review* for November, 1843,
although (according to Thoreau's letter to Emerson of August 7,
1843) only after some difficulties with the editors, who "could
not subscribe to all the opinions." Since the *Democratic Review*
was primarily a political organ, and Thoreau in his review advo-
cates individual rather than group reform, the difficulties are not
surprising.

Etzler's pamphlet propounds the theory that would man only
unite, harness the wind, the tides, and the sun, live in community
apartments, and communize most of his productive activities, he

could produce a paradise here on this earth that would relieve
him of all but the slightest necessity for labor. In many respects
his ideas closely parallel those of François Marie Charles Fourier,
which at that moment were inspiring the establishment of so many
communities across the American countryside. Thoreau's review
can be considered his reply to the many Fourierists among his
friends.

His rejection of Etzler's ideas is typically Transcendental and
Thoreauvian: "We will not be imposed upon by this vast application of forces. We believe that most things will have to be accomplished still by the application called Industry" (p. 297). "The
chief fault of this book is, that it aims to secure the greatest degree
of gross comfort and pleasure merely" (p. 302). "But a moral reform must take place first, and then the necessity of the other
will be superseded, and we shall sail and plow by its force alone"
(p. 303).

Ethel Seybold's assertion (p. 46) that this essay "is the first outward sign of social conscience" in Thoreau is overstated. But certainly the essay is a long step forward from some of the writing
of the previous years, and contains some of Thoreau's sharpest and
most caustic comments on social reform.

Thoreau's "Translations from Pindar" (W, V, 375–92) first appeared in the *Dial* for January and April, 1844. Like his translation of "The Prometheus Bound," they display no great genius
although they are more poetically rendered. Francis Allen points
out that the version now included in Thoreau's standard works is
marred by an omission and several errors. Thoreau also translated
eleven poems of Anacreon for the April, 1843, *Dial* (the number
which he himself edited) and later worked them into the text of
his *Week*.

"Herald of Freedom" (W, IV, 306–10) was a brief notice of the
New Hampshire antislavery journal edited by Nathaniel P.
Rogers, published in the April, 1844, *Dial*. As Glick points out
in "Thoreau and the 'Herald of Freedom' ": "For only three men,
of the number whom Thoreau criticized in his works prepared
for publication, is the quality of praise not strained: Nathaniel
P. Rogers, . . . Wendell Phillips, . . . and John Brown" (pp.

194–95). Glick suggests that Thoreau's praise of Rogers was inspired in part at least by his objections to Garrison's dictatorial methods in leading the antislavery movement, for Rogers was one of the leaders of the opposition to Garrison. That Rogers was pleased with Thoreau's notice is indicated by his reprinting the article in his journal with a long introductory note (reprinted in Glick, pp. 198–200). In "Thoreau and Radical Abolitionism" Glick adds: "The significant thing about Thoreau's remarks about Rogers is that they marked his first departure from the ideal of the reformer who remains aloof and apart, in communion with the moral universe" (p. 181).

"Wendell Phillips Before the Concord Lyceum" (W, IV, 311–15) was a letter written to William Lloyd Garrison, editor of the antislavery *Liberator* and first published in that journal in the issue of March 28, 1845. For some years there had been a quarrel within the ranks of the members of the Concord Lyceum between the conservative members who wished to avoid controversial issues and the liberals who in particular wished to have the antislavery problem discussed. The liberals finally won out and elected Thoreau and Emerson, among others, to the governing body of the lyceum. One of their first acts was to invite Phillips to speak, and the invitation was renewed in succeeding years. Thoreau's letter is a report on the third of Phillips' lectures. While the essay is filled with praise for Phillips, it is interesting to note that Thoreau singled out for particular praise Phillips' statement "that he was not born to abolish slavery, but to do right" (p. 313).

"Thomas Carlyle and His Works" (W, IV, 316–55) was written while Thoreau was at Walden. The few excerpts that appear in the extant *Journal* are chiefly of the period from 1845 to 1847. First used as a lecture before the Concord Lyceum on February 4, 1846, it was sent in August, 1846, to Horace Greeley, who acted as Thoreau's literary agent. A month later Greeley replied that the article had been accepted by *Graham's Magazine,* although it did not appear until the March and April, 1847, numbers, and Thoreau did not receive his pay ($75.00) for the article until Greeley, in desperation, wrote a draft on the publisher in May, 1848.

As one might expect from a Transcendentalist, it is a highly favorable review of Carlyle's life and works, perhaps one of the most understanding that Carlyle was to receive in his lifetime. Its importance to the modern scholar probably lies in its exposition of Thoreau's critical principles, and as the only extended essay by Thoreau on the literary work of a contemporary. When Carlyle received a copy of the essay, he wrote Emerson (May 18, 1847), "I like Mr. Thoreau very well, and hope to hear good and better news of him." Greeley later tried to persuade Thoreau to write a similar essay on Emerson. But Thoreau refused, apparently not wishing to presume on Emerson's friendship.

In the summer of 1846 Thoreau was arrested and jailed for non-payment of his poll tax. That evening someone, probably his Aunt Maria, paid the tax and the next morning he was released. But those few hours in jail resulted in his most famous and most influential single essay, "Civil Disobedience" (W, IV, 356–87).

John C. Broderick points out that Thoreau stopped paying his poll tax in 1842 and that, contrary to popular opinion, since this was several years before the Mexican War, the war could not have been a factor in Thoreau's original decision. It is more likely that his decision was based upon Bronson Alcott's earlier refusal, a general unpopularity of the poll tax at that time, and an opposition to slavery in particular on Thoreau's part. Thoreau's arrest was due to a complex of political factors at the time, including the fact that Sam Staples, the jailer, would have had to pay the tax himself had he not collected it.

It was apparently Thoreau's intention to bring about a test case of the poll tax law, but Aunt Maria's intervention ruined this opportunity. Instead, he turned to writing an essay to get his ideas before the people. On January 26, 1848, he delivered a lecture before the Concord Lyceum on "The Relation of the Individual to the State," and repeated the lecture there three weeks later. The essay first reached print in May, 1849, in Elizabeth Peabody's short-lived periodical *Aesthetic Papers* (pp. 189–213), under the title "Resistance to Civil Government." After his death it was included in his collected works under its present title, "Civil Disobedience."

Although the essay does tie itself down to specific political issues, it is basically more universal in its approach. "Thoreau's chief purpose in 'Civil Disobedience' was to wean men away from their adherence to an insidious relativism and to persuade them to return again to the superior standard of absolute truth" (Wendell Glick, "Thoreau's Attack upon Relativism," p. 37). When moral law and governmental law come into conflict, many argue that from expediency men should obey the government. But it is Thoreau's argument that "it is not desirable to cultivate a respect for the law, so much as for the right." Having thus established his principle, he goes on to present the most effective method of defending it, that is, by practicing "civil disobedience," refusing to pay taxes, going to jail if necessary, and thus, by clogging the meshes of governmental gears and winning sympathy through martyrdom, making an aroused citizenry aware of the wrong and willing to right it.

It was not a new idea. As I have said, Bronson Alcott had refused to pay his taxes and had been jailed only three years earlier. Emerson had theorized on the doctrine in his essay on "Politics." There had been frequent debates on the subject before the Concord Lyceum, in one of which, on January 27, 1841, Thoreau argued *against* nonresistance. And a large segment of the Abolitionist movement, that led by William Lloyd Garrison, espoused the doctrines of civil disobedience in its periodicals. Raymond Adams, in "Thoreau's Sources for 'Resistance to Civil Government' " (pp. 651 ff.), suggests William Paley's *Moral and Political Philosophy* as still another source, though Glick (p. 38) points out that Thoreau is actually arguing against and not for Paley's ideas. Edward Tinker traces the central idea back to Étienne de La Boétie's *Discourse sur la Servitude Voluntaire,* although there is no adequate proof that Thoreau was familiar with that essay.

Far more important than any study of its sources is the fact that Thoreau's presentation of the idea has been the most influential in spreading the doctrine. It was Gandhi's textbook for his civil disobedience campaign in India, was published as a handbook of political action in the early days of the British Labour party in England, and was a manual of arms for the resistance movement under Nazi occupation in Europe in the 1940's. Even more recently it has been used by the Negroes in their struggles for civil rights in the American South. It has been widely re-

printed and is perhaps more frequently read than any other work
by Thoreau. In fact, outside continental United States Thoreau
is probably more widely known as the author of "Civil Disobedience" than of *Walden*.

There is an irony about all this, that "Civil Disobedience" has
become a manual of arms for reformers, for "Civil Disobedience"
is "less a declaration of any intention to become a social reformer
than a reaffirmation of his defiant individualism" (Krutch, p. 134).
Thoreau still believed that reform could be achieved only within
the individual, not through social action.

A Week on the Concord and Merrimack Rivers (W, I) was
Thoreau's first published book. It is based on a rowboat excursion
he and his brother John took in the fall of 1839. His *Journal*
entry for June 11, 1840 (J, I, 136) would seem to imply that he
began writing the book on that date. After his brother John's
death in 1842, he determined to make it a memorial tribute.
However, other duties kept him away from the task, and his decision to go to Walden in 1845 was inspired in part at least by the
desire to write *A Week*. He progressed rapidly at the task there
and on July 16, 1846, Emerson wrote Charles King Newcomb:
"In a short time, if Wiley & Putnam smile, you shall have Henry
Thoreau's 'Excursion on Concord & Merrimack Rivers,' a seven
days' voyage in as many chapters." However, the New York publishers did not smile, nor did others that Thoreau tried at Emerson's behest, although several offered to publish it at Thoreau's
expense. Thoreau took advantage of the extra time to revise and
expand the book. As late as January, 1848, he added the "Friendship" essay to the "Wednesday" chapter (Sanborn, 1882, p. 304).
In Emerson's letter from England of December 2, 1847, he advised Thoreau to print the book at once, assuring him he would
incur no risk in underwriting its cost. Sometime in 1848 Thoreau
agreed to pay James Munroe of Boston (he had published several
of Emerson's works) to publish the book in an edition of one
thousand copies. Page proofs were in Thoreau's hands before the
end of the year (they bear the copyright date of 1848), but because
Thoreau asked for more than one thousand corrections, publication was delayed until May, 1849.

Its reception was a miserable failure (see Chapter Five). Even the printer failed him by accidentally omitting three lines of the text (p. 396 of the first edition). In four years only 218 copies were sold. Thoreau had to pay Munroe a total of $290 (J, V, 521). Munroe shipped the remainder to Thoreau on October 28, 1853, to clear the shelves, and that night Thoreau wrote in his *Journal*, "I have now a library of nearly nine hundred volumes, over seven hundred of which I wrote myself" (J, V, 459). Thoreau was not at all satisfied with the text and prepared a revised edition that included more than 400 verbal changes and 1,000 punctuation changes. But the revised edition was not published until 1868, six years after his death (Hovde, pp. 245–46).

The basic plan of the book is a day-by-day account of the voyage, a plan that George Whicher suggests (p. 35) Thoreau may have derived from Margaret Fuller's *Summer on the Lakes*. After the introductory chapter on "Concord River," there is a separate chapter for each day of the week from "Saturday" through "Friday." (Actually the excursion took two full weeks, but the period from Thursday to Thursday was used for a hike on foot to the top of Mount Washington.) The account of the voyage itself is smooth-flowing, vivid, and highly interesting. But unfortunately, either to add to the length of the book or to get material on hand into print, Thoreau inserted into the text various digressions that doubled its size. As Lowell said in his review, "We come upon them like snags, jolting us headforemost out of our places as we are rowing placidly up stream or drifting down." They include essays on the fish of Concord River (p. 23), fables (p. 58), the Christian religion (p. 65), poetry (p. 93), Sir Walter Raleigh (p. 106), reform (p. 129), the Hindoos (p. 140), history (p. 161), translations from Anacreon (p. 238), potholes (p. 261), friendship (p. 274), hiking (p. 324), Aulus Persius Flaccus (p. 327), Hannah Dustan (p. 342), Goethe (p. 347), cattle shows (p. 358), Ossian (p. 366), and Chaucer (p. 391), to mention only the longer digressions. "The *Week*," says William Drake (p. 25), "is the work of a very literary-minded young man, who is enthusiastic about books and authors"—and, one might add, about a great deal else. Thoreau also includes accounts of two excursions to western Massachusetts (pp. 189, 212) and incidents of his life on Staten Island in 1843 (pp. 190, 253). Thrown in for good measure are 48 original poems and at least 126 quotations. Fifteen of the inserts were

taken from material Thoreau had already printed in the *Dial*.
Other pieces, such as that on Sir Walter Raleigh, were culled
from his lecture manuscripts. But the great majority of the material was culled from his *Journal*, from its beginning in 1837
right up through 1848. Unfortunately, however, his technique
usually involved scissoring the passages he needed out of the
Journal, so there is now comparatively little opportunity to compare the original with the finished version. (An interesting slip-up
occurs on pp. 345–46, with the passage beginning "On beholding
an old picture of Concord." Thoreau apparently forgot that he
had used these two sentences from his *Journal* in his "A Walk
to Wachusett" [W, V, 149–50], published in the *Boston Miscellany*
six years before.) Sanborn rescued some of the *Journal* drafts
Thoreau had used for *A Week* and printed them in the first volume of *The First and Last Journeys of Thoreau.*

As usual with his excursions, Thoreau, before he started on the
journey, prepared himself by reading all the histories of the area
he could place his hands on and then carried a gazetteer with him.
And, as usual, he sprinkles liberally through his text, references
to, and quotations from, these works, including Fox's *History of
the Old Township of Dunstable*, Mirick's *History of Haverhill,
Massachusetts*, Johnson's *Wonder-Working Providence*, Gookin's
Historical Collections of the Indians in New England, and Alexander Henry's *Adventures*. In his commentary on the last-named,
Thoreau remarks, "What is most interesting and valuable in it
. . . is not the *annals* of the country, but the natural facts, or
perennials, which are ever without date." Unfortunately Thoreau
failed to take his own advice, and it is the *annals* that he includes
in this and his other volumes of excursions that date them more
than anything else. It is the high proportion of *perennials* in
Walden that make it his masterpiece.

Compared with his later books, *A Week* contains little natural
history. There is the long essay on the fish of Concord River,
already cited, and occasional mention of the flora along the banks
(p. 18, for example). But there is none of the detailed listing of
species as in *Cape Cod* or *The Maine Woods* and very little of the
natural history essay as such as in *Walden*. There are, however, a
few memorable descriptive passages, such as that of the American
bittern that "carried its precious legs away to deposit them in a

place of safety" (p. 17). In 1851, looking back at his own first
book, Thoreau was impressed with "its *hypoethral* character, to
use an epithet applied to those Egyptian temples which are open
to the heavens above, *under the ether*. . . . I trust it does not
smell [so much] of the study and library, even of the poet's attic,
as of the fields and woods" (J, II, 275).

A Week is more Transcendental than his later volumes. He
wanders into the abstract more frequently, and there are passages
vapid enough to have been written by Bronson Alcott. "The Thoreau of *A Week on the Concord and Merrimack Rivers* is primarily the mystic and the lover of the primitive, not yet much the
critic of society" (Krutch, p. 97). There are frequent passages on
the values of intuition and the conscience (p. 138, for example).
And as *Walden* does, the book closes (pp. 408 ff.) on a note of
Transcendental optimism that man will eventually develop all his
yet untried potentialities. Perhaps the most Transcendental of
all is the essay on friendship in the "Wednesday" chapter. With
the possible exception of portions of *Walden,* this is Thoreau's
most frequently reprinted excerpt. Canby is right when he says it
is an essay on love rather than friendship (p. 103), but a most
ethereal and idealistic type of love. There is no allowance made
for the passions or the senses.

It was the section on religion (included in the "Sunday" chapter) that most disturbed his contemporaries. And we need only
glance at such sentences as "In my Pantheon, Pan still reigns in
pristine glory" (p. 65), "It seems to me that the god that is commonly worshiped in civilized countries is not at all divine" (p.
65), "It is necessary not to be Christian to appreciate the beauty
and significance of the life of Christ" (p. 68), "The reading which
I love best is the scriptures of the several nations, though it happens that I am better acquainted with those of the Hindoos, the
Chinese, and the Persians, than of the Hebrews" (p. 72) to understand why the more orthodox were frightened or angered by the
book. Thoreau's willingness to tread on toes unquestionably was
a factor in the book's poor sale.

Neither does the volume have the saving grace of humor that
is found in his later books. It is true there are a few Thoreauvian
puns, such as his comment to a passerby on the river, "I shot a
buoy" (p. 212), and there are a few pithy comments, such as "He

was earthy enough, but yet there was good soil in him" (p. 218).
But the reader is so bogged down by digressions that he often
misses these. Little wonder is it, then, that this is probably Thoreau's least read book.

When, however, the book is stripped of its digressions, as in
the recent edition entitled *The Concord and the Merrimack*,
edited by Dudley C. Lunt, it becomes much more readable, and
one can then recognize the validity of H. M. Tomlinson's judgment that it is one of the best of all travel books.

In going through a miscellaneous collection of Thoreau manuscripts in the Widener Memorial Collection at Harvard College
Library, Arthur Christy discovered what was apparently the manuscript of a hitherto unknown short work of fiction by Thoreau.
However, upon further study he discovered that it actually was
a translation from the French of *The Transmigration of the Seven
Brahmans* from the *Harivansa* of Langlois, an anthology of Hindu
literature published by the Oriental Translation Fund in Paris in
1834. Thoreau borrowed the *Harivansa* from Harvard College Library in 1849 and 1850 and apparently made the translation then.
It is chiefly important as "the first extensive evidence . . . of
Thoreau's proficiency in French" (p. xvi). The "translation is not
entirely literal, but occasionally an adaptation, and . . . many
sentences were omitted entirely" (p. 15).

The essay on "Love" (W, VI, 198–204) was not published during Thoreau's lifetime. In September, 1852, he sent it to H. G. O.
Blake for critical advice, and possibly Blake's reply (which has
since disappeared) discouraged his efforts to publish it. Like the
essay on "Friendship" in *A Week*, it is highly Transcendental,
condemning any physical basis for love, and shedding far more
light on the author than on the subject. Certainly his opening
statement, "What the essential difference between man and
woman is, that they should be thus attracted to one another, no
one has satisfactorily answered," is, as Krutch suggests (p. 207)
"a real howler." F. I. Carpenter, in his *Emerson Handbook* (pp.
200–201), says, "The story of the co-ed who confided to her professor that Emerson's essay on 'Love' was very fine but not all that
she expected suggests the limitation [of Emerson's essay]." The

anecdote could be even more appropriately told of Thoreau's essay.

The essay on "Chastity and Sensuality" (W, VI, 204–9) has a similar history. Even Thoreau had his doubts about it, for he wrote Blake, "I send you the thoughts on Chastity and Sensuality with diffidence and shame, not knowing how far I speak to the condition of men generally, or how far I betray my peculiar defects" (W, VI, 197–98). If possible, it is even more vapid than the essay on love. Brooks Atkinson has best summed up both essays: "Long on idealism and short on experience—in general a silly blunder" (p. 23).

"A Yankee in Canada" (W, V, 1–101), based on an excursion Thoreau took with Ellery Channing in the fall of 1850, was first published, in part, in *Putnam's Magazine,* beginning with the issue of January, 1853. But Thoreau disagreed with his old friend, George William Curtis, the editor, who insisted upon censoring certain passages, and withdrew his manuscript after only three of the proposed five chapters had appeared. Portions of the essay had been used as lyceum lectures in 1852. Most of the text is derived from his *Journal* for the summer and early fall of 1851, but he also made a few notations in his *Journal* just after his return from Canada in 1850 and a few more in the spring of 1852. After Thoreau's death the entire essay was issued with certain miscellaneous papers in a volume entitled *A Yankee in Canada, with Anti-Slavery and Reform Papers* (1866). So far as I know, Thoreau made no revision of the essay in his last years.

A railroad offered the eleven-hundred-mile, twelve-and-a-half-day trip for $7.00, and fifteen hundred tourists responded. They visited both Quebec and Montreal, and Thoreau and Channing took the opportunity for a walking excursion along the banks of the St. Lawrence, visiting some of the notable waterfalls and observing the natives. It is one of Thoreau's least inspired "excursions." The opening sentence states, "What I got by going to Canada was a cold" (p. 3). And the objective reader will have to agree that Thoreau found little else. Even the sentence structure and vocabulary of the essay are atypical, staccato, pedestrian journalese. As Edmund Berry has observed, "We learn that he is no abstracted, airy philosopher; he can on occasion be an extremely naïve American tourist, with the self-righteousness, too, of the less attractive American tourists" (p. 74).

As usual with his excursions, Thoreau read all the history and travel books on the area he could find, referring in all to some forty-five different accounts by previous travelers to the region (John Christie, p. 97), although in this particular case he did most of his reading after his trip, rather than before (p. 93). There is in the Morgan Library a mass of unassorted notes on the discovery and later history of Canada that Thoreau apparently compiled in preparation for writing this essay. But comparatively little of it was used. "A Yankee in Canada" is a fusion of the eighty-four-page account of his trip in his *Journal* for October, 1850, with seventy pages of the notes in his Canadian notebook (p. 98). He quotes Kalm, Hontan, Cartier, Charlevoix, and others. And as soon as he arrived on the scene, he made haste to purchase two guidebooks and a map (p. 100). But never did he succeed in adapting himself to the region or its inhabitants. French Canada was a holdover from "Europe and the Middle Ages," he thought (p. 57). Its inhabitants were little better than savages, and ignoble savages at that. He resented the fact that few of them could speak English. And he spent pages denouncing the control that the Roman Catholic Church exerted over them. Perhaps in this work more than in any other Thoreau displays the violent anti-Catholicism of the mid-nineteenth-century Yankee. He could appreciate cathedrals because they were like caves, but he wanted the priests omitted (p. 14). The shrine of St. Anne, to him, was nothing more than a fraud, and he suspected the crutches suspended on the walls "had been made to order by the carpenters who made the church" (p. 51).

The domination of the British military irked him even more. He visited the various fortifications, but thought the soldiers only "one vast centipede of a man, good for all sorts of pulling down" (p. 17). He suggested that were the soldiers to receive an education, they would immediately desert (p. 27). And he could see no point to men standing guard duty in subzero weather when no enemy had approached the fortifications for centuries.

Even nature failed him here. The language difficulties with the natives were too great for him to learn the identity of certain botanical specimens that interested him, and in the whole essay there is only one brief list (p. 27) of the flowers he observed.

On the positive side, there are a few good pages devoted to the architecture of the region (pp. 44 ff.) and an enlightening comparison of French and English colonial policies (pp. 66 ff.). On the whole, however, he is the superior Yankee looking down his long nose at an inferior race. The entire essay seems out of character. Even Thoreau himself cared little for it, for on February 27, 1853, he wrote Blake, "I do not wonder that you do not like my Canada story. It concerns me but little, and probably is not worth the time it took to tell it."

"Slavery in Massachusetts" (W, IV, 388–408), delivered July 4, 1854, at an antislavery convention at Framingham, Massachusetts, was first published in the *Liberator* on July 21 of that year. It was at this convention that William Lloyd Garrison publicly burned a copy of the Constitution to symbolize his protest against the protection it afforded slavery. But his act was hardly more violent than Thoreau's words, best summarized in one of his closing sentences, "My thoughts are murder to the State" (p. 407).

Thoreau's protest was primarily against the recent arrest of the Negro Anthony Burns in Boston and his return to slavery in Virginia, and a large part of his essay is derived from his *Journal* entries at the time of Burns's arrest. But an almost equally large part of the essay is derived from his *Journal* entries from the early summer of 1851, at the time of the similar arrest of the Negro Simms. Thoreau was disturbed that his neighbors could protest slavery in the South or in Nebraska and yet overlook it in their own back yards, and he speaks out in some of his most violent language. As in "Civil Disobedience" (and the two essays are so similar in mood and tone that sentences could easily be exchanged between them), his appeal is based on obedience not to governmental law but to one's own innate sense of goodness, "They are the lovers of law and order who observe the law when the government breaks it" (p. 396).

Wendell Glick points out that Thoreau here makes a two-way attack: (1) Reform the individual, and (2) destroy those institutions that are corrupting mankind. Therefore Thoreau includes in this essay virulent attacks on both the press and the church as defenders of slavery. Despite the fact that the essay was inspired by a particular event, it is a timeless and universal appeal for a higher standard of morality. It is as timely today as the day it was written.

Walden (W, II) was Thoreau's second book, his last book to appear in his lifetime. It is based on his experiences at Walden Pond from July 4, 1845, to September 6, 1847, although it contains material from his *Journal* from as early as April 8, 1839 (W, II, 8) to as late as April 9, 1854 (W, II, 334). He apparently conceived of the idea of writing a book on his Walden experience almost as soon as he went to live there and completed a first draft of the book early enough to assure James Munroe, the publishers of *A Week,* that they could publish *Walden* soon after *A Week,* a fact they announced in the back pages of *A Week* in the late spring of 1849. But the failure of *A Week* led to cancellation of these plans, and *Walden* was not published until August 9, 1854, when it was issued in an edition of 2,000 copies by Ticknor & Fields of Boston.

Thoreau used the intervening five years to revise, expand, and polish the work considerably, so that the book of 1854 was markedly different from the manuscript of 1849. Just how much the book was changed in those years has been revealed by J. Lyndon Shanley. Although the final "fair copy" of *Walden* apparently went into the printer's wastebasket as soon as the book was published, Huntington Library owns a large collection of miscellaneous manuscripts that are obviously parts of earlier drafts of the book. In 1909 F. B. Sanborn edited a *Walden* for the Bibliophile Society of Boston based on these manuscripts. But in his usual highhanded way, he cut, added, edited, and revised to suit his own tastes, so that his final product was utterly unlike anything Thoreau conceived. All serious students have wisely avoided that edition, despite the fact that it contained some 12,000 words not in the standard edition. Since then numerous students have studied the Huntington manuscripts and have given them up as a hopeless confusion. But Shanley, by examining carefully the various types of paper and the variations in handwriting, finally solved the puzzle. He found the manuscripts consist of portions of seven different drafts of *Walden,* including an almost complete

version of the first draft. In *The Making of Walden* he published
that first draft with a detailed analysis of the changes that came
about in succeeding drafts. Shanley's book offers a superb opportunity to study the artist at work.

"The essential nature of *Walden* did not change from first to
last" (Shanley, p. 6). "It was as if after having built a modest six-
or seven-room house and living in it for a time, he found that it
was not large enough. First he began by enlarging and remodeling
most of the rooms, and then, as he did so, he decided to add new
rooms and still later he found he could improve the proportions
and disposition of the various parts of the house. But he did all
this work from the inside out, cutting apart and spreading the
foundations, walls, and roof wherever necessary to accommodate
the changes within, without destroying the fundamental character of any considerable portion of the original" (p. 6). Most of
the quotations were not added till the later versions (p. 25). The
chapter divisions were not made until 1853 (p. 4). Details were
corrected from version to version as, for example, the price of
a railroad ticket being changed from $1.00 to $.70, to $.90 in the
page proof (p. 36). But despite the changes, "the version that Thoreau might have published in 1849 . . . would have been a good
book; Thoreau did well what he first set out to do" (p. 55).

Although Thoreau spent two years, two months, and two days
at Walden Pond, he has condensed these experiences into one
year (W, II, 94, 351), and therein lies the chief unity of the book.
Early critics were prone to claim that *Walden* had no unity.
Francis H. Allen, for example, complained in 1910, in the introduction to his edition of *Walden,* "It is not an artistic composition. It lacks form. It cannot be taken as a model for the building
of a book. It disregards the rules of essay construction" (p. xix).
But more recent critics speak differently. Richard P. Adams, for
example, in "Romanticism and the American Renaissance" (*AL,*
XXIII, 1952, 425) says, "The basic structure of the book may be
most clearly understood in the fact that Thoreau, 'for convenience,' condenses his two years' experience at Walden into one,
and describes it beginning with summer and proceeding through
fall and winter to spring. The turning seasons thus define a process of symbolic death and rebirth which, for Thoreau as for other
romantics, represents the character of personal development." Not

only does he use the symbolism of the year throughout the book, but he also uses the symbolism of the day (the epitome of the year) in the individual chapters. Thus "Sounds" begins with the sounds of the afternoon, continues through the evening, the night, and ends up with the cockcrowing of dawn. "A survey of Thoreau's use of the related imagery of morning and spring in *Walden* reveals remarkable variety; he has used the imagery to criticize contemporary life, to reveal aspects of his theory of expression, to celebrate his aims in life, to emphasize the importance of man's correspondence with nature, and to argue the almost limitless possibilities of individual inspiration and achievement" (Broderick, p. 89).

The early critics thought that, as Carlyle had said of Emerson's essays, *Walden,* organizationally speaking, was a collection of duck shot in a bag. It could be read backward as easily as forward, or the pages could be shuffled and it would not be materially harmed. But Shanley has demonstrated that Thoreau had a carefully formulated blueprint of the book as a whole and that each chapter, paragraph, and sentence was put in its particular place for a precise reason. There is not space to demonstrate that fact at length here, but one need only look at the beginning sentence of each chapter to see its truth. Thus the transition sentence from "Reading" to "Solitude" begins, "But while we are confined to books . . ." and the transition sentence from "The Bean-Field" to "The Village" begins, "After hoeing. . . ." "Solitude" and "Visitors" are set up in direct antithesis to each other. And so on.

There are four related but distinct "matters" with which the book concerns itself, and they might be enumerated as follows: (1) The life of quiet desperation which most men lead. (2) The economic fallacy which is responsible for the situation in which they find themselves. (3) What the life close to nature is and what rewards it offers. (4) The "higher laws" which man begins, through some transcendental process, to perceive if he faithfully climbs the stepladder of nature whose first rung is "wildness," whose second is some such gentle and austere but not artificial life as Thoreau himself was leading, and whose third is the transcendental insight he only occasionally reached (Krutch, p. 108).

Reginald Cook finds three literary archetypes for *Walden: Robinson Crusoe* ("Man's skill in solving self-imposed economic

problems"), *Gulliver's Travels* ("A critical arraignment of so-
called civilization"), and *Pilgrim's Progress* ("An autobiographi-
cal narrative of . . . spiritūal wayfaring"). Cook might have added
a fourth: *The Natural History of Selborne,* for many there are
who still ignore *Walden's* philosophical content and think of the
book as primarily a report on the flora and fauna of Concord.

Certain it is that many of Thoreau's contemporaries thought
of the book primarily as a volume of natural history. Some even
went so far as to suggest to the reader that he skip the more philosophical chapters—"Economy," "Higher Laws," and "Conclusion." Paradoxically, it is just those chapters that have best stood
the test of time.

It is well to remember that on the title page of the first edition
Thoreau quoted from his chapter on "Where I Lived and What I
Lived For," saying, "I do not propose to write an ode to dejection, but to brag as lustily as chanticleer in the morning, standing
on his roost, if only to wake my neighbors up" (W, II, 94). Why
modern publishers omit this epigraph I never shall understand.
The book is "the most delicious piece of brag in literature" (Burroughs, *Indoor Studies,* p. 33). And unless the reader keeps this
in mind, he is likely to miss the point of the book. And finally, it
is important to remember that Thoreau wrote with a sense of
humor. It may seem like belaboring the obvious to point this out,
but unfortunately many readers have failed to see it.

Thoreau's purpose in writing *Walden* is all too frequently misunderstood. He states explicitly several times in the volume that
he is writing for a limited audience. For example:

I do not mean to prescribe rules to strong and valiant natures,
who will mind their own affairs whether in heaven or hell, and
perchance build more magnificently and spend more lavishly than
the richest, without ever impoverishing themselves, not knowing
how they live,—if, indeed, there are any such, as has been
dreamed; nor to those who find their encouragement and inspiration in precisely the present condition of things, and cherish it
with the fondness and enthusiasm of lovers . . . ; I do not speak
to those who are well employed, in whatever circumstances, and
they know whether they are well employed or not;—but mainly
to the mass of men who are discontented, and idly complaining
of the hardness of their lot or of the times, when they might im-

prove them. . . . I also have in my mind that seemingly wealthy but most terribly impoverished class of all, who have accumulated dross, but know not how to use it, or get rid of it, and thus have forged their own golden or silver fetters (W, II, 17–18).

Or, to recapitulate briefly, if you are satisfied with your own way of life, this is not a book for you. But if you are leading a life of "quiet desperation," Thoreau here offers you a way out.

Second, Thoreau is not advocating that we all abandon our cities and homes and our families, and go out into the wilderness to live in huts and meditate on nature:

I would not have any one adopt *my* mode of living on any ac- count; for, besides that before he has fairly learned it I may have found out another for myself, I desire that there may be as many different persons in the world as possible; but I would have each one be very careful to find out and pursue *his own* way, and not his father's or his mother's or his neighbor's instead (W, II, 78–79).

Third, Thoreau is not advocating that we abandon civilization. To be sure, he was discouraged at times, as all thinking people are, with some of the dark spots in modern life. He simply bewails the fact that so many of our so-called improvements of civilization are but "improved means to unimproved ends." We are in great haste to get nowhere to do nothing. Since we have invented time-savers, let us make the most of them, he suggests. But let us im- prove our spiritual natures as well as our material world.

Thoreau had talked of going to Walden Pond for a number of years before he actually moved there to live in his twenty-eighth year. He tells us that when he first saw its crystal-clear waters as a child, he wanted to live on its shores. After graduating from Harvard in 1837 and trying his hand at schoolteaching for several years, he more and more frequently talked with his friends of going off by himself for a while to experiment with life. At first he tried unsuccessfully to obtain teaching positions in distant Vir- ginia and Kentucky, but then he thought of living independently nearer home. His college classmate Charles Stearns Wheeler had lived in a hut in the woods in nearby Lincoln and Thoreau had visited him there. Ellery Channing had lived for a time alone on the Illinois prairie. From 1840 on we find constant reference in

Thoreau's *Journal* and letters to a desire to settle down in solitude for a time.

In 1845 Thoreau found the opportunity. Emerson purchased fourteen acres of woodland at Walden Pond, wishing to preserve the quiet beauty of the woods and lake. Soon after, Thoreau entered into an agreement with him. There was a small field on the land and Thoreau would render it arable. In return he would have the privilege of "squatter's rights" on the land.

Thoreau purchased the remains of a railroad shanty from an Irish immigrant named James Collins and carried its timbers to the pond to build his cabin. Most of the work on the building was his own, although he did call in a few friends for the frame-raising. The cabin was a well-built structure, fifteen feet by ten, with one room, one door, one window in each side, a cellar hole, a garret, and a closet. A few months after he moved in, he plastered the walls for winter weather and built a fireplace. The second winter he added a stove.

Explaining why he went to the pond to live, he wrote: "I went to the woods because I wished to live deliberately, to front only the essential facts of life, and see if I could not learn what it had to teach, and not, when I came to die, discover that I had not lived." There is the essence of Thoreau's experiment. He was not an escapist from civilization. His cabin was only two miles from town and twenty from "the hub of the universe." The railroad rattled by one end of the pond and the highway passed within sight of his garden. Rarely a day went by that he did not hike into town on an errand or that visitors did not come out to call on him.

His life at Walden Pond was quietly devoted to living. Each morning he took his bath in the pond and then hoed in his garden, "making the earth say beans instead of grass." Stormy days or winter mornings he read or wrote. Afternoons he spent in wandering through the Concord woods or boating on its ponds and rivers, pursuing assiduously his studies of the world about him. Evenings he devoted to his friends, with either a trip to the village for a conversation or a few guests in his cabin.

After two years he had accomplished his set task, and "left the woods for as good a reason as I went there. Perhaps it seemed to me that I had several more lives to live, and could not spare any more time for that one."

"A Plea for Captain John Brown" (W, IV, 409–40) is the first of Thoreau's three essays on Brown. Through F. B. Sanborn, who acted as Brown's agent in Concord, Thoreau met Brown twice and was greatly impressed. Although he knew nothing in advance of Brown's plans at Harpers Ferry, and although the press and even many of the abolitionists hastened to disavow and denounce Brown when word of the attack reached the North, Thoreau, almost alone, came quickly to his defense. He called a meeting in Concord Town Hall on October 30, 1859, and when the selectmen refused to ring the bell to announce the meeting, he rang it himself. The local Republicans sent him word that they thought such a meeting at the moment inexpedient, and he replied that he was not asking for advice but announcing a meeting. According to Emerson, many came who were opposed to Thoreau's opinions but found themselves listening with a surprising sympathy. Two nights later he repeated the speech at Theodore Parker's Temple in Boston, a last-minute pinch hitter for Frederick Douglass. On November 3 the lecture was delivered in Worcester under the auspices of his friend Blake. It was first printed in James Redpath's *Echoes of Harper's Ferry* in 1860.

To many people the John Brown essays have seemed to embody a complete reversal of all the principles for which Thoreau had once stood. And some, such as John Burroughs, who thought of "Civil Disobedience" as savoring of "a little bit of the grotesque and the melodramatic" (*Indoor Studies,* p. 9), found his defense of John Brown "the most significant act of his life" (p. 8). As Wendell Glick asserts: "To the impartial student of Thoreau, it is obvious at the very outset that there was much in John Brown which not only did not conform to Thoreau's fundamental theories of reform, but was in direct contradiction to them" (p. 159). "The championing of John Brown was tantamount to Thoreau's categorical rejection of his early faith in the omnipotence of the 'natural' forces for good in the universe" (p. 167). "Yet . . . in championing Brown Thoreau did not feel guilty of compromising his earlier beliefs. Instead, he saw in Brown the fulfillment of them. He made every attempt to reconcile Brown's method of reform with his own earlier theories" (p. 159). It was true that Brown was using political (that is, external) reform rather than the inward reform of the individual. But Thoreau did find that

Brown "fulfilled three of his principles—he woke man up out of his lethargy; he showed contempt for government; and he set a great personal example" (p. 168).

It was perhaps this last aspect that so much impressed Thoreau. In "Civil Disobedience" he had stressed that one *good* man could reform a nation. And in Brown, Thoreau found a man who was willing to practice that principle. Thus Brown was a major hero, on a level with Christ: "Some eighteen hundred years ago Christ was crucified; this morning, perchance, Captain Brown was hung" (p. 438). In deifying Brown, Thoreau called him "a transcendentalist above all, a man of ideas and principles" (p. 413), thus apparently rationalizing for the disparity in Brown's views and Thoreau's own.

Gilman Ostrander feels that Thoreau did not so much compromise his own principles in defending Brown as that he misunderstood or misinterpreted Brown's personality, chiefly because Brown himself purposely covered up the blackest pages of his Kansas campaigns when he talked with Emerson and Thoreau in Concord. They were thus able to picture Brown as a Transcendentalist saint, and "they assumed that if his character could be proved to be pure, it would follow that his actions must have been justified" (p. 724).

One will find many ideas in Thoreau's essay that are not contradictory to Thoreau's earlier writings: "He had the courage to face his country when she was in the wrong" (p. 411). "The only government that I recognize . . . is that power that establishes justice" (p. 430). "When were the good and the brave ever in a majority?" (p. 432.) "Is it not possible that an individual may be right and a government wrong?" (p. 437.) Any of these sentences would be appropriate in "Civil Disobedience" or "Slavery in Massachusetts." The fundamental distinction of the John Brown essays is that they apply the principles of the earlier essays to a particular man and a particular situation, even though some aspects of that man's character and action were at variance with some of Thoreau's principles.

Thoreau apparently wrote the essay under great emotional pressure. As he himself says (p. 417), "I put a piece of paper and a pencil under my pillow and when I could not sleep I wrote in the dark." The *Liberator* (November 4, 1859) was moved to comment,

"This exciting theme seemed to have awakened 'the hermit of Concord' from his usual state of philosophic indifference, and he spoke with real enthusiasm." The essay is filled with memorable epithets, such as Brown "was a volcano with an ordinary chimney flue" (p. 413). And, as usual in his later polemical writings, Thoreau expressed his indignation with the church and press for opposing rather than supporting the right.

Henry W. Nevinson (*Essays in Freedom and Rebellion*, p. 113) believes the "Plea for Captain John Brown" to be "one of the greatest speeches ever delivered among mankind, all the greater because it contains no rhetorical eloquence." In his closing paragraph Thoreau states that the "poet will sing" of John Brown's achievement. Less than three years later troops were marching southward to the tune of "John Brown's Body." Ostrander points out that Emerson and Thoreau "contributed greatly to that glorification of Brown. . . . While the writings of other nineteenth-century Brown apologists, such as Sanborn and James Redpath, are no longer widely read, the eloquent praises of Emerson and Thoreau have been incorporated into the body of their country's great literature" (p. 726).

"After the Death of John Brown" (W, IV, 451–54) was delivered by Thoreau at the memorial services for Brown held in Concord the day Brown was hanged, December 2, 1859. Except as a further indication of Thoreau's interest in Brown, the essay has little value. The closing passages are a few paragraphs from Thoreau's own translation of Tacitus.

"The Last Days of John Brown" (W, IV, 441–50) was written for the memorial services held in North Elba, New York, on July 4, 1860, at the time of John Brown's burial there. It was derived almost entirely from Thoreau's *Journal* for November and December, 1859. Thoreau was unable to make the trip to North Elba, and the paper was read for him. It was printed in Garrison's *Liberator* for July 27, 1860. Like the earlier "Plea," it is a passionate defense of John Brown and his actions. It is of interest to students of Thoreau's mind because for the first time he publicly abandoned his Transcendentalist belief that all men are innately good, with the remark, "I have known many a man who pretended to be a Christian, in whom it was ridiculous, for he had no genius for it" (p. 445). As Wendell Glick has pointed out, with the John Brown episode Thoreau adopted the principles William Lloyd Garrison had argued for in his war against slavery some years before.

"The Succession of Forest Trees" (W, V, 184–204) was first delivered as an address before the Middlesex Agricultural Society in Concord in September, 1860, and first printed in the *New York Tribune* for October 6, 1860. It is derived from the *Journal* for the period from 1852 to 1860. As Thoreau tells us, "I have often been asked, as many of you have been, if I could tell how it happened that when a pine wood was cut down an oak one commonly sprang up, and *vice versa*" (p. 185). His answer is his major contribution to scientific knowledge. "While Thoreau can not be said to have introduced the subject to science, it appears that no important studies of ecological succession were made in America for more than thirty years after his memorable lecture" (Deevey, p. 8). And when Kathryn Whitford compared his findings with a modern study made with the benefit of the development of the science of ecology in the intervening years, she found, "The similarities are too great to be obscured even by the changes which more than eighty years have made in the vocabulary of science" (p. 299). Thoreau did not discover the principle of tree succession. He himself in his essay does not hesitate to give credit for some of his ideas to William Bartram and to Loudon. (Although Thoreau does not mention it, despite the fact that he was familiar with the book, there is a further suggestion of the principle in Timothy Dwight's *Travels in New England and New York*, II, 440.) Thoreau's was the first well-formulated presentation of the idea, yet it took modern science eighty years to recognize his contribution.

The ideas behind Thoreau's "Succession of Forest Trees" grew out of his almost daily contact with wood lots as a professional surveyor. In serving as a surveyor, Thoreau "had so far yielded to expediency as to become an important instrument in the very destruction [of Concord's forests] which he necessarily regretted" (Stoller, p. 93), for surveyors were most frequently called in when a farmer was about to cut his wood lot. But "the significance of

Thoreau's silvical investigations is that they led to a reconciliation of these contradictory strains in his attitude to the forest. His
discovery of the mechanism of succession pointed to a system of
forest management which would yield lumber and profit to satisfy
man's grosser instincts and at the same time preserve nature for
the disciplining of his spirit" (p. 96).

Although the essay is scientifically accurate, it is filled with
witticisms and sly humor. Thoreau admits to his neighbors that
he is a man "distinguished for his oddity" (p. 184). And he closes
with an amusing tale of his squash that had won first prize at the
Agricultural Society fair in 1857. But his audience recognized its
value and the society's president congratulated him on "an address so plain and practical, and at the same time showing such
close observation, and careful study of natural phenomena." The
society printed the essay in its *Transactions* for 1860, and it was
reprinted (in "expurgated" form) in the *Eighth Annual Report
of the Secretary of the Massachusetts Board of Agriculture* for the
same year.

Although "Walking" (W, V, 205–48) was not published until
June, 1862, in the *Atlantic Monthly,* a month after Thoreau died,
most of the material in it was taken from his *Journal* of the years
1850–1852. He used it frequently as a lecture in 1851 and 1852
and again in 1856 and 1857, although by the time of the latter lectures, according to his letter to Blake of December 31, 1856, he
had split it into two. He then apparently revised it in the last
months of his life and submitted it to the *Atlantic* on March 11,
1862, suggesting that it could, if necessary, be again split into two
papers.

It is the least organized of his shorter works and might well
have been improved by having been split. The first portion (to
p. 224) is a delightful essay on the joys of walking, beginning with
a fanciful etymology of the term and then extolling the virtues
of spending a goodly portion of each day exploring the countryside. At times it becomes almost chauvinistic in boasting the superiority of the American landscape to the European. Thoreau
discovers that he inevitably settles upon a southwestward course
for most of his walks (p. 217) and looks upon it as a subconscious
vindication of "Westward the star of empire takes its way." But

as Raymond Adams has suggested to me, it is more simply explained by the fact that in Thoreau's native Concord all the best walking territory is southwest of the town.

The second part of the paper is an essay on "the Wild," in which Thoreau expatiates on the need of civilized men to return to nature now and then for "nourishment and vigor" (p. 225). The last few pages are a highly miscellaneous conglomeration of barely related paragraphs, but he closes with the same image he uses in the final paragraphs of *A Week, Walden,* and "Civil Disobedience": This is the dawn of a new morning. There will be "a great awakening light, as warm and serene and golden as on a bankside in autumn" (p. 248). Perhaps next to "Life Without Principle," "Walking" is the best brief exposition of Thoreau's philosophy, although it lacks the trenchancy of the former essay.

"Autumnal Tints" (W, V, 249–89), though used as a lecture as early as 1859 and derived from the *Journal* for 1851–1858, was not published until October, 1862, in the *Atlantic Monthly.* It is another of the essays Thoreau revised for publication in the last months of his life and, in this case, according to his March 11, 1862, letter to Ticknor & Fields, he was able to correct the proofs before his death. In the *Atlantic* the essay was illustrated with an engraving of a scarlet oak leaf that Thoreau submitted to the editors; this was omitted in book publication.

In his own words, it is an attempt "to describe all these bright tints [of autumn foliage] in the order in which they present themselves" (p. 251). The various trees and grasses are described in what borders on "rich, beautiful prose," and the essay lacks the pungency and wit of most of his other works. In his *Journal* (XVII, 457) he complained that his audience thought he had assumed that "they had not seen so much of them [the autumnal colors] as they had." And the essay does at times have a somewhat superior air. Along with "Night and Moonlight," "Wild Apples," "Life Without Principle," and "Walking," this essay was culled from his *Journals* of the early 1850's, but in revising them he changed the tone from discouragement to satisfaction (Seybold, pp. 86–87).

"Wild Apples" (W, V, 290–322) is Thoreau's most successful attempt at the familiar essay. It was delivered originally as a lecture before the Concord Lyceum on February 8, 1860, with exceptional success. It was considered the best lecture of the season and was followed by "long, continued applause" (Marble, p. 155). Most of it was derived from the *Journal* for 1850–1852, although there are also excerpts from the *Journal* for 1857–1860. He continued to revise it, however, as is indicated by his mentioning seeing the wild crab apple in Minnesota in 1861 (p. 301), and it was not published until November, 1862, in the *Atlantic Monthly*.

He traces the history of the apple from the Garden of Eden to his own back yard, and from the seed to the fruit, and he launches into a facetious catalogue of imaginary species that includes some of his best wordplay. The whole essay is marked by a whimsical humor, and his description of the fight of the wild apple for survival from the browsing of the cows is not only vivid writing but good natural history. Underlying the whole essay is Thoreau's basic philosophy: we get from nature only what we give. Although (or perhaps because) it lacks the sturdiness of most of his best writing, it has been one of his most frequently anthologized essays.

"Life Without Principle" (W, IV, 455–82) was published October, 1863, in the *Atlantic Monthly*, more than a year after Thoreau's death. It was another of the essays he readied for publication in his last months. But the nucleus of the paper was written many years before in his *Journal* for 1851–1855, and was delivered as a lecture, under the title "Getting a Living," at least as early as 1854. He also occasionally titled it as a lecture "What Shall It Profit [a Man If He Gain the Whole World But Lose His Own Soul]?"

It is perhaps the most central to Thoreau's philosophy of all his shorter essays and contains virtually all the fundamental principles upon which he based his life. It is too highly concentrated to be accurately condensed, but basically it is his essay on "Self-reliance." He asks us to get down to fundamental principles in life and not to be led astray by our neighbors, our nation, our churches, public opinion, the desire for wealth, or any other diverting influence. It is pure Transcendentalism, advocating that the good life be discovered within oneself. Like his other major writings, it ends with the morning symbol (p. 482) that we are at the dawn of a new day.

In this essay Thoreau is writing at his highest level, not only in content but also in style. It is filled with some of his most memorable phrases. Perhaps it is too highly concentrated to make a good introduction to his writings, but it ties together all his fundamental principles better than any other brief work.

"Night and Moonlight" (W, V, 323–36) was another essay culled from his *Journal* (chiefly from the years 1851–1852 and 1854–1855) by Thoreau, probably shortly before his death, and first published in the *Atlantic Monthly* for November, 1863. A longer version, not so well unified, and toward the end degenerating into miscellaneous sentences and paragraphs strung together, was edited by Francis H. Allen and published in 1927 as *The Moon* (Boston). Neither version is particularly remarkable as a whole, although each contains a few sentences of effective nature writing. Basically they are effusions on the beauties of a moonlit night.

The Maine Woods (W, III) was the second book to be published after Thoreau's death. (*Excursions,* a collection of his travel essays, had appeared in 1863.) Edited by his friend Ellery Channing, it appeared in 1864. Its text was derived from two magazine articles, "Ktaadn and the Maine Woods," which had appeared serially in the *Union Magazine* from July through November, 1848, and "Chesuncook," which had appeared serially in the *Atlantic Monthly* from June through August, 1858, and an unpublished manuscript, "The Allegash and the East Branch," which Thoreau had been working on at the time of his death. "Ktaadn" was derived chiefly from the *Journal* for 1847, which, although still extant, has never been published. "Chesuncook" follows the *Journal* of 1853 so closely that it has been omitted from the printed version (see J, V, 424, 456), but also includes selections from the *Journal* as early as 1850 and as late as 1858. "Allegash" follows the *Journal* of 1857 so closely that it too has been omitted from the printed version (J, IX, 485; X, 53). Thoreau had used some of this material for lectures: a portion from "Ktaadn" in January, 1848; from "Chesuncook" on December 14, 1853; and a portion of "Allegash" on February 25, 1858.

That *The Maine Woods* is not a well-integrated book but a

collection of three separate essays is obvious. The essays are frequently repetitive, and Thoreau makes explanations in the latter two which are not necessary after reading the first (for example, his definition of a "pokelogan" on p. 109, which has already been amply defined on p. 56, and his explanation that foreigners were not permitted to shoot moose, which is given on both p. 152 and p. 231), although there is some evidence that in preparing the third essay he was attempting to integrate the three (for example, his reference on p. 187 to the Indian definition of "Musketicook" given on p. 157). But it should be remembered that Thoreau died before he completed the task of editing these Maine papers.

The third paper was carelessly edited by Channing (as, for example, the misprinting of *albicola* for *albeola* in the appendix, which has been corrected in most later editions).

The book is based on three separate expeditions to the Maine woods by Thoreau with various companions: "Ktaadn" on one taken in August and September, 1846 (while he was at Walden), with his cousin George Thatcher, two friends from Bangor, and two boatmen; "Chesuncook," September, 1853, with Thatcher; and "Allegash and East Branch," with Edward Hoar of Concord, July and August, 1857. The basic form is a series of travel letters such as frequently appeared in the periodicals of Thoreau's time. In the "Allegash" section each separate day's excursion is headed by its date, but the dates have been omitted in the first two chapters, perhaps because, as Thoreau suggested in his letter to James Russell Lowell of January 23, 1858, when he submitted "Chesuncook" for publication in the *Atlantic,* the essays would otherwise appear out of date for periodical publication.

As Thoreau states in "Chesuncook" (p. 105), he went to the Maine woods primarily to study at first hand the "ways" of the Indian. The Indian community at Oldtown, Maine, was well known and the fact that Thoreau's cousins lived in nearby Bangor gave him a convenient base for operations. Although on his first expedition the Indian Louis Neptune failed to keep his promise to act as a guide and Thoreau had to turn to a white man, on the second and third trips he had able Indian guides in the persons of Joe Aitteon and Joe Polis respectively. And as Emerson pointed out in his funeral address, Polis made a particularly strong impression on Thoreau. With Polis, Thoreau made an agreement: "I would tell him all I knew, and he should tell me all he knew" (p. 186), and apparently he made a similar agreement with Aitteon, for the book is a gold mine of Indian lore and terminology, and he includes a six-page appendix of Indian words.

As usual, Thoreau read carefully in the literature of the area before making his expeditions. The book is filled with allusions to and quotations from such volumes as John Springer's *Forest Life and Forest Trees* (New York, 1851) and C. T. Jackson's various reports on the public lands of Maine; from naturalists such as André Michaux and such early historians as John Josselyn. His quotations however are far more carefully integrated into his text than they are in *Cape Cod*.

Thoreau records much about the natural history of the area and includes in his appendix lists of the trees, flowers and shrubs, plants, birds, and quadrupeds. However, these lists are somewhat inaccurate (Eckstorm, pp. 245–46).

Although this volume is supposedly one of those upon which Thoreau worked in the last years of his life to remove the humor because he could not "bear the levity" he found, there is still much punning, exaggeration, and even slapstick comedy.

There is comparatively little social criticism in the volume, although Thoreau does make a few remarks about the carelessness with which forests are harvested by the lumberers and sets up an ideal for conservation (p. 173). As usual, he cannot resist making a few gibes at the religiously orthodox and is a little irritated when his Indian guide wishes to rest on Sundays. One particular sentence about a pine tree ("It is as immortal as I am, and perchance will go to as high a heaven, there to tower above me still") so offended James Russell Lowell that he deleted it before "Chesuncook" appeared in the *Atlantic,* and so brought Thoreau's wrath down upon his head. But the sentence was restored in the book (p. 135).

Most surprising to those who think of Thoreau as an escapist from civilization are his numerous comments on the loneliness of the wilderness and his remark at the end of "Chesuncook," in which he said, "It was a relief to get back to our smooth but still varied landscape. For a permanent residence, it seemed to me that there could be no comparison between this and the wilderness" (p. 171).

Altogether, *The Maine Woods* is by no means Thoreau's best book, even though Canby (p. 373) describes it as his "most normal," yet certainly it does not deserve Robert Louis Stevenson's curt dismissal of it as "not literature." Thoreau captures the atmosphere of the coniferous forest, tells his story vividly (even though not very profoundly) and with a sense of humor, and very rarely bogs down in detail, as he does in some of his other works.

Cape Cod (W, IV) is Thoreau's sunniest book—and least profound. It provides perhaps the best introduction to his writings for those who are frightened by the "chanticleer crowing" of *Walden.* Like *The Maine Woods,* it was posthumously edited (by Ellery Channing and Sophia Thoreau) and published in 1864. It was based on excursions he had made to Cape Cod in October, 1849, June, 1850, and July, 1855, the first and last times with Ellery Channing and the second time alone. A fourth excursion, alone, in June 1857, is recounted in his *Journal,* but is not included in *Cape Cod.*

Comparatively little of *Cape Cod* still shows up in the *Journal,* although there are occasional extracts from 1850 to 1855. Thoreau had used his first excursion (and possibly his second) as the basis for lectures on Cape Cod before the lyceums in Concord, Danvers, and Clinton in 1850 and 1851. They were among his most successful lectures, and Emerson (in his February 6, 1850 letter to Thoreau) reported of one, that he heard "that Concord people laughed till they cried, when it was read to them." Portions of *Cape Cod* appeared in *Putnam's Monthly Magazine* for June, July, and August, 1855, and more was to have appeared, but the editor objected to "its tone towards the people of that region" (Francis Allen, *Bibliography,* p. 71). Still later, after Thoreau's death and immediately before its book publication, two chapters appeared in the *Atlantic Monthly* for October and December, 1864.

Basically it is a much better integrated book than *The Maine Woods.* Using the first excursion as an outline for his book, Thoreau inserts into the narrative incidents from the two later ones so skillfully that one is hardly aware of the transition. Nonetheless, as the editors of the Walden Edition point out (p. ix), "It should be borne in mind by the reader that a considerable part of this book never received its final revision at the hands of its author." Its greatest weakness is that it contains too much undigested historical source material, particularly in the final chapter (pp. 226 ff.), where there are pages and pages of quotations from early histories of Cape Cod. Thoreau evidently recognized this weakness, for when portions of the book were serialized in *Putnam's,* he wrote the editor, George William Curtis, on November 16, 1852, that he was "in doubt about the extracts" and advised Curtis he could omit them or print them in smaller type. A further indication of the unfinished state of the book lies in the note that Thoreau apparently wrote to remind himself to look up further source material, which is included as a part of the regular text (p. 199). Another weakness is that Thoreau felt impelled to intersperse the narrative with quotations in Greek. He excuses himself with the statement, "I put in a little Greek now and then, partly because it sounds so much like the ocean" (p. 67). The reaction of the modern reader is more likely to be that it was ostentation that motivated Thoreau—a charge that can rarely be brought against him.

But despite these weaknesses, *Cape Cod* is a delightful book. The humor fairly bubbles over in puns, and in anecdotes. A primary value lies in its depiction of Cape Cod before the present-day tourist invasion. Here we meet the retired sea captains, the widows, the village characters. We see the men sailing out to catch mackerel, the wives drying fish in their yards. We get accurate descriptions of the then rapidly disappearing saltworks and the newly developed cranberry industry. We learn of the battles with the storms at sea and with the sand at home. We find vivid descriptions of the flora and fauna of the area, usually better integrated than the catalogues in *The Maine Woods.* The account of the dwarf forests on the sand dunes on the tip of the cape is particularly memorable. His note that he discovered broccoli in the Wellfleet oysterman's garden (p. 100) is often cited as the earliest incidence of that plant in North America.

Although there is comparatively little social criticism, Thoreau does not miss the opportunity to take an occasional crack at the otherworldliness of the clergy, at the proneness of the natives to make an extra dollar at the expense of shipwrecked mariners, and at the habits of the men wasting their time in barrooms and taverns. But there is a saving grace in his seeing the funny side of his own appearance, and he is greatly amused when he is mistaken for a robber who had recently raided a bank in Provincetown. He even laughs at the dullness of one of his chapters and ends it with the comment, "There was no better way to make the reader realize how wide and peculiar that plain [Nauset Plain] was, and how long it took to transverse it, than by inserting these extracts in the midst of my narrative" (p. 56).

Thoreau, as usual, prepared himself well in advance with a reading of all the literature on the area he could discover. In fact, he carried along with him in his pack a gazetteer and a volume of historical collections. As I have already indicated, the book is filled with references to most of the histories of the area, from the accounts of the Norse explorers, Champlain, John Smith, the Pilgrims, and Timothy Dwight. He also reread the Cape Cod portions of the various Massachusetts natural history reports that he had reviewed some years earlier in the *Dial*.

But it is when he weans himself from these source books that Thoreau is at his best in *Cape Cod*. He writes pungent, trenchant prose in which you can "hear the sea roar, as if I lived in a shell" (p. 269). A vivid indication of the memorableness of his prose was pointed out by the *New Yorker* some years ago when it demonstrated that Robert Lowell in his Pulitzer Prize-winning "Quaker Graveyard in Nantucket" echoes word for word a lengthy passage from *Cape Cod* (pp. 6–7).

Thoreau "did not intend this for a sentimental journey" (p. 78). He portrayed Cape Cod as he saw it, omitting none of its barrenness in its physical features or in the lives of its inhabitants, but always describing it with a sense of humor. It stands, and long will continue to stand, as *the* book about Cape Cod.

Shortly after Thoreau's death, his sister Sophia asked his Worcester friend, H. G. O. Blake, to collect and edit an edition of his letters (*Daniel Ricketson and His Friends,* p. 159). When Blake refused, Emerson was asked. *Letters to Various Persons* (Boston, 1865), the resulting volume, is far from satisfactory. Since Emerson wished to emphasize Thoreau's stoic qualities, he was highly selective. He deleted many personal references and those portions of the letters that would have shown Thoreau's warmth and friendliness. When Sophia Thoreau saw the manuscript, she protested to the publisher and insisted certain passages be restored. A compromise was worked out that satisfied neither. Emerson complained that the "perfect Stoicism" of the volume had been marred and Sophia Thoreau felt that her brother had been misrepresented.

In 1894 Sanborn brought out a new edition entitled *Familiar Letters*. Although in his preface he denounced Emerson's editing, Sanborn committed even greater crimes himself. He included many more letters and restored the names and many of the expurgated passages of the Emerson edition, but he revised the punctuation, spelling, and even the wording to suit his own taste and was extremely careless in dating and annotating the letters.

Since 1894 numerous new letters have come to light. Carl Bode and I have published a new edition that includes all the known letters, based wherever possible on the original manuscripts. It also includes letters written to Thoreau. Thoreau was no Horace Walpole in either the quantity or the quality of his letters. Nonetheless, they contain some of his best writing and add to our understanding of the man and of his times.

Thoreau can hardly be considered a major poet. His *Collected Poems* contains more than two hundred, yet the number of significant poems which he wrote can be numbered on the fingers of both hands, if not of one. And rare is the anthology of American poetry that bothers to include more than two or three.

Early in his writing career Thoreau apparently thought of himself primarily as a poet. But as the years passed, he turned more and more consistently to prose. One major factor was undoubtedly Emerson's negative criticism of some of his verse, which led him at one point to burn many of his manuscript poems—an act he was later to regret. But he is joined in this regret by few others, for the simple fact is that most of his poetry is bad poetry. Much of it deserves no better name than doggerel. When it is regular, it is singsong; when it is free verse, there seems little point to the freedom. His diction is often archaic. He can commit such atrocious rhymes as "Venice" and "fen is" (p. 8), or, even worse, such a couplet as

> *I love a life whose plot is simple,*
> *And does not thicken with every pimple.* (p. 42)

But there is little point to belaboring his bad poetry. It must also be acknowledged that he did write a few good poems. The best of these are probably the nature odes, "Smoke" (p. 27), "Fog" (p. 56), and "Haze" (p. 59), all of which he himself felt worthy of including in either *A Week* or *Walden*. They are Grecian in form and mood. Emerson said of the first that it "suggests Simonides, but is better than any poem of Simonides," and the same praise might well be given to the others.

Other notable and popular poems include "My Prayer" (p. 10), "A Gentle Boy" (pp. 64–66), written about Edmund Sewall and not his sister Ellen, as some have suggested, "Sic Vita" (pp. 81–82), and "Inspiration" (pp. 230–33). The last, especially in its central stanzas beginning

> *I hearing get who had but ears,*
> *And sight, who had but eyes before,*

is one of the best expositions of the Transcendental experience in all Thoreau's writings.

Henry Wells, in the only lengthy discussion of Thoreau's poetry, discerns the influence of many schools of poetry from medieval times to Thoreau's own, and even anticipations of twentieth-century poetry. Strangely enough, Thoreau imitated most frequently either Skelton or the seventeenth-century metaphysical poets, none of whom were popular in his day. "Scarcely a single poem from his hand can be associated with American fashions soon to be securely established by Longfellow, Whittier, and Lowell" (p. 100).

Perhaps the greatest value of his poetry is that it often presents in epitomized form those ideas he expounded at greater length in his prose. Thus,

> *Tell Shakespeare to attend some leisure hour,*
> *For now I've business with this drop of dew.* (p. 76)

or

> *He's governed well who rules himself,*
> *No despot vetoes him.* (p. 199)

Thoreau's best poetry, paradoxically enough, as Harry Lee and

Langley Keyes have demonstrated in their biographies in poetry, is in his poetic prose.

In 1905 the Bibliophile Society of Boston issued *The First and Last Journeys of Thoreau* in a limited edition edited by Sanborn. Its source was described as some unpublished fragments "lately discovered among his unpublished journals and manuscripts." (At least some of the material Sanborn used is now part of HM 13182 in Huntington Library.) The book shows every sign of Sanborn's tampering and revision. A highly miscellaneous group of manuscripts is included, and these are tossed about with little regard for chronological (or any other) order. Because the volumes give hitherto unpublished portions of early drafts of *A Week* and the only detailed account of Thoreau's journey to Minnesota, they could have been invaluable source material. But Sanborn's highhandedness puts all scholars into a quandary, and his editions can be used only with the greatest caution.

The first volume is made up of excerpts from the Ward family correspondence of 1839 (pp. 1–7); Thoreau's diary of his voyage on the Concord and Merrimack Rivers (pp. 7–62); excerpts from his *Journal* while on Staten Island in 1843 (pp. 63–113); a fragmentary essay on "Conversation" (pp. 113–17); and an appendix of *Journal* fragments and poems accompanied by facsimile reproductions of the manuscripts (pp. 121–46). The second volume is devoted to the trip to Minnesota and includes excerpts from his journey notebook, fragments of the Mann family correspondence, Thoreau's botanical lists for the journey, and excerpts from letters Thoreau wrote while in the West. The many faults and errors of this volume have been adequately pointed out by Evadene Burris Swanson.

I suppose it is better to have these manuscripts in print in this condition than not at all, since the first volume does shed a little light on the composition of *A Week* and the second records virtually all we know about the Minnesota journey. But they contain nothing that adds appreciably to Thoreau's stature as a writer and are of value only to the Thoreau specialist.

On October 22, 1837, just a few months after Thoreau graduated from Harvard, he purchased a blank notebook and entered on the first page, " 'What are you doing now?' he asked. 'Do you keep a journal?' So I make my first entry to-day" (J, I, 3). Thus, probably at Emerson's suggestion, he began a task that was to last a lifetime, for nearly every day until a few months before his death he faithfully entered his thoughts into his journal, occasionally only a brief entry, such as "Went to Boston," but more frequently a page or two pages, or even five or six, recording his thoughts, beliefs, and aspirations, to a final total of about two million words.

Thoreau, originally at least, had no intention of publishing his *Journal*. " 'Says I to myself' should be the motto of my journal," he wrote in it on November 11, 1851 (J, III, 107). But others thought otherwise. In 1853 Emerson hired Ellery Channing to compile a volume of excerpts from the journals of Emerson, Channing, and Thoreau, to be entitled *Country Walking*. But that effort died a-borning. Sometime after Thoreau's death, when Thomas Wentworth Higginson "endeavored to enlist Judge Hoar, the leading citizen of Concord, in an effort to persuade Miss [Sophia] Thoreau to allow her brother's journals to be printed, he heard me partly through, and then quickly said, 'But you have left unsettled the preliminary question, Why should any one care to have Thoreau's journals put in print?' " (*Cheerful Yesterdays*, p. 170.)

As early as 1872 Bronson Alcott suggested (in his *Concord Days*, p. 264) that "A delightful volume might be compiled from Thoreau's Journals by selecting what he wrote at a certain date annually, thus giving a calendar of his thoughts on that day from year to year." And it was this plan Thoreau's Worcester friend, H. G. O. Blake, who had inherited the manuscript journals from Sophia Thoreau, followed when he issued *Early Spring in Massachusetts* (Boston, 1881). So immediate was the success of this volume that he followed it with *Summer* in 1884, *Winter* in 1888, and *Autumn* in 1892. Unfortunately, Blake's selections gave no really adequate indication of the content of the *Journal* as a whole since they concentrated almost entirely on Thoreau's nature writing. Nonetheless, they served their purpose in stimulating interest and paved the way for publication of the full *Journal*.

It was in 1906 that Houghton Mifflin issued the so-called "complete" *Journal*, in an edition of fourteen volumes, as part of the twenty-volume Manuscript or Walden Edition of Thoreau's works

(J, I–XIV). Although the title page assigns the credit for editing the *Journal* to the then well-known nature writer Bradford Torrey, most of the work was done by Francis Allen, of the Houghton Mifflin staff. (When the *Journal* was reissued in 1949, Allen at long last received the credit he deserved of having his name appear on the title page.) The work of transcription and editing was no easy task, as anyone who has worked with Thoreau's manuscripts will quickly concede. But the editors proceeded carefully and conscientiously. The editorial practices they followed are stated in their preface (J, I, vii–ix; xiii–xiv in the 1949 reprint).

The printed *Journal* as it now stands is, however, not complete. As the editors indicate in their preface, they have omitted long quotations, certain of the Maine woods material, which was incorporated in *The Maine Woods,* and some extended lists of plants. In a later footnote (J, XII, 219n) they acknowledge the omission of many tables and charts of the river's depth made by Thoreau for the dam controversy of 1859. And occasionally they omit a proper name "out of regard for the feelings of possible relatives or descendants of the persons mentioned." More questionable is the fact, pointed out by Perry Miller in *Consciousness in Concord,* that they were lamentably inconsistent in recording Thoreau's editorial revisions.

More important, however, is the fact that two early volumes of the *Journal* were not available to the editors. The first of these covers the period from July 30, 1840, to January 22, 1841, and consists of more than 16,000 words. This volume was available to Blake, and he used nearly two-thirds of it in his seasonal volumes. However, he omits important material shedding further light on Thoreau's romance with Ellen Sewall. Fortunately this volume has recently been acquired by the Morgan Library and edited by Perry Miller as *Consciousness in Concord.* Miller, in his introduction and footnotes, has made a very worth-while study of Thoreau's editorial technique. The second volume, covering part of the year 1846, consists of more than 42,000 words. It is devoted chiefly to the first trip to Maine. This volume is now in the New York Public Library and it is to be hoped that it will eventually be published.

Still another omission is the "Supplement" to the *Journal,* apparently a volume filled with pertinent clippings, which Thoreau mentions (J, XII, 439). I have been unable to discover if it is extant. It is doubtful in any case if it would be worth publishing, but it might prove helpful to scholars studying Thoreau's sources.

There also exist many pages of rough drafts of *Journal* material, drafts Thoreau made before entering his fair copy into the bound volumes. Most of these that I have seen differ only slightly, if at all, from the fair copy. Although they offer an interesting opportunity to study Thoreau's methods of composition, they are now unfortunately so widely scattered in private collections and in libraries that it would be virtually impossible to reassemble any large number of them.

Finally, the text of the first fourteen years of the *Journal* (that is, from 1837 to 1850) is Thoreau's own condensation of the much longer original, which no longer exists. As I have pointed out above, Thoreau used his *Journal* as a mine from which to extract material for his essays and books. Although in later years he usually simply drew a line through the *Journal* version to be sure that he didn't extract it again for another essay, in the earlier years he scissored it out. Eventually the original evidently became so mutilated that he copied what was left and, I suspect, edited still further material he thought not worth the copying. This editing may account for the lack of lists of species of birds, flowers, and so forth, in the *Journal* before 1850. The meat of the scissored-out fragments is, of course, not completely lost. It may be found woven into the pages of *A Week, Walden, The Service, Sir Walter Raleigh,* and other early writings.

It is virtually impossible in a few words to summarize the contents of the *Journal*. As Thoreau himself said, the ideas for it came "from all points of the compass, from the earth beneath and the heavens above" (J, I, 413). The first volume is in large part simply a commonplace book, filled with favorite quotations from his reading, alternated with Transcendental aphorisms in the vein of Bronson Alcott's "Orphic Sayings." William Drake says: "The striking thing about his own early work is the preponderance not of observed fact but of highly generalized speculation" (*A Formal Study of Thoreau,* p. 4). There is comparatively little nature writing in these pages, although what there is occasionally equals the best writing of his later years. Here too are embedded

many of his poems and drafts of some of his early lectures for the
Concord Lyceum.

From 1850 on we find a quite different work. It is "one of the
most complete records extant of the inner life of an individual"
(Canby, p. 79). Late in 1857 Thoreau wrote: "Is not the poet
bound to write his own biography? Is there any other work for
him but a good journal? We do not wish to know how his imaginary hero, but how he, the actual hero, lived from day to day"
(J, X, 115). Such a record of himself Thoreau presents in his
Journal. It reports "all his joy, his ecstasy" (J, IV, 223). There are
still occasional quotations from his reading, a few aphorisms, and
numerous lists of natural phenomena (these latter increasing
noticeably as the years progress), but there are also added many
character sketches of his neighbors and, most important of all,
a remarkably full record of his thoughts on man, life, society, and
government. When the full *Journal* was published in 1906, many
critics expressed their amazement that so large a portion of the
work was thus devoted to his thoughts. They had considered him
primarily a nature writer; now they discovered that he was more
fundamentally a thinker. It is surprising that with all the research
on Thoreau in the past half century, and with all this primary
material available in the *Journal,* no one has embarked on a serious study of the development of Thoreau's mind. Many have
winnowed out anthologies of his comments on birds or music or
ferns or his neighbors, but no one has attempted to study the man
as a whole through his *Journal*. That is the greatest need of Thoreau research today.

There are still a good many unpublished Thoreau manuscripts
extant, but few, if any, of them are of interest to anyone other
than the specialist. Thoreau's surveying papers are in the Concord
Free Public Library. Many pages of nature notes are scattered
in various libraries and private collections. The Canadian notebooks are in the Morgan Library. Other miscellaneous items are
scattered elsewhere.

Thoreau's commonplace books are a different story. Throughout his life he kept large notebooks of extracts from his reading
and then used many of them in his writing. None of these com-

monplace books has been published, and yet they afford basic research material for a study of his sources. They include the "Index Rerum" and the 1841–1873 Notebook (it was used after Thoreau's death by his sister Sophia) at Huntington Library, eleven volumes of Indian notes and a volume of miscellaneous extracts at the Morgan Library, a Literary Notebook at The Library of Congress, a volume of extracts, mostly on natural history at the Berg Collection and another (sometimes referred to as the "Fact-Book") at Harvard, and finally a volume of extracts from early English authors and Oriental authors, which is now in private hands.

SOURCES FOR CHAPTER TWO

The standard edition of Thoreau's works is the Manuscript Edition of *The Writings of Thoreau* (Boston, 1906, 20 vols.). The Walden Edition (also Boston, 1906, 20 vols.) is printed from the same plates. In 1949 the last fourteen volumes of this set were reissued as *The Journal of Thoreau* (Boston) and were printed from the same plates.

The second best edition is the Riverside Edition (Boston, 1893, 10 vols.), with an eleventh volume added in 1894. It omits the complete *Journal* but includes in its stead the four volumes of seasonal selections from the *Journal* edited by H. G. O. Blake. The Concord Edition (Boston, 1929, 5 vols.) was reprinted from the Riverside Edition.

There are many volumes of selections from Thoreau. Among the best are *The Works of Thoreau*, edited by H. S. Canby (Boston, 1937), reissued as the Cambridge Edition (Boston, 1948); *Walden and Other Writings of Henry David Thoreau*, edited by Brooks Atkinson (New York, 1937); *The Portable Thoreau*, edited by Carl Bode (New York, 1947); *Walden and Selected Essays*, edited by George F. Whicher (Chicago, 1947); *The Living Thoughts of Thoreau*, edited by Theodore Dreiser (New York, 1939); *Thoreau, Reporter of the Universe*, edited by Bertha Stevens (New York, 1939); *Thoreau: Representative Selections*, edited by Bartholow V. Crawford (New York, 1934); *Little Essays from the Works of Henry David Thoreau*, edited by Charles R. Murphy (Boston, 1931); *Thoreau: Philosopher of Freedom*, edited by James MacKaye (New York, 1930), and *Thoreau Today*, edited by Helen Barber Morrison (New York, 1957).

The best general commentary on the editing of Thoreau's writings is Francis H. Allen, *Thoreau's Editors: History and Reminiscence* (*TSB* VII).

Although Sanborn includes "The Seasons" in his 1917 biography of Thoreau (pp. 51–52), a more authoritative edition is that by E. B. Hill (Mesa, Ariz., 1916; reprinted Ysleta, Tex., 1940[?]). This has been reprinted in *ESQ* (IX, 1957, 4).

Twenty-seven of Thoreau's college essays have been printed in corrupt versions in Sanborn's 1917 biography of Thoreau (pp. 54–189) and one ("The Commercial Spirit") in *Familiar Letters* (pp. 8–10) in part. There is an accurate transcription of the twenty-ninth (on "Moral Excellence") in R. L. Cook, *Concord Saunterer* (pp. 60–61). Edwin I. Moser, "Henry David Thoreau: The College Essays" (New York University, M.A., 1951) gives accurate transcriptions for all those for which the manuscripts are still available (23), plus the remaining six derived from the Sanborn versions. Some enterprising publisher would do well to get Moser's work into print. Three of the book reviews are included in Wendell Glick, "Three New Early Manuscripts by Thoreau" (*HLQ*, XV, 1951, 59–71), and the fourth in Carl Bode, "A New College Manuscript of Thoreau's" (*AL*, XXI, 1949, 311–20). The best analysis of the college essays is Joseph Kwiat, "Thoreau's Philosophical Apprenticeship" (*NEQ*, XVIII, 1945, 51–69). Facsimile reproductions of and annotations on many of Thoreau's college writings are included in "Thoreau's Notes on Harvard Reading," in Kenneth Cameron, *The Transcendentalists and Minerva* (Hartford, Conn., 1958, pp. 130–358).

Cameron recently discovered "Died" and reprinted it with transcripts of two early drafts of the text in "Thoreau's Three Months Out of Harvard and His First Publication" (*ESQ*, V, 1956, 2–12).

The Service was edited by F. B. Sanborn (Boston, 1902). The manuscript and Sanborn's transcription are reprinted in Kenneth Cameron, *The Transcendentalists and Minerva* (Hartford, Conn., 1958, 935–70). F. O. Matthiessen gives a detailed analysis in *American Renaissance* (New York, 1941, 83 ff.).

A good discussion of the "Natural History of Massachusetts" may be found in Robert Welker, *Birds & Men* (Cambridge, Mass., 1955, p. 106).

For details of Thoreau's difficulties in collecting payment for

"A Walk to Wachusett," see his letters to Emerson of June 8 and August 7, 1843, and Emerson's letter to him of July 20, 1843.

For the background of Thoreau's translation of "The Prometheus Bound," see Ethel Seybold, *Thoreau: The Quest and the Classics* (New Haven, Conn., 1951); Leo Kaiser, "Remarks on Thoreau's Translation of the Prometheus" (*CW*, XLVI, 1953, 69–70); Walter Harding, "Thoreau's Professor Has His Say" (*TSB* 46); and Channing's 1902 biography (p. 50).

Sir Walter Raleigh was edited by F. B. Sanborn (Boston, 1905). Thoreau's literary criticism therein is discussed at length in chapter xii of Raymond Adams, "Henry Thoreau's Literary Theories and Criticism" (University of North Carolina, Ph.D., 1928).

Sherman Paul has written a brief but provocative analysis of "The Landlord" in "Thoreau's 'The Landlord'; 'Sublimely Trivial for the Good of Men' " (*JEGP*, LIV, 1955, 587–91).

Emerson's criticism of "A Winter Walk" may be found in his letter to Thoreau of September 8, 1843. An unpublished fragment of the essay will be found in *First and Last Journeys of Thoreau* (I, 142–46). Welker's observations are in *Birds & Men*.

When "Paradise (to be) Regained" was incorporated in Thoreau's works, it was considerably revised from the magazine version. Bartholow Crawford, *Thoreau: Representative Selections* (pp. 32–56), prints the original version and in his annotations (pp. 355–56) points out the revisions.

Francis H. Allen, "Thoreau's Translations from Pindar" (*TSB* 26), points out errors and omissions in the transcription of this work in the standard editions. "The Origin of Thera," included in the *Dial* (IV, 385), has for some inexplicable reason been dropped from the collected works.

For discussions of "Herald of Freedom," see Wendell Glick, "Thoreau and Radical Abolitionism" (Northwestern University, Ph.D., 1950) and Glick, "Thoreau and the 'Herald of Freedom' " (*NEQ*, XXII, 1949, 193–204).

The vicissitudes of publishing "Thomas Carlyle and His Works" are covered in the correspondence between Thoreau and Greeley from August 16, 1846, to May 17, 1848. A detailed analysis of the essay may be found in Raymond Adams, "Henry Thoreau's Literary Theories and Criticism" (chap. xi) and in Frederick W. Lorch, "Thoreau and the Organic Principle in Poetry" (*PMLA*, LIII,

1938, 300–302). When this essay was incorporated in Thoreau's works, it was considerably revised from the magazine version. Crawford, *Thoreau: Representative Selections,* points out the variations (pp. 186–215, 372–73).

Raymond Adams, " 'Civil Disobedience' Gets Printed" (*TSB* 28), gives the publishing history of Thoreau's essay. Adams, "Thoreau's Sources for 'Resistance to Civil Government' " (*SP,* XLII, 1945, 640–53), gives some of the sources but it is challenged by Wendell Glick, " 'Civil Disobedience': Thoreau's Attack upon Relativism" (*WHR,* VII, 1952, 35–42). Glick has further material in "Thoreau and Radical Abolitionism" (see above). Edward Larocque Tinker, "New Editions, Fine and Otherwise" (*The New York Times Book Review,* Mar. 29, 1942), suggests another source. John C. Broderick, "Thoreau, Alcott, and the Poll Tax" (*SP,* LIII, 1956, 612–26), gives a full historical background for the essay. Samuel Arthur Jones, "Thoreau's Incarceration" (*Inlander,* IX, 1898, 96–103, reprinted in *TSB* IV), gives the fullest account of Thoreau's arrest. Two favorable discussions of the practicality of Thoreau's ideas are John Haynes Holmes, "Thoreau's 'Civil Disobedience' " (*Christian Century,* LXVI, 1949, 787–89) and Walter Harding, "Thoreau: Pioneer of Civil Disobedience" (*Fellowship,* XII, 1945, 118 ff.). Two negative appraisals are C. Carroll Hollis, "Thoreau and the State" (*Commonweal,* L, 1949, 530–33) and Heinz Eulau, "Wayside Challenger: Some Remarks on the Politics of Henry David Thoreau" (*Antioch Review,* IX, 1950, 509–22).

One should note that there are between 1,200 and 1,300 changes (mostly minor) between the first edition of *A Week* and the 1868 edition, now considered standard. The edition edited by Odell Shepard (New York, 1921) has a particularly good introduction. The shortened version, *The Concord and the Merrimack,* edited by Dudley Lunt (Boston, 1954), has helpful notes and a detailed map. Another map can be found in Robert Stowell, *Thoreau Gazetteer* (Calais, Vt., 1948). Carl Hovde, "The Writing of Henry D. Thoreau's A Week on the Concord and Merrimack Rivers" (Princeton University, Ph.D., 1956), is the most thorough analysis of the book. It has been published in part as "Nature into Art: Thoreau's Use of His Journals in *A Week*" (*AL,* XXX, 1958, 165–84). E. E. Leisy, "Sources of Thoreau's Borrowings in *A*

Week" (*AL,* XVIII, 1946, 37–44), identifies most of the quotations in the book. James P. Wood, "Mr. Thoreau Writes a Book" (*New Colophon,* I, 1948, 367–76), is the fullest account of the first publication of *A Week.* Raymond Adams, "The Bibliographical History of Thoreau's *A Week on the Concord and Merrimack Rivers"* (*PBSA,* XLIII, 1949, 1–9), gives data on the various editions. Christopher McKee, "Thoreau's First Visit to the White Mountains" (*Appalachia,* XXXI, 1956, 199–209), fills in the details of the mountain-climbing interlude. Walter Harding, "The Influence of Thoreau's Lecturing upon His Writing" (*BNYPL,* LX, 1956, 74–80), presents an early draft of a portion of the manuscript.

Thoreau's translation of *The Transmigration of the Seven Brahmans* was edited by Arthur Christy (New York, 1932).

Thoreau's correspondence with Greeley about "A Yankee in Canada" and with Curtis about the censoring of it are summarized in W, V, xi–xii. Lawrence Willson, "The Influence of Early North American History and Legend on the Writings of Henry David Thoreau" (Yale University, Ph.D., 1944, pp. 175–81), discusses Thoreau's attitude toward the French in this essay. Two brief general discussions are Edmund Berry, "Thoreau in Canada" (*DR,* XXIII, 1943, 68–74), and Max Cosman, "A Yankee in Canada" (*CHR,* XXV, 1944, 33–37).

Wendell Glick, Thoreau and Radical Abolitionism (see above), discusses "Slavery in Massachusetts."

There is unfortunately no thoroughly annotated edition of *Walden,* although I have one under way which I hope someday to see in print. Francis Allen's edition (Boston, 1910) has the most helpful annotations to date. The best introduction, by far, is that by Sherman Paul (Boston, 1957). Thoreau's own suggested revisions of the text, many of which have never been included in any printed edition, are recorded in Reginald Cook, "Thoreau's Annotations and Corrections in the First Edition of *Walden"* (*TSB* 42). Scholars should use F. B. Sanborn's Bibliophile Society edition (Boston, 1909) with great care, even though it contains much material not in the regular editions. See M. E. Cryder, "An Examination of the Bibliophile Edition of Thoreau's Walden" (University of Chicago, M.A., 1920). J. Lyndon Shanley, *The Making of Walden* (Chicago, 1957), is an essential tool for anyone attempting to study the composition of the book; it supersedes his earlier "Study of the Making of *Walden*" (*HLQ,* XIV, 1951, 147–70). A helpful work is Joseph Jones, *Index to Walden* (Austin, Tex., 1955). A much more detailed word index is now being compiled by Richard Reynolds and J. Stephen Sherwin of the State University of New York. The following provide helpful annotations to particular sections of *Walden:* John H. Briss, "Thoreau and Thomas Carew" (*N&Q,* CLXIV, 63); Edith Peairs, "The Hound, the Bay Horse, and the Turtle-Dove: A Study of Thoreau and Voltaire" (*PMLA,* LII, 1937, 863–69); Frank Davidson, "Thoreau's Hound, Bay Horse, and Turtle-Dove" (*NEQ,* XXVII, 1954, 521–24); Kenneth Cameron, "Thoreau and the Folklore of Walden Pond" (*ESQ,* III, 1956, 10–12); Walter Harding, "The Apple-Tree Table Tale" (*BPLQ,* VIII, 1956, 213–15); T. Y. Davis, "The Death of Hugh Coyle" (*TSB* 33); Joseph Leach, "Thoreau's Borrowings in 'Walden' " (*American Notes & Queries,* II, 1943, 171); Edward Deevey, "A Re-examination of Thoreau's 'Walden' " (*Quarterly Review of Biology,* XVII, 1942, 1–11); Adrian Hayward, "The White Pond Tree" (*Nature Outlook,* IV, 1945, 29–36); and Howard Schultz, "A Fragment of Jacobean Song in Thoreau's *Walden*" (*MLN,* LXIII, 1948, 271–72). For analyses of the structure of *Walden,* see Shanley, *The Making of Walden;* William Drake, "A Formal Study of H. D. Thoreau" (University of Iowa, M.A., 1948, chap. v); Sherman Paul's introduction to his edition of *Walden;* and F. O. Matthiessen, *American Renaissance* (New York, 1941, pp. 168 ff.). For studies of imagery in *Walden,* see John Broderick, "Imagery in *Walden*" (*UTSE,* XXXIII, 1954, 80–89), and Stanley Hyman, "Henry Thoreau in Our Time" (*Atlantic,* CLXXVIII, 1946, 137–46). One of the best general discussions of *Walden* is Reginald Cook, "This Side of Walden" (*English Leaflet,* LII, 1954, 1–12). Others include Raymond Adams, "Thoreau at Walden" (*University of North Carolina Extension Bulletin,* XXIV, 1944, 9–22); Adams, "Thoreau's Growth at Walden" (*Christian Register,* CCXXIV, 1945, 268–70); Lewis Leary, "A Century of 'Walden' " (*Nation,* CLXXIX, 1954, 114–15); Sherman Paul, "Resolution at Walden" (*Accent,* XIII, 1953, 101–13); and E. B. White, "Walden—1954" (*YR,* XLIV, 1954, 13–22). Roland Robbins, *Discovery at Walden* (Stoneham, Mass.,

1947), gives a pleasant account of Robbins' archaeological work at Walden Pond. Walter Harding, *A Centennial Check-List of the Editions of Henry David Thoreau's Walden* (Charlottesville, Va., 1954), lists and describes 132 different editions. I am indebted to the editors of the *Colorado Quarterly* for permission to reprint in my discussion of *Walden* a portion of my "Century of Walden" (III, 1954, 186–99) and to the editors of the *Humanist* for permission to reprint a portion of my "Significance of Thoreau's Walden" (Autumn, 1945, 115–22).

For discussions of the John Brown essays, see Wendell Glick, Thoreau and Radical Abolitionism (see above); Gilman Ostrander, "Emerson, Thoreau, and John Brown" (*MVHR*, XXXIX, 1953, 713–26); Leo Stoller, "Thoreau and the Economic Order" (Columbia University, Ph.D., 1956, 169–203), published in revised form as *After Walden* (Stanford, Calif., 1957); F. B. Sanborn, *Recollections of Seventy Years* (Boston, 1909); and James Redpath, *Echoes of Harper's Ferry* (Boston, 1860). For a facsimile of the broadside announcing the meeting at Concord on December 2, 1859, see *TSB* 54.

We are fortunate in having a number of excellent studies of "The Succession of Forest Trees." They include Leo Stoller, "Thoreau and the Economic Order" (see above); Kathryn Whitford, "Thoreau and the Woodlots of Concord" (*NEQ*, XXIII, 1950, 291–306); and Edward Deevey, "A Re-Examination of Thoreau's 'Walden' " (see above).

For Thoreau's interest in "the Wild" ("Walking") see John Burroughs, "Thoreau's Wildness" (*Literary Values*, Boston, 1902, 197–202, *TCC*), and Howard Zahniser, "Thoreau and the Preservation of Wildness" (*TSB* 60).

The only annotated edition of *The Maine Woods* is that edited by Dudley Lunt (New York, 1950), which unfortunately takes great liberties in reorganizing the text. A map of the Maine journeys is available in Robert Stowell, *Thoreau Gazetteer* (see above; also in *TSB* 16). The most authoritative study of the book is Fannie Hardy Eckstorm, "Thoreau's 'Maine Woods' " (*Atlantic Monthly*, CII, 1908, 245–50, *TCC*). But see also Eckstorm, *The Penobscot Man* (Bangor, Me., 1924), Eckstorm, *Old John Neptune* (Portland, Me., 1945), and Eckstorm, "Notes on Thoreau's

'Maine Woods'" (*TSB* 51). John W. Worthington, "Thoreau's Route to Katahdin" (*Appalachia*, XXVI, 1946, 3–14), clears up some details of that trip.

By far the best edition of *Cape Cod* is that edited by Dudley Lunt (New York, 1951), for not only is it the only annotated edition but it is also the only one to append the *Journal* materials about the fourth journey. Lovers of fine books will appreciate the edition illustrated with water colors by Amelia Watson (Boston, 1896). A map of Thoreau's journeys is included in Robert Stowell, *Thoreau Gazetteer* (see above). Edward Hinckley disparages *Cape Cod* in "Thoreau and Beston: Two Observers of Cape Cod" (*NEQ*, IV, 1931, 216–29). See also "Preliminary Reading in Cape Cod Background (1848–1850)" in Kenneth Cameron, *The Transcendentalists and Minerva* (Hartford, Conn., 1958, 378–88), for Thoreau's source material.

The earliest edition of Thoreau's letters is *Letters to Various Persons*, edited by Ralph Waldo Emerson in 1865. A more inclusive edition is F. B. Sanborn, *Familiar Letters* (Boston, 1954), enlarged slightly as W, VI. I have discussed Sanborn's arbitrary editing of the letters in "Franklin B. Sanborn and Thoreau's Letters" (*BPLQ*, III, 1951, 288–93). Carl Bode and I have compiled "Henry David Thoreau: A Check List of His Correspondence" (*BNYPL*, LIX, 1955, 227–52). We have also edited *The Correspondence of Henry David Thoreau* (New York, 1958).

The earliest collection of Thoreau's poetry was F. B. Sanborn and Henry Salt, *Poems of Nature* (Boston, 1895). But this has been completely superseded by Carl Bode, *Collected Poems of Henry Thoreau* (Chicago, 1943). Students should be warned that two editions, a "critical edition" and one without notes, were issued at the same time. The "critical edition" is far superior. Francis Allen made some corrections of this text in "Thoreau's *Collected Poems*" (*AL*, XVII, 1945, 260–67) and Bode replied to Allen in "Rejoinder" (*AL*, XVII, 1945, 267–69). Further additions to the text were made in Kenneth Cameron, "Four Uncollected Thoreau Poems" (*ESQ*, V, 1956, 13–16). Henry Wells, "An Evaluation of Thoreau's Poetry" (*AL*, XVI, 1944, 99–109, *TCC*), has made the only lengthy critical study of the poems. William S. Thomas, in "Thoreau as His Own Editor" (*NEQ*, XV, 1942, 101–3), studies the genesis of one of the poems.

The First and Last Journeys of Thoreau was edited by F. B. Sanborn (Boston, 1905). Further studies of the Minnesota material therein can be found in John Flanagan, "Thoreau in Minnesota" *(MH*, XVI, 1935, 35–46); Robert L. Straker, "Thoreau's Journey to Minnesota" *(NEQ*, XIV, 1941, 549–55); and Evadene Swanson, "The Manuscript Journal of Thoreau's Last Journey" *(MH*, XX, 1939, 169–73). I am at the moment preparing for publication a verbatim transcription of the Minnesota journal.

The standard edition of the *Journal* is that in the fourteen volumes in the Manuscript and Walden editions (Boston, 1906), reprinted in 1949 (Boston). H. G. O. Blake printed many selections (some of which are not in the standard edition) in his four seasonal volumes *Early Spring In Massachusetts* (Boston, 1881), *Summer* (Boston, 1884), *Winter* (Boston, 1888), and *Autumn* (Boston, 1892). The "missing" volume for 1840–1841 has been edited by Perry Miller as *Consciousness in Concord* (Boston, 1958). Miller's introduction raises many thorny biographical problems which will have to be considered by any further biographer of Thoreau. "Contents of Thoreau's Lost Notebooks" in Kenneth Cameron, *The Transcendentalists and Minerva* (Hartford, Conn., 1958, pp. 883–86), reconstructs the indexes of the early lost volumes. There are also some ungathered fragments in *The First and Last Journeys of Thoreau* (see above). For the background of Ellery Channing's "Country Walking," see Rollo Silver, "Ellery Channing's Collaboration with Emerson" *(AL*, VII, 1935, 84–86) and Walter Harding, "Two F. B. Sanborn Letters" *(AL*, XXV, 1953, 230–34). There are many volumes of selections from the *Journal*. The best is Odell Shepard, *The Heart of Thoreau's Journal* (Boston, 1927). Francis H. Allen, *Men of Concord* (Boston, 1936), concentrates on Thoreau's comments on his fellow townsmen. Allen, *Notes on New England Birds* (Boston, 1910; reissued as *Thoreau's Bird-Lore*, Boston, 1925), is a handbook of Thoreau ornithology. Herbert Gleason, *Through the Year with Thoreau* (Boston, 1917), anthologizes many of the nature comments. Some of the notes on ferns have been gathered in "Fern Notes from Thoreau's Notebooks" *(Nature Study Review*, XIX, 1923, 187–93). The late William Thomas compiled a collection of Thoreau's comments on music that remains unpublished. Edwin Way Teale has made a compilation (also unpublished) of Thoreau's com-

ments on writing. Joseph Wade has gathered together many of
the entomological notes in "Some Insects of Thoreau's Writings"
(Journal of the New York Entomological Society, XXXV, 1927,
1–21). Francis Allen has gathered together Thoreau's notes on
fishes, batrachians, invertebrates, and reptiles, and they are on
deposit in the Thoreau Society Archives.

Catalogues of the major collections of Thoreau manuscripts include Abernethy Library, Viola White, "Check List of the Thoreau Items in the Abernethy Library," in Reginald Cook, *The
Concord Saunterer* (Middlebury, Vt., 1940), reprinted in White,
Check List: Abernethy Library of American Literature (Middlebury, Vt., 1940); see also White, "Teacher's Avocation" *(TSB*
13); for the Henry W. and Albert A. Berg Collection in the New
York Public Library, *TSB* 43; for the Concord Antiquarian Society, *TSB* 47; for Harvard University Library, *TSB* 43 and *TSB*
53; for Huntington Library, *TSB* 43; for the Pierpont Morgan
Library in New York City, *TSB* 19; for the Alfred Hosmer Collection in the Concord Free Public Library, Herbert Hosmer, *The
Thoreau Library of Alfred W. Hosmer* (Concord, Mass., 1949);
see also Raymond Adams, "Fred Hosmer, the 'Lerned Clerk'"
(TSB 36). Two large private collections, the Stephen H. Wake-
man Collection and the William Harris Arnold Collection, were
dispersed at public auctions in New York City in 1924. Their
catalogues contain many important details. The private collection
of Raymond Adams is listed in *The Thoreau Library of Raymond
Adams* (Chapel Hill, N. C., 1936) and its *Supplement* (Chapel
Hill, N. C., 1937). A small portion of the invaluable collection
of Albert Lownes, of Providence, Rhode Island, is listed in [Frank
Walters'] *Catalogue of a Collection of Books by or Pertaining to
Henry David Thoreau* (New York, n.d.). Arthur Christy, "A Thoreau Fact-Book" *(Colophon*, XVI, 1934), gives a detailed description of one of the commonplace books. All the commonplace
books are described in Anne Whaling, "Studies in Thoreau's
Reading of English Poetry and Prose" (Yale University, Ph.D.,
1946, Appendix A). The Indian notebooks are discussed in Albert
Keiser, "Thoreau's Manuscripts on the Indians" *(JEGB*, XXVII,
1928, 183–99).

CHAPTER THREE

Thoreau's Sources

I

Thoreau was an inveterate reader and haunter of libraries. Despite his frequent protestations that he preferred the out of doors to the scholar's cell, he was rarely without a book in hand. He seldom, if ever, read for amusement. He avoided novels as a waste of time. He paid little attention to contemporary belles-lettres. But before he explored any new field, whether in science, history, philosophy, or the site of a new excursion, he prepared careful reading lists and devoured every book on the subject he could lay hands on.

Because he was not basically an original thinker—Canby (p. 151) says quite rightfully, "His ideas are all borrowed; the originality is in the blending"—it is important to the student to know Thoreau's sources. Fortunately the record of his reading is fairly near complete. We know what libraries he used, and most of them still have available the records of his book withdrawals. We know from his own catalogue the books he had in his own library. We know what texts were required reading for the courses he took at Concord Academy and Harvard. And Thoreau kept voluminous commonplace books of his favorite quotations and made frequent notations on his reading in his *Journal*.

There is one major difficulty, however—a difficulty that holds true for all of the American Transcendentalists: they were all highly eclectic in their reading. They read widely but took from their reading only those ideas that particularly appealed to them and ignored the rest. In his *Journal* Thoreau once commented, "I do not the least care where I get my ideas, or what suggests them" (J, VIII, 135). He could, and often did, extract from a particular source an idea quite at variance with the philosophy of its original author. And what he said of Oriental literature—"Like some other preachers, I have added my texts . . . long after my discourse was written" (W, II, 192)—is true of most of his other reading.

It is even more dangerous than usual to ascribe Thoreau's ideas to specific sources. He did, however, have certain fields of interest —Oriental literature, the classics, English literature, American history, the American Indian, travel literature, and natural history— that must be considered, although it is difficult to evaluate their relative importance.

II

It is obvious to any serious student of Thoreau that a sympathy with, and knowledge of, the great works of Oriental literature permeates his writings. In *A Week,* he says: "The reading which I love best is the scriptures of the several nations, though it happens that I am better acquainted with those of the Hindoos, the Chinese, and the Persians, than of the Hebrews" (W, I, 72). In his August 10, 1849, letter to H. G. O. Blake he writes: "Depend upon it that, rude and careless as I am, I would fain practice the yoga faithfully. . . . To some extent, and at rare intervals, even I am a yogi." And in *Walden* he adds, "I bathe my intellect in the stupendous and cosmogonal philosophy of the Bhagavat-Gita" (W, II, 328).

Still further evidence of his interest in Oriental literature may be found in the fact that when he edited portions of the "Ethnical Scriptures" for the *Dial,* he chose his selections from "The Laws of Menu" (January, 1843), the "Sayings of Confucius" (April, 1843), the "Chinese Four Books" (October, 1843), and "The Preaching of Buddha" (January, 1844). He translated *The Transmigration of the Seven Brahmans* from a French translation of the Harivansa of Langlois. And when in 1855 Thomas Cholmondeley searched for the most appropriate gift to send his friend Thoreau, he chose a collection of forty-four Oriental volumes.

Helen Snyder has pointed out the frequent paralleling of

Thoreau's ideas with those of the Oriental mystics. Citing passage after passage from the major Hindu works, she then quotes remarkably similar passages in Thoreau's works. Kurt Leidecker demonstrates conclusively that Thoreau's writings are not only filled with Oriental ideas but that they are also shot through with Oriental symbols and images. Pine pollen on Walden reminds him of "rills dyed yellow with the golden dust of the lotus." A mirage on Cape Cod doesn't amount to what in Sanskrit is called "the thirst of the gazelle." And flowers in the fields stand "like Brahminical devotees."

Thoreau was late in acquiring this interest in the Orient. "It is a singular fact that not a single Oriental volume appeared on the record of Thoreau's reading as an undergraduate at the Harvard College Library. . . . It was during the residence in his friend's [Emerson's] home in the year 1841 that Thoreau's extravagant outpouring of praise for the Eastern books commenced" (Christy, p. 188). It was in Emerson's library that he first discovered Oriental literature. Later, when he had exhausted this supply, he turned to Harvard College Library for further books.

Thoreau made a different use of his Oriental reading from Emerson. "Natural objects were what appealed to Thoreau" (p. 191). And "when his scorn was aroused . . . he used the Hindus to bolster his own thought" (p. 193). "The common denominator of all that Thoreau took from the Hindus, Chinese and Persians was a mystical love for Nature. This reading, to be sure, was but a small portion of his wide literary interests . . . but it was the most important of his reading in religious and philosophical literature" (p. 199).

However, one must be cautious not to overemphasize the significance of the Oriental influence. "Of course the word *Yogi* suggests certain very definite things that Thoreau never intended: . . . ascetic self-torture, the bed of nails, sun-gazing, limbs withered from long dis-use" (p. 207). Thoreau could never accept the pessimism of the Hindu (p. 21). And "a last definite sense in which Thoreau probably never accepted the Yoga is in the Hindu insistence that the man who has reached a stage of true enlightenment is freed from the consequences of his works" (p. 212).

Yet on the positive side Thoreau came very close to the kind of

Hindu asceticism described in the *Bhagavadgita*. "The Hindu
Yogi wrapt in his contemplations is not a far cry from the picture
Thoreau gives of himself, sitting in his sunny doorway lost in
reverie, oblivious of time from sunshine till noon, oblivious even
of the songs of birds" (p. 221). "He was a New England Yogi,
conditioned by his nativity and his moral and religious heritage"
(p. 206).

Finally, it is important to realize that what Thoreau found in
the Oriental literatures was a reflection and a confirmation of
ideas and attitudes already achieved. It is significant that by the
time the Cholmondeley collection of Oriental books arrived in
Concord he was no longer vitally interested in reading them.

Thoreau has been called "the best Greek scholar in Concord"
(Van Wyck Brooks, *The Flowering of New England*, p. 284).
There is no question but that he had a thorough training in the
classics. "The Concord Academy . . . offered training in the
classics, especially Greek, that was the equal of that to be had in
any other preparatory school in New England" (Adams, "Henry
Thoreau's Literary Theories," p. 6). And the curriculum at Harvard in Thoreau's time was predominantly classical. But unlike
most college graduates, Thoreau continued to read the classics
throughout his life. Ethel Seybold, *Thoreau: The Quest and the
Classics*, has discovered a definite pattern to that reading:

His postcollege reading fell generally into three periods. The
first was a literary period; he began by rereading authors which he
had read in college and by making little explorations into fields
suggested by that reading. Among the Greeks he read Homer and
Orpheus, the Greek lyrists, especially Anacreon and Pindar; in
drama, Aeschylus' *Prometheus Bound* and *Seven Against Thebes*.
He investigated also Plutarch's *Lives* and *Morals*, Jamblichus' *Life
of Pythagoras*, and Porphyry's *On Abstinence from Animal Food*.
Among the Latin authors he read Vergil, Horace, Persius, and
Ovid. In the second period, after Walden, in the early 1850's, he
made the acquaintance of the agricultural writers, Cato, Varro,
Columella, and Palladius, and confined himself to them with two
exceptions, Sophocles' *Antigone* and a brief excursion into Lucre-
tius. He did no new reading in Greek during this period. In the
late 1850's he discovered the early naturalists: the Roman Pliny
and among the Greeks, Aristotle, Theophrastus, and Aelian. His
last reading was in Herodotus and Strabo (pp. 15–16).

Miss Seybold asserts: "When a man who defined the cost of a thing as the amount of life one had to give in exchange for it was willing to spend 'youthful days and costly hours' in classical study, it may be assumed that for some reason he found the classics indispensable" (p. vii). But unfortunately Miss Seybold over-stresses the classical influence on Thoreau:

The classics had gone a long way with Thoreau and had served him in many ways. In utilitarian fashion they had provided ma-terial for translation and models for imitation. In them he had found the source, the corroboration, or the extension of most of his favorite theories: of language, of government, of history and myth, of poetry and music, of the sameness of the universe. As a whole they had been for him originally a reference work which he might consult in his search for truth. From a source of infor-mation concerning his ideal world they had become a kind of symbol of that world, an encouraging glimpse and a proof of the existence of a still greater and yet surely attainable world. In Thoreau's youth Homer and Vergil had given him such encour-aging glimpses; at Walden it was Homer who offered him a work-ing pattern and a relaxed philosophy of living, who permitted him through the reconstruction of the Homeric life to live in part his ideal life; in the depression of the post-Walden years Thoreau found sanative value in the husbandry writers and a gleam of hope in that vision of the Grecian Era evoked by the telegraph harp. When he knew at last that he would not in this world attain the world which he had dreamed, the Golden Age of the Greeks became an acceptable substitute, a vista on which his eyes might rest with pleasure. During the last years of his life the naturalists, geographers, and anthropologists contributed to that view and helped him pursue his piecemeal investigation of the universe. He came back at last to Homer but at secondhand and with a scientific rather than a poetic approach (p. 85).

Unquestionably much of this is true. And if Thoreau had read nothing but the classics, we could perhaps accept all of it. But throughout his life he read in many other literatures as well, and many of the influences Miss Seybold ascribes to the classics could be as easily attributed to these other literatures. Weakest of all is her lengthy discussion of his life at Walden as a Homeric experi-ment. It is true he says in *Walden,* "I kept Homer's Iliad on my table through the summer"; but he completes that sentence with, "though I looked at his page only now and then" (W, II, 111). There is more to Walden than simply a Homeric experiment.

One fact Miss Seybold does not seem to take into consideration is that Thoreau's classicism was forced upon him by the educational practices of his time. We suspect Gohdes is nearer to the truth when he says, "Thoreau was a romanticist by nature, and a classical scholar by mere force of circumstances" (p. 329). It is true that Thoreau continued to read the classics after his school days were over. But by that time he was thoroughly acquainted with the great body of classical literature, and instead of concentrating on those authors who had been stressed in his classes, he turned to such lesser known men as the agriculturalists Cato, Varro, and Columella, whom he read not because they were classical authors but because they offered him confirmation of many of the ideas he had already independently achieved. Thoreau was much too eclectic to follow completely the dictates of any school or any individual author.

Although Thoreau read French as readily as English and knew "German, Italian, and Spanish more or less" (Sanborn, *The Life of Henry David Thoreau*, 1917, p. 260), his acquaintance with Continental literature was surprisingly slight. Raymond Adams has overstated the case when he says: "I can find no evidence that Thoreau read any continental philosophical works, or any French books save the French translations of the Oriental bibles or, in one instance, a French translation of a Chinese novel; nor did he read any German books save the poems of Goethe and J. R. von Zimmermann's *Thoughts on the Influence of Solitude on the Heart*" ("Thoreau's Literary Theories," p. 36), but he has not overstated it by much.

While it is widely recognized that all the American Transcendentalists derived much of their inspiration from the German Transcendentalists, most of it came at second hand through Coleridge and Carlyle. Thoreau learned to read German with the help of Orestes Brownson in the winter of 1835, but he apparently never really felt at home with the language. He read Goethe intensively just after graduating from college and included a tribute to him in *A Week* (W, I, 347–53). Thoreau was probably repelled by what he considered the immorality of Goethe's personal life, but he found his mature writings worth study.

Paul Elmer More, in "Thoreau's Journal," thought he found

"almost the whole body of [German] romanticism . . . reflected, explicitly or implicitly" in Thoreau's *Journal* (p. 106). "Often a passage in the Journal bears the stamp of German romanticism so plainly upon it, that we stop to trace it back in memory to Tieck or Novalis or one of the followers of the earlier Storm and Stress" (p. 108). But More found no evidence of direct reading in these authors and concluded that most of the influence was at second hand. Further, he discovered there was a basic difference in outlook: "The freedom of the romantic school was to the end that the whole emotional nature might develop; in Thoreau it was for the practice of a higher self-restraint" (p. 114).

The similarity of Thoreau's ideas to those of Johann Ritter von Zimmermann, the author of *On Solitude,* has been frequently commented on and it is known that Thoreau owned an English translation of Zimmermann's book. Grant Loomis, in pointing out the ideas the two men held in common, concludes, "Basically, the ideas of the two men are alike at many points, but if Thoreau was an advocate of the principles [of Zimmermann], he was an original disciple" (p. 792).

Although Norman Foerster ("Intellectual Heritage of Thoreau," p. 197) says, "It is perfectly obvious that no French writers meant much to Thoreau," many have thought him a follower of Rousseau. There is no evidence that he ever read Rousseau directly. He was acquainted with his ideas only through secondary sources (Anton Huffert, "Thoreau as a Teacher," pp. 151 ff.). Thoreau was undoubtedly repelled by Rousseau's moral laxity.

The tormenting desire of European, especially Continental romanticism—the sighs, the aching void, the meltings, the sweet abandon, the boundless longing and utter weariness were more remote from his experience than the moral integrity of the Puritans and the serene reason of the Greeks. . . . It is entirely certain that when Thoreau speaks, in the romantic vein, of following his genius, or instincts, he does not unwittingly urge, as romanticism too often does, obedience to the instincts of his temperament, but the very opposite—the subjection of these instincts to the instincts of a higher, and peculiarly human, self (Foerster, *Nature in American Literature,* pp. 128–29).

According to Sanborn, Thoreau's favorite Italian author was Tasso, but that he was also familiar with Dante both in the original and in translation has been indicated by J. Chesley Matthews.

That he was also somewhat interested in an almost forgotten Italian contemporary, Silvio Pellico, has been pointed out by John C. Broderick.

Thoreau's interest in Scandinavian literature was threefold. He read widely in the writings of the scientists Linnaeus, Kalm, and to a lesser extent, Biberg and Fries. He was familiar with Swedenborg, probably through Emerson, though he wrote B. B. Wiley (December 12, 1856), "I cannot say that Swedenborg has been directly and practically valuable to me." And finally, he read extensively in Norse mythology and the records of Norse exploration in North America: an English version of *Heimskringla*, the *Prose Edda*, Rafn's *Antiquitates Americanoe*, and Samuel Laing's *Sagas of the Norse Kings*. Of the literatures of the other Continental peoples Thoreau apparently knew virtually nothing.

That the early English writers held a particular fascination for Thoreau has long been accepted as an axiom by scholars. His friends Channing and Sanborn frequently attested to it. There was a legend that he had read the entire set of Chalmers' *English Poets* (twenty-one large volumes) before he entered college and later a second and possibly a third time. Frequent mention was made of the influence of the seventeenth-century writers, particularly Browne and Donne, upon his style.

Anne Whaling ("Studies in Thoreau's Reading"), however, has made the only extended study of Thoreau's interest in the early English writers, and she has come to a quite different conclusion. She was able to find no conclusive evidence that Thoreau displayed any extensive interest in these authors before the last two months of his college career and theorizes that the reading he did then was probably a classroom assignment (p. 47). She does agree that he read fairly thoroughly in these authors in the six years after he graduated from college, entering many extracts in his commonplace books. But "after November, 1843, there is no clear evidence . . . of any sustained reading of early English writers except in the special fields of natural history and exploration" (pp. 127–28). "He did not, on the evidence available, have any deep general interest, historical or critical, in the seventeenth century. He had no precocious interest in its poetry or prose, nor do the extracts made in college and immediately after reflect anything that could be called a 'strong fascination.' Even his interest in the older English poetry and prose, as they were defined in his day, was limited" (p. 170). The many quotations from the period that flavor his published writings, particularly *A Week,* were virtually all taken from the extracts he had made in his commonplace books. The evidences of stylistic influence that have been frequently pointed out are so tenuous and generalized as to have no real significance. However, Miss Whaling does admit that "even though his acquaintance with the older English poetry and prose was somewhat less extensive than tradition has implied, . . . the reading remains a considerable achievement and a significant factor in the modest excellence of Thoreau's work" (p. 193).

Of the earlier English writers, he was quite understandably most attracted to the major figures—Chaucer, Shakespeare, and Milton. There are extended tributes to Chaucer in *A Week* (W, I, 391–400), fairly frequent references to his works in his *Journal,* and a misquotation of him in *Walden* (W, II, 234). Thoreau "picked up the reverent manner toward Shakespeare which was in the air. . . . But Thoreau's actual feeling about Shakespeare seems not to have been very warm and intimate" (Dunn, *Shakespeare in America,* p. 260). There are frequent allusions to, and quotations from, the plays that indicate a familiarity with the Shakespeare canon, but there is little of the adulation of the bard that one finds in Emerson's works, for example.

For Milton, however, Thoreau held an "exaggerated reverence" (Whaling, p. 41). He wrote a "volunteer essay" on *L'Allegro* and *Il Penseroso* in college and quoted from *Paradise Lost* and *Lycidas* so extensively throughout his writings that one suspects he must have committed large portions of Milton to memory. Crawford's supposition (*Thoreau: Representative Selections,* p. xix) that Thoreau's "preference for Milton over Shakespeare was likely a Puritan inheritance, and based on moral grounds," is undoubtedly correct. But perhaps Milton's greater intimacy with the world of nature was another factor.

Of the lesser writers, Sir Walter Raleigh stood high in Thoreau's esteem. He delivered an essay on Raleigh before the Concord Lyceum on February 8, 1843, and incorporated portions of this essay in *A Week* (W, I, 106 ff.). Though Thoreau admired

Raleigh's style, he was far more interested in the man. It is significant, I think, that he included "The Soul's Errand" among his tributes to John Brown read at the memorial service in Concord (W, IV, 452), for his attitude toward the two men was much the same.

Thoreau did not discover the writings of Francis Quarles until his visit to Staten Island in 1843, which gave him the opportunity of using some of the New York libraries. But that his enthusiasm was aroused is indicated by the fact that there are no less than thirteen quotations from Quarles in *A Week*.

His interest in Sir Thomas Browne has been frequently cited, and it has been pointed out that the last paragraph of "The Pond in Winter" in *Walden* mimics Browne. It has also been noted that a paragraph in the final chaper of *Walden* closely parallels Browne. Walter Gierasch has found similar parallels with the writings of Bishop Joseph Hall (1574–1656).

Students of Thoreau's poetry have frequently cited the influence of the seventeenth-century poets, particularly George Herbert. Many of Thoreau's poems are best described as "metaphysical." It is not surprising that he was interested also in the early English ballads and songs. He read Percy and several other similar collections and made occasional quotation from, or allusion to, them in his works.

And finally, perhaps more than any other English work, the King James Bible exerted a profound influence on Thoreau's style. Although he often belittled his knowledge of the Scriptures and declared he was more familiar with the Oriental Bibles, his familiarity with the King James Bible is obvious on almost every page he wrote. His allusions to the Bible are frequent, and the word choice and sentence structure of the King James Bible are integral parts of his style.

Thoreau had surprisingly little interest in the later English literature. As Norman Foerster ("Intellectual Heritage of Thoreau," p. 212) has said, "In the entire long procession from Dryden to Matthew Arnold, Thoreau had but a handful of friends." His lack of interest in eighteenth-century English literature is outstanding. A notable exception is Ossian. Thoreau read the Ossianic poems while on Staten Island, delivered a lecture on the "Ancient Poets," particularly Ossian, on his return to Concord in November, 1843, and included fifteen quotations from Ossian in *A Week*. But since he thought the Ossianic poems genuine, his interest in them could hardly be considered a demonstration of an affinity for eighteenth-century literature.

One other eighteenth-century English author did arouse Thoreau's interest. That was the Rev. William Gilpin, the leader of the vogue for the "picturesque." Thoreau not only read most of his available works and recommended them highly to his friend Daniel Ricketson, but he discussed Gilpin at greater length in his *Journal* than he did any other noncontemporary figure. Thoreau's continued interest in the "picturesque" landscape can be traced in large part to his reading of Gilpin, although, as William Templeman points out, he was often disappointed that Gilpin failed to display a moral as well as an aesthetic interest in nature.

When we turn to the English romanticists, we find surprisingly little explicit comment in Thoreau's writings. He owned the works of Shelley, Keats, and Byron, but almost never mentioned them in his writings. It is obvious that he read widely in Wordsworth, for, though again he does not quote him frequently, he does make many an allusion to, or echo of, Wordsworth, particularly the "Ode on Intimations of Immortality." He admired Wordsworth's genius but thought he lacked talent (J, I, 431). "Thoreau saw nature as he did because of his own inherent emotional make-up, but . . . he found a kindred and stimulating spirit in Wordsworth" (James Southworth, "Reply to W. D. Templeman," *PMLA*, XLIX, 1934, 974).

Coleridge was of interest to Thoreau not as a poet but as the translator and exponent of the German Transcendentalists. James Marsh's American edition of Coleridge's *Aids to Reflection* was one of the bibles of the American Transcendentalists, and Thoreau read it with avidity. Carlyle served much the same purpose for Thoreau. Thoreau's essay "Thomas Carlyle and His Works" is one of his few explicit attempts at literary criticism. "For Carlyle's themes, Thoreau cared little enough, for his ideas little more, at least in the form which Carlyle gave them; but for his style he cared a great deal" (Norman Foerster, "Intellectual Heritage of Thoreau," p. 200).

There is occasional reference to Tennyson in Thoreau's works, a rather surprising interest in De Quincey and Felicia Hemans, and, in the late 1850's, some interest in Ruskin. Dickens and Scott are mentioned halfheartedly. And there, for all practical purposes, Thoreau's interest in later English literature ends.

Thoreau's interest in American literature was primarily historical. He read avidly everything he could lay his hands on concerning early America. As I have already pointed out, he studied the records of the early Norse explorations. He continued with the writings of the French and English explorers. He searched the documents of the first settlers—and here he was fortunate in that the various state historical societies and commissions, Massachusetts, New York, and New Hampshire in particular—were reprinting many of the rarer pieces just when his interest in the field was at its height. And he read thoroughly in the local histories, not only of Concord and eastern Massachusetts or the areas which he visited on his excursions (although he was particularly conscientious about reading these), but any local histories he could find. "If it should prove at all possible—and he [Thoreau] saw no reason why it should not, apparently—he wished to know every place as he knew Concord: completely, both as it was in the present and as it had been in the past" (Lawrence Willson, "The Influence of Early North American History," p. 106). "No man in his time, or perchance in any other, was so thoroughly informed on purely local history as he" (p. 115).

"Josselyn [*Account of Two Voyages to New England*] should head the list of Thoreau's authorities on early America, because he apparently read him first and certainly refers to him most often" (p. 102). Edward Johnson's *History of New England . . . or Wonder-Working Providences* was another favorite. The many volumes of Jesuit Relations, which Thoreau had to read in the French, were often turned to. But it would be idle to attempt to list all the volumes in the field with which he was familiar. He himself has cited most of them in his various "Excursions." Willson has discussed their influence fully, although he too overstates his case when he asserts: "His [Thoreau's] reading in the literature of early American history was the most important element by far in all his reading, for the ultimate solidification of his mind and character" (pp. 202–3).

In later American literature Thoreau was less widely read. His dislike of fiction kept him away from Cooper, although there are indications that he read some of Irving and at least Melville's *Typee*. There are numerous allusions to Hawthorne's tales in his *Journal*. In poetry, only Whitman interested him. Thoreau read little more than the early essays and poetry of Emerson. It was Emerson the man, not the author, who attracted him.

Another field of intense interest to Thoreau was the lore of the American Indian. Although he had been interested in the Indian from childhood and early started collecting Indian relics on his walks through the countryside, it was not until 1848 that he began an intensive reading on the subject. But in the last fourteen years of his life, he read at least two hundred works on the subject, according to Albert Keiser (*The Indian in American Literature*, p. 211), and filled eleven manuscript notebooks, containing about 2,800 pages, with more than half a million words, mainly extracts from books, pamphlets, and magazine articles on the American Indian. It was his intention to write a book on the Indian, and he worked out a tentative table of contents. But illness forced him to abandon the project.

The various Jesuit Relations were probably his major source of information, and Lawrence Willson, in "Thoreau and Roman Catholicism," has pointed out how closely, carefully, and thoroughly he read these many documents, showing none of the prejudice against them displayed by most New England historians. Thoreau also found much of interest in the writings of Henry Rowe Schoolcraft, George Henry Loskiel, and John G. E. Heckewelder. The range of material he included in his notebooks is tremendous. He was interested in virtually anything pertaining to the Indian, whether from New England, the West, or even the Arctic regions. But he made no attempt to organize the material as he gathered it. The Indian notebooks are a heterogeneous mass, now valuable only as a literary curiosity.

One of the many paradoxes about Thoreau, according to John Christie, is that he is "a man who reiterates his disdain for travel while he peppers his writings with its products; . . . a writer who urges his readers to concentrate upon a knowledge of their own local plot of ground while he makes sure in his writings that their acquaintance with the world be nothing less than global; . . . the seemingly contented provincial who is all the while devouring the accounts of other men's farthest travels" ("Thoreau, Traveler," p. 48). "In his published writings (including the *Journal*) Thoreau directly refers to his reading in at least eighty-three different travel works" (p. 38). "We are able to identify . . . a minimum of one hundred and seventy-one separate travel accounts read by Thoreau" (p. 41).

Thoreau was particularly interested in books about Canada (many of them read in preparation for the writing of "A Yankee in Canada"), American exploration (including many of the government reports on various Western expeditions), sea voyages (such as Darwin and Cook), South America, Africa, Asia (often in conjunction with his Oriental studies), and the Arctic regions (pp. 92–139). What is even more surprising is that while many of the travel books he read were old (Thoreau was always interested in the records of the past), a large proportion of them were contemporary, many of which he read almost as soon as they were published.

Thoreau's reading in travel literature was not wasted. He peppered his writing with references to distant places, mentioning at least 443 foreign locales and 95 American (pp. 18–19 n.). These references were not made in any attempt to display ostentatiously his own wide reading, but rather to add a universality to his books, "to make local objects suggest their global counterparts" (p. 186).

It is surprising that no one has made an extended effort to study Thoreau's reading in natural history. Miss Seybold has examined his acquaintance with the classical natural history writers, and Benson has mentioned his interest in the Scandinavian natural scientists, but that is all. Yet Thoreau read widely in the English natural histories—White, Walton, Howitt, and Evelyn, to mention only a few. He owned an exceptionally good collection of British natural history textbooks for his time. In American literature he was familiar with Audubon, Bartram, Agassiz, Baird, Michaux, Wilson, Brewer, Gray, and many of the state and federal natural history reports that were issued in his lifetime. And he opened his essay on the "Natural History of Massachusetts" with the comment, "Books of natural history make the most cheerful winter reading" (W, V, 103). Surely this is a field worthy of further study.

It has been impossible in these few pages to do any more than roughly indicate some of Thoreau's areas of interest and to attempt to explain what attracted him to these fields and what he derived from them. There is still much room for further research, although one must always remember: "No man can be explained in terms of his reading. . . . There was in him [Thoreau] . . . a personal element that was inborn, that determined largely the direction and degree of growth, that helped him to choose his books and his friends, that, probably more than anything else, made him what he became" (Foerster, "Intellectual Heritage of Thoreau," p. 212).

III

When we turn to the influence of Thoreau's educational experience, we find we know so little about his early schooling that it is useless to attempt to draw any conclusions. We can guess that his primary education was similar to that of most of his contemporaries in New England schools and that it apparently provided him with an adequate background in the three R's.

As to his secondary education, Thoreau himself wrote, "I was fitted, or rather made unfit for college at Concord Academy and elsewhere, mainly by myself, with the countenance of Phineas Allen, Preceptor" (Canby, p. 40). Fortunately many of Allen's records for the Concord Academy have recently come to light. They reveal that Thoreau received, despite his comment, a better-than-average training in the classics, mathematics, and languages in preparation for his matriculation at Harvard and that he also received noteworthy training in composition and public speaking.

It is Christian P. Gruber's contention that "Harvard College contributed more to the intellectual and literary evolution of Henry Thoreau than he or any of his biographers has admitted" ("The Education of Henry Thoreau," p. 1). "No other four year period in his life is marked by such rapid and significant development, particularly in the very areas of his enduring fame. Surely it is nonsense to imply or assume that the college, whose sole reason for existence was to foster intellectual and moral growth, retarded such growth or merely provided him a place to live while he developed independently" (p. 4).

"Whatever limitations characterized Harvard in 1833, this much is perfectly obvious. To a village youth like Thoreau, life at Cambridge will be a new and broadening experience, both intellectually and socially. He will sit under men who have lived and studied in Europe, some of them political exiles from monarchical tyranny there; and under men who edit and write books, publish scholarly and critical articles on philosophy, science and religion in various journals; he will have free access to the best and most extensive library in America; he will live with boys of diverse backgrounds, some with well-defined professional and literary aspirations unlike those that characterized his own beloved Concord; and he will live under an institutional regimen different from any he had known" (p. 21).

While the curriculum at Harvard "reflected the principles of President Quincy, who was instinctively conservative" (p. 25), showed little change from pre-Revolutionary days (with the exception of voluntary courses in modern languages and in science) (p. 27), and featured a recitation system and a grading system that emphasized memory work at the expense of creative thought, it did develop "skilled readers" (p. 34), encouraged the student to read widely "for his edification or pleasure" in the open stacks of the largest library in the country (p. 34), and through the department of rhetoric and oratory "emphasized the importance of communicating ideas, and demanded that he [the student] do so on a variety of subjects, philosophical, literary, and ethical" (p. 37).

Gruber also points out that many of the most typical Thoreauvian ideas (most notably those on "the pleasure of solitary or semi-solitary communion with nature") are common to the college themes and articles contributed to the undergraduate magazine *Harvardiana* by Thoreau's classmates (p. 49). And despite the fact that "neither the curriculum nor the teaching in many departments had kept abreast of the philosophical, social, or literary movements which had produced the work of Kant, Wordsworth, or Carlyle," such members of the faculty as Francis Bowen and Edward Tyrrel Channing actively read, wrote, and talked about their work (pp. 23–24).

In the years Thoreau was in college, Harvard was "far more interested in nurturing Christian ethics than in pushing specific Christian doctrines" (p. 92). Henry Ware, the Hollis Professor of Divinity, was noted for his tolerance, his intellect, and his cultured tastes, but he was neither metaphysical nor emotionally spiritual in his temperament. His ideas were well represented by the two textbooks he used in his classes: Paley's *View of the Evidences of Christianity* and Butler's *Analogy of Religion*. But these books probably "increased his [Thoreau's] distaste for formal Christianity and for the traditional Christian view of man's role in the scheme of nature" (p. 97) because their "concept of man's journey through life clashed with Thoreau's deepest instincts" in that "the general tone of [their] analysis of the human condition is very pessimistic"; they are "devoid of passion, paradox, or emotional heightening of any kind" (p. 98), and they display no evidence of any real acquaintance with nature. However, Thoreau "would have sympathized with [their] basic conception that natural, moral, and spiritual elements are indissolubly linked together" (p. 101) and "that reason and conscience are the final test of the truth or falsehood of any doctrine" (p. 102).

In philosophy Thoreau's Harvard texts were Dugald Stewart's *Elements of the Philosophy of the Human Mind*, Locke's *Essay Concerning Human Understanding*, Paley's *Principles of Moral and Political Philosophy*, and Say's *Political Economy*. There seems to be "little evidence" to show that these books "exerted much influence" on Thoreau's philosophy (p. 113). But they "could not help increasing Thoreau's sensitivity to the infinite possibilities and the rich complexity of language as a tool for communicating ideas and recording experience" (p. 114). "He was encouraged by these texts to use his god-given senses at their full capacity" (p. 116).

Both Edgeley W. Todd, "Philosophical Ideas at Harvard College," and Joseph J. Kwiat, "Thoreau's Philosophical Apprenticeship," disagree strongly with Gruber's findings at this point. Todd points out that the Harvard curriculum of Thoreau's day presented "in metaphysics two divergent streams, . . . English empiricism systematized by Locke, and the natural realism or 'common sense' Scottish philosophy. . . . . Thus, Harvard students in the formation of their own philosophical outlook were made acquainted with two opposing tendencies in respect to the problem of knowledge" (pp. 67–68). "In general it may be said that the two philosophies represented, on the one hand, a denial, and on the other, a moderate affirmation of the existence of innate ideas" (p. 69). Locke had been the patron saint of the early Unitarians. But "the Scottish philosophers suggested to Harvard students the inadequacy of Locke's theory of knowledge. . . . The general direction in which the 'common sense' philosophers pointed would conceivably encourage the formation of ideas preparatory to later ones more accurately termed transcendental. . . . This is not to imply any extensive synonymity between Scottish philosophy and New England Transcendentalism, but rather to suggest that the philosophy of Reid, Stewart, and Brown possibly served as a useful transition between Locke and Transcendentalism" (pp. 88–89). Joseph J. Kwiat, examining Todd's thesis with particular reference to Thoreau, comes to the conclusion: "The prominent position of the Scottish philosophy in the Harvard curriculum, the Scottish philosophical inclinations of the instructors, Thoreau's direct references to representatives of the Scottish school [particularly in his college essays], and the correspondence between his ideas and their own indicate a major influence, particularly in aesthetic and ethical matters, by the end of his junior year" (p. 59).

"Chemistry, mineralogy, zoology, and botany were considered important enough to be offered at an elementary level [at Harvard], but not important enough to be considered more than addenda to the really important core of liberal studies," says Gruber (p. 152). In natural history, T. W. Harris, the college librarian, used Smellie's *Philosophy of Natural History* and Nuttall's *Introduction to Systematic and Physiological Botany*. But both texts emphasized an aesthetic rather than a scientific approach to nature. They "made it unlikely that Thoreau or any Harvard graduate of his time would make any significant contributions to natural science as either a botanist or zoologist" (p. 159). In the then so-called "mixed mathematics" Thoreau studied mechanics, electricity, optics, and astronomy (p. 161). The courses were primarily lectures, with only a cursory glance at laboratory work. "And yet in spite of its limitations, Harvard did manage to insinuate a good bit of science and scientific method into Thoreau's consciousness" (p. 164), even though it lacked any "really first rate teacher of the mixed sciences" (p. 165). "In surveying he found an occupation which solved his problem of earning a living and at the same time living close to nature. The course in mechanics no doubt furnished him technical knowledge that made it easier for him to design a more efficient plumbago mill" (p. 167). "But more important than these purely practical results of his education are the surprising uses which Thoreau as a writer makes of the information picked up in the Department of Mathematics and Natural Philosophy" (p. 167). They provided him with a great number of concepts and a large storehouse of tropes for his future literary use (p. 169).

All Thoreau's biographers have belittled the influence of the Boylston Professor of Rhetoric and Oratory, Edward Tyrrel Channing, and Canby went so far as to state: "It took him [Thoreau] approximately ten years to put his Harvard rhetoric behind him, and write steadily on his own" (p. 50). But Gruber concludes, "It is an inescapable fact that . . . development certainly occurred under Channing" (p. 204). Channing's text in his course was Whately's *Elements of Rhetoric*. And "Channing, like Whately, encouraged a liberal philosophy of rhetoric" (p. 207). "He did attempt to get students to think logically and organize their thought effectively" (p. 209). "The truth seems to be that Thoreau learned his lessons in logic very well, for, when he argues he does so logically" (p. 211). "Under his [Channing's] wise criticism and encouragement, a student was free to shape an individual style, a style that would adequately and freshly express his own thought. The conclusive proof that Thoreau, under Channing, did make bold progress in achieving such a style is to be found in the college essays" (p. 230). And it is quite apparent to the reader that in these essays "Thoreau demonstrates beyond doubt that he has learned very well how to express himself with sincerity, with originality, and with the energy so often stressed by Whately and carefully nurtured by Channing" (p. 275). "Thoreau's debt to the liberal education he received at Harvard was greater than has generally been acknowledged" (p. i).

IV

There is more to the making of Thoreau than his books and his formal education, however. He had no further formal schooling after 1837, and even though he was an inveterate reader throughout his life, he found many other sources for ideas and attitudes. There has been comparatively little attempt to place Thoreau against the background of his times, and yet we must do it if we would attempt to understand what made him what he was.

Although his biographers, Sanborn in particular, have attempted to trace the influence of his Scottish and French ancestry on his ideas, their findings have been so tenuous and problematical that I think them of little significance. There is slight indication of any great intellectual activity on the part of any of his ancestors. They were, for the most part, simple, everyday, ordinary people, although some of his maternal ancestors (the Dunbars and the Joneses) did display a willingness to go against the crowd when they asserted their Tory leanings during the American Revolution.

Thoreau's father was as little out of the ordinary as most of the rest of his ancestors, though his knowledge of local history (J, XI, 437) undoubtedly whetted Thoreau's interest in early Americana. His father's long series of business failures during Thoreau's youth must have had a profound influence on Thoreau's outlook toward society. Would Thoreau have been so critical of the economic structure, for example, if he had not been raised in an atmosphere of financial insecurity?

Although Sanborn out of personal prejudice created a picture of Thoreau's mother as a small-minded gossip that has been accepted by most of the biographers, she was actually a woman of broad interests and intellectually alert. I suspect that she was one of the major formative factors in Thoreau's life. She was so interested in natural history that according to legend one of her children was nearly born out in the fields on one of her nature walks. As I have already pointed out (see p. 2), she was not one to accept her religious beliefs without serious question, although she was orthodox enough to compel her son, when he was young, "to pass my Sundays in the house without the aid of interesting books"

(J, III, 427). And she took an active part in both abolitionist activities and in social work.

Thoreau always thought that he had "been born into the most estimable place in all the world, and in the very nick of time, too" (J, IX, 160). Surely, had he a choice, he could not have picked a better spot than Concord, Massachusetts. In his classbook at Harvard he wrote: "I shall ever pride myself on the place of my birth. . . . If I forget thee, O Concord, let my right hand forget her cunning. . . . To whatever quarter of the world I may wander, I shall deem it good fortune that I hail from Concord North Bridge." It was a town filled with intellectual ferment. "There was more vital awareness [there] of the best that was being said and thought in the contemporary civilized world than in any university town in America today" (Canby, p. 12).

Foremost of the local influences outside his family was, of course, Emerson. For many years it was the fashion to deride Thoreau as an imitator of Emerson. James Russell Lowell charged that Thoreau's works were but "strawberries from his [Emerson's] own garden." Many of their contemporaries accused Thoreau of imitating Emerson's voice and mannerisms, and some even went so far as to accuse him of imitating Emerson's nose. Their handwriting was so much alike that I often find it difficult to distinguish between the manuscripts of the two. I am not alone in this, for the editors of the first edition of *A Yankee in Canada, with Anti-Slavery and Reform Papers* (Boston, 1866) included Emerson's essay on "Prayers" as one of Thoreau's. And Sanborn, in his 1917 biography, included some of Emerson's *Journal* as Thoreau's. One would not find it at all difficult to transpose occasional sentences back and forth between the works of the two without arousing the suspicions of any but the most careful scholars.

But both men quite understandably resented these charges of imitation, and Emerson in particular frequently spoke out against them. In his *Journal* for June 24, 1863, Emerson points out most distinctly the difference between the two: "In reading him [Thoreau], I find the same thought, the same spirit that is in me, but he takes a step beyond, and illustrates by excellent images that which I should have conveyed in a sleepy generality" (IX, 522). In other words, in their prose Emerson tends toward the abstract, Thoreau toward the concrete; Emerson toward the ideal, Thoreau toward the practical. "Even if he [Thoreau] were insignificant in that he took all of his ideas from Emerson, he would still be significant in that he reduced them to their practicable and visualizable essence" (Van Doren, p. 10).

Yet it must be remembered that Emerson's influence was exerted primarily through his personal association rather than through his books. *Nature,* Canby feels (pp. 97 ff.), was a major influence. And certainly Emerson's early essays played an important part in Thoreau's life. But by 1851 Thoreau was commenting in his *Journal* (III, 134) that he rarely looked at Emerson's books. It was through their daily association in the streets and woods of Concord and through Thoreau's two lengthy residences in Emerson's house that Emerson exerted his chief influence. It must also be remembered, as Walt Whitman (*Complete Prose,* New York, 1910, p. 317) pointed out: "The best part of Emersonianism is, it breeds the giant that destroys itself. Who wants to be any man's mere follower? lurks behind every page. No teacher ever taught, that has so provided for his pupil's setting up independently—no truer evolutionist."

Nor was the influence one-sided. It was Thoreau who provided Emerson with his knowledge of the world of nature around him. "Remove the details of material nature from Emerson's essays, and you will rob them of much of their charm and power, since the author would be in perpetual danger of soaring aloft, balloon-fashion, among his 'Circles' in worlds unrealized" (Foerster, *Nature in American Literature,* p. 37). Emerson, in his *Journals,* devotes at least ninety-seven paragraphs to Thoreau. Thoreau in his much longer *Journal* makes only forty references to Emerson, and most of those simply in passing.

"It is an important and frequently unrecognized fact that with respect to his defiance of church and state Thoreau was far more radical than Emerson and perhaps had a considerable influence on him" (Glick, "Thoreau and Radical Abolitionism," pp. 10–12). Emerson liked to preach self-reliance and nonconformity, but he hesitated to practice them. Thoreau, on the other hand, practiced before he preached. When Thoreau was jailed for his civil disobedience, Emerson "thought it mean and skulking, and in bad taste" (Alcott, *Journals,* p. 183). In later years Emerson thought more highly of Thoreau's "escapade." When the Fugitive Slave

Law was passed, Emerson wrote in his *Journals* (VIII, 179) that he would do all he could do "in opposition to the execution of the law." But it was Thoreau who delivered a lecture on "Slavery in Massachusetts" (W, IV, 388). In 1859, when word was received of John Brown's ill-fated expedition against Harpers Ferry, it was Thoreau, not Emerson, who called a meeting in Concord to defend Brown. Emerson did not come to Brown's defense until Thoreau had paved the way. "In the sage of Concord Thoreau soon began to suspect that there was too much of the merely genteel, too little of the genuine wildness which he valued so much in himself and which he cultivated by direct association with physical nature" (Krutch, p. 49).

That great upsurge of idealism in New England of the 1830's, known popularly as Transcendentalism, was also a formative influence. "Instead of being a precursor or an inaugurator of New England Transcendentalism, he [Thoreau] was in a sense a product of that movement—a child and not a parent" (Foerster, "Intellectual Heritage of Thoreau," p. 192). It was through Emerson, through personal contact and through *Nature,* that Thoreau first learned of the Transcendentalist philosophy. He attended meetings of the "Hedge Club" at Emerson's home and worked closely with him in the editing of the *Dial,* thereby meeting most of the leaders of the movement and reading their major pronouncements. By 1840 "it is evident that Thoreau was rapidly breaking away from the tyranny of the earth-creeping quality of the Scottish common sense school and that he was arriving at a more complete acceptance of the intuitive principles of Transcendentalism" (Kwiat, p. 67). The first volume of Thoreau's published *Journal* is filled with echoes of Transcendental idealism. Thoreau received from Transcendentalism "a mysticism that insists the truth comes through inspiration and is more valid than any truth arrived at through reason and understanding, a regard and heed for all nature and all men, for divinity may be found in the least of these" (Adams, p. 55). It was Transcendentalism, with the transitional help of the Scottish common-sense school that led him away from Locke, although ironically, "Thoreau continued throughout life to approach the study of nature through the senses rather than through abstract reasoning" (Huffert, pp. 149–50).

In his junior year at Harvard Thoreau interrupted his studies with an interlude of schoolteaching at Canton, Massachusetts, under the direction of Orestes Brownson. It is Gruber's contention that since "Thoreau's flight from orthodoxy was complete before Emerson's personal influence became strong" (p. 186), and since "various of Thoreau's college essays of his senior year contain ideas so similar to Brownson's that one can only conclude that he was making use of what his new friend and mentor had taught him" (p. 192), "the impact of Brownson was in quickening Thoreau's reaction to orthodox views of Christianity and to society as presently constituted, and in strengthening his reliance upon his own faculties and perceptions" (Gruber, p. 198). "There is no question that [Orestes Brownson] opened Thoreau's eyes to the intellectual tumult of the age as they had never been opened before" (Glick, "Thoreau and Radical Abolitionism," p. 14).

Less tangible, but equally important, was the impact of New England Puritanism upon Thoreau. "No son of a Dunbar, no native of Concord in 1817 could have escaped an inheritance of Puritanism. Nor did Thoreau escape" (Adams, "Henry Thoreau's Literary Theories," p. 32). "The constantly reiterated demand that the writer be sincere is a part of this Puritan integrity" (p. 33). "The fact that he denounced what he did not believe in— for example, money—as not only foolish but sinful" was another indication of the Puritan influence (Van Doren, pp. 55–56). F. W. Lorch sees a further sign of it in his deep concern "in his own life to subject passion to discipline" (p. 25). "The impulse which sent him off to study nature in order to discover the unifying thread which binds God to man was a Puritan impulse" (Willson, p. 25). "His also was a salvation religion and the empathy he sometimes felt was the assurance which his soul gave him that he was among the elect. Indeed it would be easy to interpret certain phases of his thought as merely a secularized puritanism, since, though he had discarded almost completely most of the vocabulary of puritanism, he had kept some of the conceptions as well as a few of the words" (Krutch, p. 197). And finally, that sense of guilt and sin that is woven throughout the fabric of Thoreau's writings sounds at times like echoes from a Puritan journal.

Closely allied to the Puritan sense of sin was Thoreau's Victorian sense of morality. At times he was a prig. He was shocked that nature "imitated" the male organs in the *phallus impudicus* fungus (J, IX, 115–17). He berated Channing for telling off-color jokes and added piously, "I lose my respect for the man who can make the mystery of sex the subject of a coarse jest. . . . I would preserve purity in act and thought, as I would cherish the memory of my mother" (J, III, 406–7). Yet he was among the few who were not shocked by Whitman's *Leaves of Grass,* and praised the Hindus for their frankness in discussing sexual relations. Most surprising of all, for his times, was his frequent practice of wading along the streams of Concord in the nude. Modern sunbathers have hailed him as "the pioneer American nudist."

Although I have already ascribed some of Thoreau's radicalness to the economic insecurity of his childhood, it is important to remember that, paradoxical as it sounds, radicalness and resistance are essential parts of the American tradition. Henry Adams has said in his *Education:* "Resistance to something was the law of New England nature; the boy looked out on the world with the instinct of resistance; for numberless generations his predecessors had viewed the world chiefly as a thing to be reformed, filled with evil forces to be abolished."

One of the predominant intellectual ideas of Thoreau's time, as R. W. B. Lewis has so effectively demonstrated in *The American Adam,* was that in America man was offered a new opportunity to break away from the past and begin all over again as an innocent man in paradise, as a new Adam. "Probably nobody of his generation had a richer sense of the potentiality for a fresh, free, and uncluttered existence [than Thoreau]; certainly no one projected the need for the ritual burning of the past in more varied and captivating metaphors. This is what *Walden* is about; it is the most searching contemporary account of the desire for a new kind of life" (p. 20).

New England in the 1830's and 1840's was a hotbed of reform. As Emerson wrote to Carlyle: "We are all a little wild here with numberless projects of social reform. Not a reading man but has a draft of a new Community in his waistcoat pocket" (letter of October 30, 1840). Talk of Fourierism, vegetarianism, the water cure, phrenology, and mesmerism filled the air. But Thoreau found few reformers to his liking. He was more interested in self-reformation than in social reformation.

A notable exception was the abolitionist movement. As Wendell

Glick has pointed out, Concord sponsored one of the most active antislavery societies in the country. Seven members of Thoreau's household were dues-paying members. The periodicals of the movement were subscribed to by members of his family. Leading abolitionists dined at his mother's table whenever they visited town. He numbered among his intimate friends such antislavery men as Alcott, Ricketson, and Parker Pillsbury, and he met at one time or another virtually all the leaders from Garrison down. The Concord Lyceum, by the mid-1840's, was open frequently to antislavery lecturers. "Thoreau never joined the Abolitionist organizations. So deeply ingrained was his feeling that organizations were the breeders of all 'unnatural' restraints upon human liberty that he could not trust even an organization with aims which were almost exactly like his own" (Glick, p. 155). However, he did not remain uninfluenced. Abolitionism from 1835 to 1855, under the leadership of William Lloyd Garrison, gradually evolved its philosophy of action from concentration on individual reform to attacks on the institutions of church and government, which abolitionists felt were retarding reform, and finally to active social reform. And Glick has found a strange coincidence in the similar evolution of Thoreau's social theory. "Almost invariably the radical positions which Garrison took up before 1855 became those of Thoreau a few years later" (Glick, p. 23).

The interest in natural history, so widespread in New England, had a lasting influence on Thoreau. Even today there is hardly a New England town without its local bird watchers, mineral collectors, and amateur botanists. Thoreau was never at a loss to find neighbors interested in discussing the blossoming of a rare azalea or an unseasonal flight of geese.

The mid-nineteenth century was marked by a great surge of scientific discovery. Thoreau kept abreast of his times not only by reading the works of Darwin and Lyell, for example, but through his contact with Agassiz and Harris at Harvard. If at times he seems obsessed with the classification of species, it was because his contemporaries were equally obsessed. "The only official science of which he [Thoreau] had any knowledge was of the sort least likely to stimulate philosophical thought. . . . He was living toward the end of the heyday of the anatomist and the taxonomist, when natural history did not mean primarily either the study of habits and life histories . . . or, still less, those attempts to understand man as part of nature" (Krutch, pp. 181–82).

Henry David Thoreau was in a large part the product of his times. "It is doubtful that he [Thoreau] could have lived and flourished after his particular fashion in any other section of the world than New England, in the nineteenth century. It is equally doubtful that, had his ancestors settled in any other corner of the land, he would have been quite the person he was" (Willson, p. 10). Surely Thoreau was right in thinking that he had "been born into the most estimable place in all the world, and in the very nick of time, too" (J, IX, 160).

SOURCES FOR CHAPTER THREE

The major study of Thoreau's sources is by Arthur Christy, who devoted many years to tracking down the quotations and allusions in Thoreau's writings. Unfortunately his study was left only 90 per cent complete on his death and has never been published. The manuscript is available at Columbia University Library, and it is hoped that it will eventually be completed by some competent student in the field.

A number of lists of Thoreau's borrowings from libraries have been published by Kenneth W. Cameron. These include "Books Thoreau Borrowed from Harvard College Library," in *Emerson the Essayist* (Raleigh, N. C., 1945, pp. 191–208); "Thoreau Discovers Emerson: A College Reading Record" (*BNYPL*, LVII, 1953, 319–34), listing the books he borrowed from the "Institute," an undergraduate club at Harvard; and "Emerson, Thoreau, and the Society of Natural History" (*AL*, XXIV, 1952, 21–30), listing the books he borrowed from the Boston Society of Natural History. Cameron, *The Transcendentalists and Minerva* (Hartford, Conn., 1958, 3 vols.), reprints the "Institute" list (pp. 81–89) and adds "Thoreau's Notes on Harvard Reading" (pp. 130–358), which includes facsimile reproductions of many of Thoreau's reading lists and notes with helpful annotations and identifications by Cameron; "Ungathered Thoreau Reading Lists" (pp. 359–88), which includes among others his Cape Cod, surveying, and Oriental reading lists; "The Concord Social Library in 1836" (pp. 496–506), the catalogue of a library Thoreau probably used; "The Concord Town Library in 1852" (pp. 818–27), the catalogue of another library Thoreau likely used; and "Thoreau's Index at Harvard College" (pp. 871–82), some more reading notes. Walter

Harding, *Thoreau's Library: A Catalog* (Charlottesville, Va., 1957; *TSB*, II), lists and describes the books in Thoreau's library. Emerson's library is intact in the Concord Antiquarian Society, but no catalogue of it has yet been published.

The best brief survey of Thoreau's reading is Norman Foerster, "The Intellectual Heritage of Thoreau" (*Texas Review*, II, 1917, 192–212). Another study is Raymond Adams, "Thoreau's Literary Apprenticeship" (*SP*, XXIX, 1932, 617–29). Virtually all the major biographies and critical studies have also devoted space to the subject. Leonard Gray, "Thoreau's Reading" (*Concord Enterprise*, December 31, 1953), raises a dissenting voice, asserting that Thoreau could not possibly have had the time to do the omnivorous reading that most scholars imply.

The most comprehensive study of the Oriental influence on Thoreau is Arthur Christy, *The Orient in American Transcendentalism* (New York, 1932). Its appendix of Oriental books available to Thoreau is particularly important. Christy also gives a good brief summary of the Oriental influence in his introduction to Thoreau, *Transmigration of the Seven Brahmans* (New York, 1932). Other studies include H. A. Snyder, *A Study of Henry D. Thoreau's Philosophy of Life with Special Reference to the Influence of Hindoo Philosophy* (Heidelberg, Ph.D., n.d.); Kurt Leidecker, "That Sad Pagan Thoreau" (*Visva-Bharati Quarterly*, 1951, 218–59); Li Wang, "The Orient in Henry David Thoreau" (Ohio University, M.A., 1949), a mosaic of Thoreau's remarks on the Orient; and two brief studies: Frances Fletcher, "Henry D. Thoreau, Oriental" (*Open Court*, XLIV, 1930, 510–12) and Egbert S. Oliver, "Thoreau Finds the Dawn in Asia" (*Korean Survey*, II, 1953, 6 ff.).

The most authoritative study of Thoreau's classicism is Ethel Seybold, *Thoreau: The Quest and the Classics* (New Haven, Conn., 1951). Most valuable is its appendix identifying the particular editions Thoreau used and indexing his references to classical authors. Clarence Gohdes, "Henry Thoreau, Bachelor of Arts" (*CJ*, XXIII, 1928, 323–36), is a good brief summary. John Paul Pritchard, "Cato in Concord" (*CW*, XXXVI, 1942, 3–5), summarizes Thoreau's many references to the author of *De Re Rustica*. Leo M. Kaiser, "Remarks on Thoreau's Translation of the Prometheus" (*CW*, XLVI, 1953, 69–70), concludes that "the work today has significance pretty much as a philological curiosity only." John Paul Pritchard, *Return to the Fountains* (Durham, N. C., 1942), points out the influence of Horace on Thoreau's critical theories. Francis L. Utley, "Thoreau and Columella: A Study in Reading" (*NEQ*, XI, 1938, 171–80), comments on Thoreau's interest in the Roman agriculturist. Its findings are challenged in Odell Shepard, "Thoreau and Columella: A Comment" (*NEQ*, XI, 1938, 605–6). Hubert Hoeltje, "Thoreau and the Concord Academy" (*NEQ*, XXI, 1948, 103–9), describes in detail his classical training in Concord Academy. See also K. W. Cameron "Thoreau's Early Compositions in the Ancient Languages" (*ESQ*, VIII, 1957, 20–29) and Cameron, "Ralph Cudworth and Thoreau's Translations of an Orphic Hymn" (*ESQ*, VIII, 1957, 31–36).

For Thoreau's acquaintance with German literature, see Stanley M. Vogel, *German Literary Influences on the American Transcendentalists* (New Haven, Conn., 1955) and Paul Elmer More, "Thoreau's Journal" in *Selected Shelburne Essays* (New York, 1935; reprinted frequently as "Thoreau and German Romanticism"). For his interest in Goethe, see Anton Huffert, "Thoreau as a Teacher, Lecturer, and Educational Thinker" (New York University, Ph.D., 1951, pp. 176–200); in Zimmermann, Grant Loomis, "Thoreau and Zimmermann" (*NEQ*, X, 1937, 789–92); in Rousseau, Huffert, *op. cit.* (pp. 151 ff.); in Dante, J. Chesley Matthews, "Thoreau's Reading in Dante" (*Ital.*, XXVII, 1950, 77–81); in Pellico, John C. Broderick, "Thoreau and *My Prisons*" (*BPLQ*, VII, 1955, 48–50); and in Scandinavian literature, Adolph B. Benson, "Scandinavian Influences in the Writings of Thoreau" (*SS*, XVI, 1941, 201–211, 241–56).

The major work on Thoreau's interest in the early English writers is Anne Whaling, "Studies in Thoreau's Reading of English Poetry and Prose, 1340–1660" (Yale University, Ph.D., 1946). Caroline Spurgeon, *Five Hundred Years of Chaucer Criticism and Allusion* (Cambridge, England, 1925), cites some of Thoreau's major references to Chaucer, but omits at least ten. Esther Cloudman Dunn, *Shakespeare in America* (New York, 1939, pp. 260–63), discusses Thoreau's interest in Shakespeare. There has been no separate study of Thoreau and Milton, but see Sanborn's 1917 biography (pp. 98–105). Thoreau's interest in Raleigh has been rather inadequately covered in the preface to Sanborn's edition of Thoreau, *Sir Walter Raleigh* (Boston, 1905). A good discussion of his interest in Quarles is Ernest Leisy, "Francis Quarles and Henry D. Thoreau *(MLN,* LX, 1945, 335–36). Thoreau and Browne are discussed in Van Doren (p. 81), F. O. Matthiessen, *American Renaissance* (New York, 1941, pp. 110–30), and Joseph Wood Krutch, "Thoreau and Sir Thomas Browne" *(TSB* 29). Walter Gierasch, "Bishop Hall and Thoreau," is in *TSB* 31. For evidences of Thoreau's interest in the metaphysical poets, see Carl Bode, *Collected Poems of Henry Thoreau* (Chicago, 1943; "Textual Notes," *passim*). Raymond Himelick, "Thoreau and Samuel Daniel" *(AL,* XXIV, 1952, 177–85), is a perceptive study of how Thoreau wrenched quotations from the Elizabethan poet to serve his own purposes. Thoreau's interest in early English ballads and songs has not received the attention it deserves, but there are brief notes in Joseph Leach, "Thoreau's Borrowings in *Walden*" *(Amer. N. & Q.,* II, 1943, 171) and Howard Schultz, "A Fragment of Jacobean Song in Thoreau's *Walden*" *(MLN,* 1948, 271–72). There is no completed study of Thoreau's use of the Bible, though I understand that a doctoral dissertation on the subject, by the Rev. Carl Weller, is in progress at Notre Dame University. For Thoreau's interest in Ossian, see Ernest Leisy, "Thoreau and Ossian" *(NEQ,* XVIII, 1945, 96–98). For his reading of Gilpin, see William Templeman, "Thoreau, Moralist of the Picturesque" *(PMLA,* XLVII, 1932, 864–89), but note also James Southworth, "Reply" *(PMLA,* XLIX, 1934, 971–74). There have been no extended studies of Thoreau's interest in the nineteenth-century English literary figures.

The definitive study of Thoreau's interest in early American literature is Lawrence Willson, "The Influence of Early North American History and Legend on the Writings of Henry David Thoreau" (Yale University, Ph.D., 1949); and see also Willson, "Thoreau and Roman Catholicism" *(Cath HR,* XLII, 1956, 157–72).

Albert Keiser presents a careful discussion and evaluation of the Indian notebooks (now in the Morgan Library) in "Thoreau's Manuscripts on the Indians" *(JEGP,* XXVII, 1928, 183–99); reprints a brief essay by Thoreau on "big things and little," found imbedded in the Indian notebooks in "New Thoreau Material"

(*MLN,* XLIV, 1929, 253–54); and evaluates Thoreau's attitude toward the Indian in "Thoreau—Friend of the Native" (*The Indian in American Literature,* New York, 1933, pp. 209–32). Lawrence Willson discusses Thoreau's reading in Indian literature in his Yale dissertation cited above (pp. 211–91). See also Reginald Cook, "An Indian Memory" (*Passage to Walden,* Boston, 1949, pp. 80–98) and Jason Almus Russell, "Thoreau: The Interpreter of the Real Indian" (*QQ,* XXXV, 1927, 37–48). Kenneth Cameron prints a list of "Books on Indians Which Thoreau Did Know or Might Have Known by November, 1837" as an appendix to "Thoreau's Three Months Out of Harvard" (*ESQ,* V, 1956, 10–11).

For Thoreau's interest in travel literature, see John Christie, "Thoreau, Traveler" (Duke University, Ph.D., 1955). Walter Harding, "Thoreau and Timothy Dwight" (*BPLQ,* X, 1958, 109–15), discusses the influence of one particular travel writer on Thoreau.

Hubert Hoeltje, "Thoreau and the Concord Academy" (*NEQ,* XXI, 1948, 103–9), presents the newly discovered records of Phineas Allen's teaching. See also Gladys Hosmer, "Phineas Allen, Thoreau's Preceptor" (*TSB* 59). The most intensive study of the influence of Thoreau's Harvard education is Christian Gruber, "The Education of Henry Thoreau, Harvard 1833–1837" (Princeton University, Ph.D., 1953). Edgeley Todd's study is entitled "Philosophical Ideas at Harvard College, 1817–1837" (*NEQ,* XVI, 1943, 63–90), and Joseph Kwiat has discussed Todd's findings with particular relation to Thoreau in "Thoreau's Philosophical Apprenticeship" (*NEQ,* XVIII, 1945, 51–69). See also Raymond Adams, "Thoreau's Literary Apprenticeship" (*SP,* XXIX, 1932, 617–29).

Sanborn devotes the opening chapter in each of his biographies to the influence of Thoreau's ancestry. Samuel A. Jones, *Thoreau: A Glimpse* (Concord, Mass., 1903, pp. 30–31), stresses the influence of Thoreau's mother and father. Ruth R. Wheeler, *The Concord Friendly Aid Society* (Concord, Mass., 1950), points out Mrs. Thoreau's charitable activities. Townsend Scudder, *Concord: American Town* (Boston, 1947), gives a vivid picture of the intellectual activity of the town in Thoreau's day.

For the relationship of Thoreau and Emerson, see the Sources for Chapter One (p. 34); see also Alice Hazard, "The Reciprocal

Relations of Emerson and Thoreau" (Boston University, M.A., 1935); Percy W. Brown, "Was Thoreau a Disciple of Emerson?" *Middlesex Monographs* (Cleveland, 1941); Leonard Gray, "Emerson and Thoreau" (*Unity*, CXXXVII, 1952, 88–92); and W. Stephen Thomas, *Emerson and Thoreau: A Relationship* (Rochester, N. Y., 1954); the last work stresses the influence of Thoreau on Emerson.

There is no good study of American Transcendentalism, although Perry Miller, *The Transcendentalists* (Cambridge, Mass., 1950) and *American Transcendentalists* (New York, 1957), collect the major documents of the movement. Raymond Adams, "Henry Thoreau's Literary Theories and Criticism" (University of North Carolina, Ph.D., 1928), discusses some of the influence of Transcendentalism on Thoreau. An amusing but unscholarly picture of the reform movements of Thoreau's time is Grace Adams and Edward Hutter, *The Mad Forties* (New York, 1942). Joseph Jones, "Transcendental Grocery Bills: Thoreau's *Walden* and Some Aspects of American Vegetarianism" (*UTSE*, XXXVI, 1957, 141–54), demonstrates that Thoreau's ideas on vegetarianism were fairly common in his time. Wendell Glick, "Thoreau and Radical Abolitionism" (Northwestern University, Ph.D., 1950), presents the definitive account of the effect of Garrison and his followers on Thoreau. For the influence of Puritan morality on Thoreau, see Raymond Gozzi, "Tropes and Figures" (New York University, Ph.D., 1957). For the American Adamistic theories, see R. W. B. Lewis, *The American Adam* (Chicago, 1955). There is some discussion of the influence of scientific theories of the time upon Thoreau in William Drake, "A Formal Study of H. D. Thoreau" (Iowa University, M.A., 1948).

CHAPTER FOUR

Thoreau's Ideas

Before any attempt can be made to examine Thoreau's philosophy and present an organized analysis of his ideas, it is important to recognize that he never made any such attempt himself. "Thoreau will remain forever baffling if we insist on resolving into perfect harmony all his ideas and impulses, since there is every reason to believe he did not himself harmonize them" (Foerster, *Nature in American Literature*, p. 119). Thoreau, like most of the other Transcendentalists, was essentially an eclectic. He picked up his ideas from hither and yon, accepting what interested him and ignoring the rest. As he grew older, many of his ideas inevitably changed, but that did not disturb him. In any one period of his life he was usually consistent. Contradictions can be found only if one places in juxtaposition statements Thoreau made at wide intervals of time. Unfortunately there is not space in a brief treatment such as this to indicate in any detail the development of his thought and his changes of attitude. There is a real need for a detailed study devoted to that subject. But until that study is made, we shall have to be content with attempting to understand his most prevalent or most familiar ideas.

Although this problem does raise a serious obstacle to presenting accurately Thoreau's ideas per se, it does offer, on the other hand, an almost unequal opportunity to study the development of a man's mind, since Thoreau's writings, particularly his *Journal,* are so voluminous. "Thoreau's principal achievement was not the creation of a system but the creation of himself, and his principal literary work was, therefore, the presentation of that self

in the form of a self-portrait" (Krutch, p. 11). The very fact that
Thoreau never crystallized his ideas into a set form, Krutch also
suggests, adds immensely to the charm of his writing. Thoreau
was always on the search for an answer, and his enthusiasm in that
search carries the reader along with him.

But unfortunately altogether too many students of Thoreau
have not been willing to accept the fact that Thoreau did not
formulate and unify his thinking. Approaching his writings with
a preconceived notion that there was a unity to his ideas, they
have attempted to impose a consistency where no consistency existed. They have accepted those ideas of his that fitted their own
particular orthodoxy and silently rejected the rest. Thus they have
been able to "prove" that Thoreau was a stoic or an epicurean,
a pacifist or a militarist, a pessimist or an optimist, an individualist
or a communist. There is hardly an ism of our times that has not
attempted to adopt Thoreau—and yet was there ever a man who
so consistently renounced all isms, all preconceived or institutionalized views of the universe?

Perhaps the most popular misconception of Thoreau is that he
was a stoic. "He was an ascetic who reveled in self-denial." "He
could more easily say no than yes." "He preferred to do without."
These are the most frequent reactions to Thoreau. It is easy to
discover the basis for this misconception. It was popularized by
Ralph Waldo Emerson. Emerson delighted in seeing Thoreau as
"the perfect Stoic." It mattered little to him that Thoreau's sister
Sophia protested, "Henry never impressed me as the Stoic which
Mr. E. represents him" (*Daniel Ricketson and His Friends,* p.
155). To Emerson, Thoreau was a stoic. When he composed Thoreau's funeral address, he overemphasized the negative elements
in Thoreau's personality. When he edited Thoreau's *Letters to
Various Persons,* he purposely omitted all homely, personal remarks because they did not conform to his preconception. Sophia
again protested, this time to the publisher James T. Fields, but
Emerson was permitted to have his way. Thus there has been built
up in the minds of the people the picture of Thoreau as a stoic,
and no amount of evidence to the contrary seems to convince
them that their conception is false. I do not wish to imply that
Emerson was malicious in his misinterpretation. On the contrary,

he was trying his best to emphasize what he thought were Thoreau's greatest values.

Mary Edith Cochnower has examined Thoreau's stoicism at length and has concluded: "He was perhaps as true a Stoic as could have been in his day or any day. He was surprisingly like his ancient prototypes" ("Thoreau and Stoicism," p. 94). But I, for one, feel that she has been highly selective in choosing her evidence and that, as she herself admits, the term "stoicism" has become so broadened and so watered down as to render it virtually meaningless.

F. O. Matthiessen (*American Renaissance*, p. 122) presents the diametrically opposite viewpoint: "In the broad use of the terms, he [Thoreau] is much more of an epicurean than a stoic." It would be foolish to try to epitomize Thoreau's philosophy as "Eat, drink, and be merry, for tomorrow we die." Nothing was much further from his attitude. But if we define (as the dictionary does) an epicurean as one who delights in sensuous pleasure, we do come much closer to certain aspects of Thoreau's outlook. Thoreau was basically sensuous. "See, hear, smell, taste, etc., while these senses are fresh and pure," he says (J, II, 330). When he denied himself sense stimulation—as often he did—it was not through any stoic belief in asceticism for its own sake but through his desire to keep his senses "free and pure" for the higher levels of perception. "I do not take snuff," he says (J, IX, 197). "In my winter walks, I stoop and bruise between my thumb and finger the dry whorls of the lycopus, or water horehound . . . and smell that. That is as near as I come to the Spice Islands."

"However much Thoreau wished always to walk in the pure empyrean, he could not check for long his sensuous love for solid earth" (Willson, p. 27). And that sensuous love is obvious throughout his writings. It is because he expresses himself sensuously rather than abstractly that he is so readable. When we read Thoreau at his best, we bring every sense into play. "My body is all sentient," he says. "As I go here or there, I am tickled by this or that I come in contact with, as if touched by the wires of a battery" (J, VIII, 44). And so we the readers see, hear, smell, and taste vicariously through Thoreau. As F. O. Matthiessen has pointed out (*American Renaissance*, p. 87), it is what separates Thoreau most from Emerson and what makes him more readable today. Emerson gives us abstract ideas; Thoreau makes us experience. Perhaps it was because Emerson did not comprehend this difference (maybe it was something beyond his ken) that he misinterpreted Thoreau as a stoic.

But one must be careful not to go too far in depicting Thoreau as an epicurean. He was not interested (theoretically, at least) in sense stimulation for its own sake. It was only a means toward an end. His ultimate goal was to find his place in the universe. He developed his senses to ascertain more accurately where that place was.

Thoreau classified himself as a Transcendentalist. If we use the popular definition that a Transcendentalist is one who believes that one can (and should) go beyond Locke in believing that all knowledge is acquired through the senses, that in order to attain the ultimate in knowledge one must "transcend" the senses, we can unquestionably classify Thoreau as a Transcendentalist. "It is not the invitation which I hear, but which I feel, that I obey," he said at one point (J, II, 181); at another, "My genius makes distinctions which my understanding cannot and which my senses do not report" (J, II, 337). His *Journals,* particularly up to approximately 1850, are filled with avowals of the Transcendental philosophy. The "Higher Laws" chapter of *Walden* is one of his most explicit statements of these beliefs. The account of his reverie on the doorstep of his Walden cabin, which opens the chapter on "Sounds" (W, II, 123–24), is perhaps his best-known account of the Transcendental experience.

But unfortunately as he grew older he found that he was "transcending his senses" less and less frequently, that he was depending more and more on sensuous rather than Transcendental inspiration. Over and over again in his *Journal* of the early 1850's he laments this change: "I fear that the character of my knowledge is from year to year becoming more distinct and scientific; that, in exchange for views as wide as heaven's scope, I am being narrowed down to the field of the microscope. I see details, not wholes nor the shadow of the whole. I count some parts, and say, 'I know'" (J, II, 406).

Thoreau realized that he attained Transcendental insight not through excitement but through serenity. But as the moments of inspiration became fewer and farther between, he paradoxically intensified the search. "What more than anything else brought him out in all weathers—rain, snow, sleet, fog—alone or with a more than superfluous companion, ever and again to the old forest shrines and hillcrest temples, was the mystic's hope of detecting some trace of the Ineffable" (Norman Foerster, *Nature in American Literature*, p. 101). "Ah, those youthful days!" Thoreau lamented, "are they never to return? when the walker does not too curiously observe particulars, but sees, hears, scents, tastes, and feels only himself,—the phenomena that show themselves in him,—his expanding body, his intellect and heart. No worm or insect, quadruped or bird, confined his view, but the unbounded universe was his. A bird is now become a mote in his eye" (J, V, 75). But the search continued. "The birding and botanizing were not so ill a thing," he rationalized, according to Foerster, "affording just enough occupation—save when they amounted to a tyranny of observation—to prevent his too insistently asking Nature to give him 'a sign.' Even 'the slight distraction of picking berries is favorable,' he found, 'to a mild, abstracted, poetic mood, to sequestered or transcendental thinking'" (*Nature in American Literature*, p. 104).

In Thoreau's later years one will find more and more space in his writings devoted to an external record of nature and less and less to a recounting of Transcendental experiences. It seems at times—and it has led some observers to believe—that in those later years Thoreau abandoned his earlier Transcendentalism for purely scientific observation. But such an interpretation, I believe, is not correct. Never did he completely abandon his belief in the Transcendental approach to knowledge. In his *Journal* for 1856 he wrote: "It is by obeying the suggestions of a higher light within you that you escape from yourself and . . . travel totally new paths" (J, IX, 38); in 1858, "In all important crises one can only consult his genius" (J, IX, 379).

It is almost universally agreed that Thoreau is America's greatest nature writer. It was as a nature writer that he first achieved fame, and it is as a nature writer that he is still most widely known.

Thoreau has had a remarkable influence on the development

of the natural history essay. Thoreau was "the first of the American writers upon Nature to be concerned with the workmanship of his product" (Hicks, *The Development of the Natural History Essay in American Literature,* p. 88); that is, the first to realize that the natural history essay could be something more than a mere reporting of natural phenomena observed, that it could in fact be a full-fledged type of belles-lettres. He was the first to make the natural history essay "a definite, and separate, literary form as contrasted to the 'Letters' of White and Crèvecœr, the 'Episodes' of Audubon, the 'Rambles' of Godman, and the various 'Journals' and 'Travels' of earlier writers" (Hicks, pp. 88–89). He established the pattern that most nature writers since his day have followed.

But there are certain characteristics of Thoreau's nature writing that neither his predecessors nor his imitators have ever succeeded in duplicating. He gives his readers a unique sense of immediacy. "Most nature writers appear limited, an eye or an ear or a taste or a touch, but in Thoreau the senses are integrated and focussed" (Cook, *Passage to Walden,* p. 51).

Further, Thoreau has a contagious enthusiasm. Up to the moment of his death he succeeded in retaining that sense of wonder and awe in the beauty of the world around him that most of us associate with our childhood. Clifton Fadiman is supposed to have remarked that Thoreau could get more out of ten minutes with a chickadee than most men could get out of a night with Cleopatra. What is even more remarkable, he almost succeeds in convincing us that the chickadee is preferable to Cleopatra.

But the most significant difference between Thoreau and other nature writers is that natural history was never his primary interest. It was always a means toward an end. His basic concern was not with nature itself but with man's place in nature. "It is narrow to be confined to woods and fields and grand aspects of nature only," he says in his *Journal* (J, II, 421). "The greatest and wisest will still be related to men."

Thoreau's greatest scorn, in fact, was directed at those who were "mere accumulators of facts" about nature (J, I, 18). "The anecdotes of science affect me as trivial and petty," he said (*The Moon,* p. 24). He was disturbed that scientists were willing to kill even a snake to ascertain its species. "I feel that this is not the means of acquiring true knowledge" (J, VI, 311). "This haste to kill a bird or a quadruped and make a skeleton of it, which many young men and some old ones exhibit, reminds me of the fable of the man who killed the hen that laid golden eggs, and so got no more gold. It is a perfectly parallel case" (J, XIV, 109). When an ornithologist said to him, "If you hold the bird in your hand . . . ," he replied, "I would rather hold it in my affections" (J, VI, 253). He was not so much interested in the bird, as "a bird behind the bird,—for a mythology to shine through his ornithology" (Burroughs, *Indoor Studies,* p. 40).

It was this mystical approach that has led many scientists to distrust Thoreau. (Paradoxically, as Willson has pointed out [p. 33], philosophers have distrusted him because he was too scientific.) Havelock Ellis (*The New Spirit,* p. 94) has perhaps been the most vehement in his denunciation of Thoreau's science: "He seems to have been absolutely deficient in scientific sense." Lowell, in his well-known 1865 essay on Thoreau, said, "He discovered nothing. He thought everything a discovery of his own." Bradford Torrey, the editor of Thoreau's *Journal,* thought that he "leaves the present-day reader wondering how so eager a scholar could have spent so many years in learning so comparatively little" (J, I, xliii), and the coeditor of the *Journal,* Francis Allen, in *Thoreau's Bird-Lore,* devoted much space to pointing out Thoreau's errors in ornithology. Fannie Hardy Eckstorm, in her essay on "Thoreau's 'Maine Woods,' " went to some length to emphasize his weakness as a naturalist. W. L. McAtee denounced him as naïve for accepting some of the theories of protective coloration. And even John Burroughs, who, as I have shown above, realized that natural history was not Thoreau's major interest, delighted in disparaging his observations on nature.

Thoreau himself realized that the scientists would not understand his aims. When he was invited by Spencer Fullerton Baird to join the [American] Association for the Advancement of Science, he noted in his *Journal* that he was declining the invitation because "The fact is I am a mystic, a transcendentalist, and a natural philosopher to boot. . . . I should have told them at once that I was a transcendentalist. That would have been the shortest way of telling them that they would not understand my explanations. . . . If it had been the secretary of an association of which Plato or Aristotle was the president, I should not have hesitated to describe my studies at once and particularly" (J, V, 4–5).

Thoreau's errors of observation in natural history are not difficult to understand. In the first place, he lacked adequate scientific equipment. He owned no bird glasses at all until 1854, and then he acquired a telescope rather than the far more efficient binoculars. He used his hat as a botany box. And apparently he had to borrow a microscope when he wanted to use one. But he deliberately did without scientific instruments, frequently because he believed they gave a distorted picture of nature. Then too there were few adequate reference books available in his time. Most of the natural history books in his library were British, simply because there were no comparable American counterparts, although he did own Gray's botany, Wilson's ornithology, Harlan's and Audubon's fauna, and Jaeger's entomology, among others.

What was even more important was that American science was still in its most elementary stages. The pioneering work of classification under such men as Agassiz and Gray had just begun. Taxonomy was the major field of science in Thoreau's day. Thoreau was willing to help in laying these important foundations. In the late 1840's he supplied Agassiz himself with many new specimens, including several new fish, a mouse, and more than one tortoise (Channing, p. 264). And he also assisted Thaddeus William Harris in his entomological researches. But taxonomy could never be Thoreau's major interest. He was not so much interested in the individual species as in the interrelation of all species, and particularly in their relation to man. After reporting a new species of fish to the Boston Society of Natural History, he commented: "What is the amount of my discovery to me? It is not that I have got one in a bottle, that it has got a name in a book, but that I have a little fishy friend in the pond" (J, XI, 360). Nearly a century ahead of his time, he was fundamentally an ecologist. He would have had fewer complaints about the narrowness of the scientific view if he could have read some of our twentieth-century ecological studies. And, reciprocally, twentieth-century scientists have begun to realize the values of his broader approach.

Though as an ecologist Thoreau "perhaps never quite attained what could be called real competence in analyzing the relative effects of all of environment," still he "was acutely aware of the complexity of factors which go to make up the living conditions of a plant" (Nash, "Ecology in the Writings of Henry David Thoreau," p. 15). "The remarkable thing about Thoreau's plant ecology is that he *noticed* so complete a list of environmental effects with so little professional guidance" (p. 27). In his ecological studies Thoreau found "a clue to an explanation of the unity and the completeness of nature which [he] had so long accepted in his transcendental faith" (p. 80). "Certainly ecology with its emphasis upon natural law and the study of vital inter-relationships represented the most logical scientific position from which Thoreau could rise to defend his more transcendental convictions as to the greater unities and the essential completeness of Nature" (p. 80).

Thoreau's major specific contribution to science was his discussion of the theory of the succession of forest trees. It is true that his discovery was anticipated by several other scientists. But Thoreau did his work independently, and his essay is still a standard treatise on the subject. Edward Deevey believes that Thoreau was the first American limnologist and that he made an independent discovery of thermal stratification of water. Aldo Leopold has accorded Thoreau the title of "the father of phenology in this country." But Leo Stoller, after extensive study, has concluded that "Thoreau was by no means a pioneer in American phenology and that his observations probably had no part in the development of this aspect of science" (p. 172). And Anna Botsford Comstock, the leader of the nature study movement in American education, has said, "Thoreau is the ideal toward which those of us engaged in nature study have been working" (p. 54).

Since the publication of Thoreau's complete *Journal* in 1906 scientists have come more and more to recognize it as an important source book for studies of American natural history. It was primarily the records available in these books that led Ludlow Griscom to choose the town of Concord as the setting for his study of changing bird populations, *Birds of Concord*. Arthur Bent and Edward Forbush cited Thoreau regularly in their ornithological studies. Dame and Collins used his records in their *Flora of Middlesex County, Massachusetts* (Malden, Mass., 1888), even though the full *Journal* was not available then. I understand that the American Meteorological Society is now combing the *Journal* for early weather records. And the authors of many other natural history textbooks have found his records useful.

In recent years much has been made of the new type of field handbooks in natural history popularized by Roger Tory Peterson. Their primary value is that they epitomize and emphasize the distinctive marks of the various species. It is interesting to discover that a century ago Thoreau called for just such handbooks: "The object should be to describe not those particulars in which a species resembles its genus, for they are many and that would be but a negative description, but those in which it is peculiar, for they are few and positive" (J, V, 189).

But despite Thoreau's insistence that he was not a natural scientist, and apparently quite against his own will, he found himself in the last fifteen years of his life more and more concerned with scientific data for their own sake—a fact well evidenced by the details on the temperature of the water in Walden Pond in *Walden* (W, II, 330–31) and the pages and pages of lists of species in the later *Journal* (many of which were omitted in the printed version). He was quite conscious of this change of attitude and frequently bewailed it with such comments as "I feel I am dissipated by so many observations" (J, V, 45). But he continued increasingly to concern himself with such data. Ironically enough, as I have indicated above, it is just such information that has proved of value to modern scientists. Finally,

Amateur though he may have remained in any single field, and protester throughout his life that science's perspective was untrustworthy, yet Thoreau's microscope, spy-glass, charts, weather-tables, presses, and collections, his geological surveys, "Zoological Notes," Reports of the Smithsonian Institute, of the Massachusetts [*sic*] Society of Natural History, of the Massachusetts Agricultural Society, his reading of Audubon, Wilson, Mcgillivray, Bergstein, Littel, and Nuttal, of Loudon, Gray, Harlan, and Lovell, of Fitch, Harris, Kirby, and Spence, of Agassiz and Gould, Abbott, Sowerby, and Chambers, his own field notes and his essays, all attest to the respect and interest which he showed for the natural scientist's acute eye and practice of induction (Christie, p. 81).

There is a widespread confusion as to Thoreau's religious beliefs. When George Ripley reviewed *A Week* for the *New York*

Tribune, he denounced Thoreau as a pantheist. I have been told that each spring an elderly lady makes a pilgrimage to Sleepy Hollow Cemetery to place bouquets on the graves of Emerson and Hawthorne and, turning to Thoreau's grave, ends her ceremony by shaking her fist and saying, "None for you, you dirty little atheist." On the other hand, John Sylvester Smith has hailed him as "an American spiritual genius" ("The Philosophic Naturism of Henry David Thoreau," p. 220) and "a man seeking the salvation of his soul" (p. iv). Wherein does the truth lie?

Thoreau never subscribed to any sectarian creed. "We are wont foolishly to think that the creed which a man professes is more significant than the fact he is," he said (J, IX, 144). The Unitarians frequently claim him as one of their own on the basis of the fact that he was baptized by a Unitarian minister and buried from a Unitarian church. But Thoreau specifically renounced membership in the Unitarian Church. When he was invited to deliver a lecture in the basement of an orthodox (that is, Congregational) church, he "trusted he helped to undermine it" (J, IX, 188).

Although he numbered many clergymen among his friends, he disliked ministers in general, complaining that they were men who could not butter their own bread and yet who combined with a thousand like them to "make dipped toast for all eternity" (J, IX, 284). When one clergyman told Thoreau that he was going to dive into his inmost depths, Thoreau replied, "I trust you will not strike your head against the bottom" (J, V, 265). He complained: "The church! it is eminently the timid institution, and the heads and pillars of it are constitutionally and by principle the greatest cowards in the community" (J, XI, 325). He wished that "ministers were a little more *dangerous*" (J, XII, 407).

Neither was he interested in homiletics or sectarian theology. "In the main, one may say he was uninterested in the deity" (Drake, "A Formal Study of Thoreau," p. 32). Metaphysics, said Channing, was Thoreau's aversion. His more orthodox maiden aunts were exasperated with him because he would take no interest in theological literature and yet found plenty of time to observe frogs (J, V, 58).

Although Thoreau often belittled his own knowledge of the Bible, he was far better read in it than many, perhaps most, professed Christians. It is difficult to read more than a few pages of his writings without finding a biblical quotation or echo. But "he was among the first to see Christian literature as only the purest and most inspiring of the fables about the relation of man to nature and about the infinite capacities of the unaided human spirit" (Lewis, *American Adam,* p. 22).

Thoreau was critical of the effect that religion had upon his contemporaries. He could not see that it made them superior morally to any other race or nation (J, III, 21). In fact, he thought that conversion was often a "blast" upon youth that prevented their full development (J, V, 210). As he grew older he became more and more convinced that the institutionalized churches were a blight on society. Their opposition to abolitionism in particular antagonized him, and in his various antislavery papers he denounced their conservatism roundly.

Yet it is entirely false to think of Thoreau as irreligious. The Rev. John Sylvester Smith recognizes that although Thoreau rejected orthodox theology and dogma,

He saw what the religious thinkers of his time did not see—that their religion was too much indoors, that it was too often a logical and abstract verbalism only, that it possessed a great vocabulary of orthodox thinking and a minimum of classic Christian experience ("The Philosophic Naturism of Henry David Thoreau," p. 276). [He] held immediate religious feeling of the aesthetic quality of the world to be superior, as a means of religious revelation, to scientific investigation on the one hand and to traditional dogma on the other (p. 95). Thoreau believed man was meant to experience God, not to theologize about him. . . . Thoreau's "theology" was not a branch of metaphysics, it was an experience of life (p. 263). Thoreau was seeking for himself and for his fellowmen . . . a fuller and more nearly natural self-realization, a fulfillment more in harmony with the constituted quality of man's own being (p. 29).

Unlike some of his fellow Transcendentalists, Thoreau did not naïvely deny the existence of evil.

His thought does not share in that tendency of typical American Transcendentalism (of which Emerson is patron saint) to retreat from experience into the cloud-land glories of subjective idealism (Smith, p. 112). But it was really only social and universal maladjustment that he admitted, and not categorical evil. It was nothing that a good reformation could not cure (p. 265).

Yet

Thoreau's thinking must be distinguished from that of Rousseau. The latter held that all social forms corrupt men. Thoreau held that the organization of society *as he knew it in his time* was corrupting. He did not despair of social life, although without question he denounced the value of any society as being inherently greater than that of the individual (p. 264). Thoreau's thinking is clear enough. He believed in God; he believed in man; but he did not believe in "civilization" as he found it because it is not organized for the natural and moral good of man (p. 141). For Thoreau, orientation in nature is not "back to nature" in the Rousseauistic sense, but rather is it the transcendental idea, "through nature to God" (p. 182).

Thoreau went to Walden not to escape from civilization but to discover the true civilization that would permit and foster the greatest development of man's spiritual nature.

Finally, Thoreau was interested in a universal religion, an ethical religion that would be based on the high points of all the Bibles of the world. When Moncure Conway, then a student at Harvard Divinity School, told Thoreau he was "studying the Scriptures," Thoreau replied, "Which Scriptures?" He found as much of value in Confucianism, Buddhism, and the other major Oriental religions as in Christianity. One of his important contributions to the *Dial* was his series of selections from these other Bibles, entitled "Ethnical Scriptures." As he said, "To the philosophers, all sects, all nations, are alike. I like Brahma, Hari, Buddha, the Great Spirit, as well as God" (J, II, 4).

From the beginning of his life to the very end, Thoreau believed that all reform must come from within and cannot be imposed by any outside force. We cannot reform society; we can reform only the individual. When each individual reforms himself, then the reformation of society will automatically follow. Reformation through legislation may achieve temporary results, but lasting reformation will be achieved only when each individual convinces himself of its desirability. Such is the basic belief of Transcendentalism. Thoreau was one of the few Transcendentalists to remain true to that belief throughout his life.

Thoreau, in fact, was as suspicious of reformers as a class as he was of clergymen. One of the most amusing passages in his *Journal* is the oft-quoted description of the three reformers who by coincidence landed at his house in Concord at the same time (J, V, 263–65). He thought them "slimy" and did his utmost to make them ill at ease. He questioned their motives and feared that often they were more interested in forwarding their own careers than their reforms. "They cannot tolerate a man who stands by a head above them," he complained (J, V, 365). It is important to remember, however, "though he lacked a whole-hearted sympathy for those who advocated far-reaching reforms, Thoreau preferred them vastly to the smug and timid conservatives (Kirchner, "Henry David Thoreau as a Social Critic," p. 237).

Far more than the individual reformers, he mistrusted the reform societies. No matter what their purpose, societies tended to in-stitutionalize themselves. They destroyed rather than developed the strength of the individual:

Speaking of Fourier communities with Bellew, I said that I sus-pected any enterprise in which two were engaged together. "But," said he, "it is difficult to make a stick stand unless you slant two or more against it." "Oh, no," answered I, "you may split its lower end to two or three, or drive it single into the ground, which is the best way; but most men, when they start on a new enterprise, not only figuratively, but really, *pull up stakes*. When the sticks prop one another, none, or only one, stands erect" (J, VII, 500).

Thoreau, said Emerson in "Life and Letters in New England," "was in his own person a practical answer, almost a refutation to the theories of the socialists."

Of all the reform movements of his time, the one that came the closest to leading Thoreau astray from his basic principles of individual reformation was the abolitionist movement. It was the most vocal, the most active. Thoreau agreed that slavery was *the* problem of his time. He spoke out frequently and vociferously against it. He aided Negro slaves to escape to freedom in Canada. He was one of the first to come to the defense of John Brown after Harpers Ferry. But never did he officially join any antislavery movement. And although he wavered at times, I do not believe he ever completely abandoned his original principles.

Wendell Glick believes differently:

For at least eight years—from 1837 . . . to 1845 . . . he [Thoreau] believed implicitly . . . that the reform of society should be intrusted solely to the forces for good within man and the universe ("Thoreau and Radical Abolitionism," p. 105). While Thoreau was at Walden Pond, he and his government had a disagreement [the "Civil Disobedience" episode] which left its mark and hastened the day of his willingness to aid radical Abolitionists in their attempt to destroy it (p. 143). When he left Walden Pond . . . the evil which lurked in institutions, he concluded, was more malevolent than he had ever suspected as a youth. It was so malevolent that it would have to be fought by every means available, and that meant, of course, by attempting to decrease the strength of institutions while at the same time appealing to the conscience of man (pp. 133–34). The method of reform from within, which he had advocated so staunchly to 1845, had not been enough to arrest the trend, any more than the combination of appeals to the conscience and attacks on institutions to which he resorted after his stay at Walden. The result was that by the end of the 1850's, Thoreau was in a quandary, and willing to embrace any method which seemed to have the least prospect of success (p. 158). Though his close friends and admirers used the [John Brown] incident in his defense [that through it he fulfilled his social obligations], had they understood him they would have gone to any length to play it down. For its real meaning was that Thoreau's long cherished faith in the adequacy of the Moral Law to satisfy all man's individual and collective needs was slipping precariously (p. 215).

Since I have already discussed some of these points in an earlier chapter, I will not amplify them here. But I am not convinced that Thoreau ever more than wavered from his original principles. To the very end he held to his belief that reform must come from within.

With government, as with reform, Thoreau's principles were almost purely Transcendental. "There are, for Thoreau, only individuals and the only fundamental law is the law of morality, and if political expedience and the law of morality clash it becomes the duty of the individual citizen to follow the divine law— that is, the voice of his conscience within" (West, *Rebel Thought*, p. 206). He did not want "no government, but *at once* a better government" (W, IV, 357), a government that would "recognize the individual as a higher and independent power, from which all its own power and authority are derived" (W, IV, 387).

The government he idealized was not a government by force but a government by co-operation. He fully realized that certain functions could best be conducted by society rather than by the individual. "In passage after passage of his published works and journal, Thoreau makes specific proposals for legitimate governmental activity, often proposals for new state or local laws or improvements of existing ones" (John C. Broderick, "Thoreau's Proposals for Legislation," p. 285). "With Thoreau the individual comes first, but the welfare of the community is also important" (Broderick, "Thoreau's Principle of Simplicity," p. 286). Thoreau suggests compulsory education laws, supplemented by government-sponsored adult education. He asks that the government improve roads, issue adequate maps, further crime detection, prevent fires, and conserve natural resources. Thus, such a statement as that by James MacKaye (*Thoreau: The Philosopher of Freedom,* p. x), that Thoreau was "an extreme individualist, he never grasped the potentialities of cooperation in promoting efficient production," is belied. "It must be observed that almost all of Thoreau's proposals fall into a general grouping not unjustifiably described as welfare legislation" (Broderick, "Thoreau's Proposals for Legislation," p. 288). "The specific proposals in the journal, however, suggest Thoreau's acceptance of the principle of governmental activity, legislation for human welfare, so long as increased, abusive authority over the individual is not its inevitable companion" (p. 289).

Thoreau constantly kept in mind the danger of centralized government. No matter for what good purpose a government was established, it too soon became institutionalized. Founded to serve the individual, it inevitably ended in subordinating the individual to its own purposes. Founded to establish justice, it ended by preserving injustice. The protection of the institution of slavery by the federal, state, and even local governments of Thoreau's own time was to him convincing evidence of the inherent danger. It was the duty of the good citizen, he believed, to be ever on the watch to prevent the expansion of the powers of the state. Most, if not all, of his political essays were written to call the attention of his fellow citizens to this danger and to encourage them in their duty to fight it in specific instances.

At times, he found, one must be in outright revolt against the state. If the laws of the state came in conflict with the "higher laws" of the conscience, it was the conscience, not the state, that must be obeyed. It became a "duty of civil disobedience," and his essay on that subject has become, through the years, a manual of arms for those who are so led to revolt. It is significant that Thoreau, unlike his friends Hawthorne and Whitman, when he was faced with the dilemma of choosing between abolishing slavery and saving the Union, without hesitation chose the former.

Howard Floan complains that Thoreau's information about the true nature of slavery in the South was "both limited and distorted" (*The South in Northern Eyes,* p. 63) because he had never visited the area and because he accepted prejudiced (that is, abolitionist) sources of information as accurate. But unlike most of his Northern contemporaries, Thoreau directed his attack not at the "far-off foes" in the South, "but at those in the North who were so enslaved by commerce that they were not capable of helping the Negro or the Mexican" (p. 66).

Far more important to Thoreau than government was liberty. That government he would respect that not only frees man from civil restraint but also fosters and encourages a true moral freedom:

I please myself with imagining a State at last which can afford to be just to all men, and to treat the individual with respect as a neighbor; which even would not think it inconsistent with its own repose if a few were to live aloof from it, not meddling with it, nor embraced by it, who fulfilled all the duties of neighbors and fellow-men. A State which bore this kind of fruit, and suffered it to drop off as fast as it ripened, would prepare the way for a still more perfect and glorious State, which also I have imagined, but not yet anywhere seen (W, IV, 387).

Thoreau was even more critical of the prevailing economic system and for the same reason: means had become substituted for ends. It had become the major aim of business not to better mankind but to accumulate wealth for its own sake (W, II, 29). Thoreau thought the accumulation of surplus wealth was pointless. Not only that, it was dangerous. It "needlessly complicated existence and enslaved those who fell a prey to its allurements," Thoreau felt (William Kirchner, "Henry David Thoreau as a Social Critic," p. 42). The unfair distribution of wealth left many in dire need (J, III, 191), and ostentatious display of wealth was a direct incentive to crime (J, VII, 43).

Thoreau's measure of the value of money was "the amount of what I will call life which is required to be exchanged for it, immediately or in the long run" (W, II, 34). Thus he did not wish to purchase anything until he was convinced that it would produce for him ample reward for the labor required to pay for it. It was on this basis that he established his philosophy of the simple life.

The simple life, by whose gauge Henry Thoreau measured men and economies, aims at the most complete realization of the perfectibility innate in every person. . . . In his youth, Thoreau sought the conditions for such a life in an idealized distortion of the economic order then being displaced by the industrial revolution. After his experiment at Walden Pond, he moved toward a reconciliation between simplicity and an economy of machines and profit. This goal he never reached. But he left behind elements of a critique of our society and intimations of an undiminishable ideal to be fought for (Stoller, "Thoreau's Doctrine of Simplicity," p. 443).

Thoreau did not fear toil. Unlike most intellectuals, he was perfectly willing to perform manual labor if it were necessary to earn money to fulfill his needs. For a large portion of his adult life he earned his own living by surveying, manufacturing pencils, building chimneys, or even shoveling manure. But by reducing his wants, he found it was necessary to devote to such labor only a small portion of his time. Six weeks of labor produced funds sufficient to supply his wants for a year. As he said in his Harvard commencement essay, "The order of things should be somewhat reversed; the seventh should be man's day of toil, wherein to earn his living by the sweat of his brow; and the other six his Sabbath of the affections and the soul" (W, VI, 9). But even this one day of labor was to be chosen carefully. "The aim of the laborer should be, not to get his living, to get a 'good job,' but to perform well a certain work" (W, IV, 459). For "every man . . .

should love his work as much as the poet does his" (J, XIII, 20). "He advocated a leisure not in which to idle, but in which to seek self-improvement" (Kirchner, p. 117). The six days he spent, not in loafing but in pursuing his interests—observing nature and writing. The twenty volumes of his collected works are adequate proof of his industry.

✳ For those who persisted in pursuing business and accumulating needless wealth, Thoreau had only contempt. "In my experience, nothing is so opposed to poetry [and to Thoreau poetry was the ideal]—not crime—as business" (J, IV, 162). Business led man astray, led him to ignore his higher nature, because it was not "simple, but artificial and complex" (J, V, 445). "If a man has spent all his days about some business, by which he has merely got to be rich, as it is called, *i.e.*, has got much money, many houses and barns and wood-lots, then his life has been a failure, I think" (J, XIV, 281).

Years ahead of his time, Thoreau saw the psychological dangers of division of labor. "However vital to industry division of labor might be, Thoreau was convinced that it thwarted that well-rounded self-culture he sought" (Kirchner, pp. 104–5). Visiting Sam Barrett's mill in Concord, Thoreau commented: "You come away from the great factory saddened, as if the chief end of man were to make pails; but, in the case of the countryman who makes a few by hand, rainy days, the relative importance of human life and of pails is preserved, and you come away thinking of the simple and helpful life of the man" (J, XI, 227).

One of the most common stereotypes of Thoreau is that he was against civilization and wished to return to a primitive life. Like most such stereotypes, it is misleading. "Thoreau did not turn from the multiplicity of a modern world of mechanics, electricity, and radium, to look backward wistfully toward the age of faith in the Middle Ages, symbolized for Adams by the Virgin. . . . The setting of Walden is a geographical present" (Cook, *Passage to Walden*, p. 112). Over and over again Thoreau reiterated his love for the here and now: "We cannot afford not to live in the present" (W, V, 245). "Think of the consummate folly of attempting to get away from *here!* When the constant endeavor should be to get nearer and nearer *here*" (J, XI, 275).

Thoreau was satisfied to live in his own day and time, just as he would have been satisfied to live in any day or time he found himself in. But this did not prevent his being critical of the follies of his time. The Industrial Revolution was in full swing. Mechanization was the theme of the day. The railroad reached Concord just before Thoreau moved to Walden Pond, and before his death it had covered most of the eastern half of the United States. Mills were being established on every accessible water privilege in New England. New inventions were pouring into the patent office and on to the market. Paeans in praise of progress were being sung in every direction. Thoreau himself joined in the chorus when he could honestly admit the values of the accomplishments, but altogether too often, he saw, the new inventions were but "improved means to an unimproved end" (W, II, 58). Worse yet, we become so involved in the development of new improvements that we come to worship them for their own sake rather than for the better life they afford us. "Thoreau's originality was in accepting the advantages of civilization without sacrificing the benefits of the wild" (Broderick, "Thoreau's Principle of Simplicity," p. 279).

"There is no evidence that Thoreau ever held a brief for primitivism, beyond a recognition of its help in exposing the elementary necessaries for survival" (Christie, pp. 162–63). Indeed, quite in contrast with the popular concept of Thoreau as a primitivist is his own belief in progress. It is significant that so many of his works end on this note. Thus the closing words of *Walden*: "There is more day to dawn. The sun is but a morning star"; of "Life without Principle": "Why should we not . . . congratulate each other on the ever-glorious morning?"; and of "Civil Disobedience": "Prepare the way for a still more perfect and glorious State." These surely are not the words of one who has lost faith in the progress of civilization.

Thoreau's lifetime was a period of urbanization. Large cities were a comparatively new phenomenon in America. But Thoreau was not pleased with their development. "Almost all our improvements, so called, tend to convert the country into the town," he complained (J, XIV, 57). He avoided cities whenever possible and said that the only places in Boston which appealed to him were the wharves, where he could look at the ocean, and the railroad station, where he could return to Concord. "He was convinced that cities, in their anxiety to exclude nature from within their limits and to impose the urban pattern upon the surrounding region, were destroying their own source of vitality" (Broderick, "Thoreau's Principle of Simplicity," p. 107). He noted that "artificial, denaturalized persons cannot handle nature without being poisoned. If city-bred girls visit their country cousins,— go a-berrying with them,—they are sure to return covered with blueberry bumps at least" (J, VIII, 448–49). Cities, by separating man from nature, worked an irreparable harm. "At the same time that we exclude mankind from gathering berries in our field, we exclude them from gathering health and happiness. . . . We strike only one more blow at a simple and wholesome relation to nature" (J, XIV, 56). There is a constant need for the urbanized man to return to nature to fulfill his spiritual needs. The symbol of Romulus and Remus, the founders of Rome, being raised by a wolf, was a favorite in Thoreau's mythology.

However, it should be noted, as Broderick has pointed out, in his later years Thoreau came to accept the value of cities as repositories of human knowledge in their libraries and museums.

In *Walden* particularly Thoreau made much of his desire for solitude. But one must be careful not to think him antisocial. When he traveled through the Maine woods and discovered true hermits living miles from any neighbor, he was appalled. He wanted merely to be able to be alone when he felt the need to be by himself, not to dwell in complete solitude.

Actually, Thoreau was a man of many friendships. First and foremost were the members of his own family. The closeness of his ties with them is emphasized in his letters. Both his sisters and his parents always spoke of him as a most devoted brother and son.

Second, he had a large number of intellectual companions, particularly among the Transcendentalists. His friendship with Emerson is well known. He was on even closer terms of intimacy with Ellery Channing, who accompanied him on his daily walks. There is no need of listing here the many others he turned to for intellectual stimulation.

Third, there were the children. Edward Emerson, in his *Henry Thoreau as Remembered by a Young Friend,* has left adequate evidence of the esteem in which he was held by the small folk of Concord. Thoreau's later *Journals* are filled with notations of visits from children, telling him of their discoveries of wild flowers or birds. When he died, the local schools were closed so the children might follow his cortege and place wild flowers on his grave.

And, finally, there were the townspeople of Concord. Thoreau here exerted his individuality in his choice of friends. In his *Journal* we find comparatively little mention of the leading citizens. They did not interest him. He had little more interest in the typical farmers of his neighborhood. Their lives were too mean; like the businessmen, they were too concerned with making money (J, XII, 366). "The farmer accustomed to look at his crops from a mercenary point of view is not aware how beautiful they are" (J, XIII, 414). He was more concerned with the "poetical farmers"—Hosmer, Minott, and Rice (J, III, 41)—because they seemed to be living closer to the life he idealized. And perhaps even more he was attracted to the social outcasts—Melvin, Goodwin, and Alek Therien, the French-Canadian wood chopper. These men had the courage to live the life they wanted, and for that he admired them, even though some of them drank to excess and lived outside the bounds of Victorian standards.

Included with the social outcasts were the Irish. The modern liberal is occasionally offended by Thoreau's critical comments on the Irish immigrants who flocked into New England in the 1840's. He criticized their uncleanliness, their shiftlessness, and their lack of veracity. He thus reflected the strong prejudice of the old Yankee stock, a prejudice based in large part on the fact that the Irish were Roman Catholics. But as time went by and he became better acquainted, his attitude changed and he learned to admire their industry. He helped the illiterate to write back to the old country, defended one laborer when he was unjustly deprived by his Yankee employer of a prize he had won at the local cattle show, and collected subscriptions to enable another Irishman to bring his family across the Atlantic. "Although Thoreau's portrayal of the Irish is less important than his experiences with nature or his lessons in economic values, it has a significance that cannot be overlooked. In its freedom from religious and political bias it is almost unique as a contemporary record" (Buckley, p. 400).

Thoreau's whole life was a search. "His life was a quest of the Holy Grail, undertaken in all purity of body and mind and soul, and in the fullness of faith and devotion" (Norman Foerster, "The Humanism of Thoreau," p. 9). As Thoreau himself says in *Walden*: "I wished to live deliberately, to front only the essential facts of life, and see if I could not learn what it had to teach, and not, when I came to die, discover that I had not lived" (W, II, 100–101).

Although he would have been the first to admit (as he does in his parable of the hound, bay horse, and turtledove in *Walden*) that the perfect life was an unattainable ideal, he was convinced at an early age of the direction in which to aim. It was "the perfect correspondence of Nature to man, so that he is at home with her" (J, X, 127). "I love to see anything that implies a simpler mode of life and a greater nearness to the earth" (J, XIV, 88). "In society you will not find health, but in nature. You must converse much with the field and woods, if you would imbibe such health into your mind and spirit as you covet for your body. . . . Without that our feet at least stood in the midst of nature, all our faces would be pale and livid" (J, I, 306). It was for this that he wished to live a life of leisure—so that he might spend as much time as possible with nature.

Thoreau frequently said: "I think that I cannot preserve my health and spirits, unless I spend four hours a day at least—and it is commonly more than that—sauntering through the woods and over the hills and fields, absolutely free from all worldly engagements" (W, V, 207). It was for this reason he disliked cities. They denied man his opportunity of communing with nature. It was for this also that he condemned the businessmen and upstanding citizens of his community. They were too busy to commune with nature. The world was too much with them, or rather, they were too much with the world.

He saw a close association with nature as a means toward a fuller life. It was a purgative, a panacea for the ills of civilization: "I have come to this hill to see the sun go down, to recover sanity and put myself again in relation with Nature" (J, VI, 329). "Nature, the earth herself, is the only panacea. They bury poisoned sheep up to the necks in earth to take the poison out of them" (J, XII, 350). "It is important, then, that we should air our lives from time to time by removals, and excursions into the fields and woods,—starve our vices" (J, XII, 343).

It was an almost inevitable corollary of Thoreau's search for the ideal life that he should become involved in a search for the ideal man; that is, the man in perfect correspondence with nature: "It is the marriage of the soul with Nature that makes the intellect fruitful, that gives birth to imagination" (J. II, 413).

Wherever Thoreau traveled in history he was in search of men who had fulfilled his vision of manhood, who lived close to nature and understood it (Lawrence Willson, "The Influence of Early North American History and Legend," p. 181). His concern to know just how far men *had* taken advantage of their opportunities perhaps explains better than anything else . . . the reason for his historical research (p. 149). In the last analysis, all of Thoreau's excursions into antiquarianism and history were inspired by the same motive that inspired his excursions into the woods and up and down the rivers; to learn more about the basic relationship in which man and nature stood to each other (p. 86). When he considered the Concord Fight, it was to discover the manhood displayed in it; when he read the "Wast Books" of Ephraim Jones, it was to discover the independence of general stores and the merchandise of the eighteenth century villager (p. 83).

He investigated the history of the Pilgrims and the Jesuit missionaries and the *coureurs de bois* [because] in their lives he thought he would be able to see more clearly than in the lives of his contemporaries the workings of divine law, because they had perforce lived closer to nature, where the permanency of that law and its inexorableness were most openly demonstrable. But in each of these studies he failed in some degree to discover what he wished to discover. The men of old Concord were brave, to be sure, but their bravery was expended merely in an effort to reduce the tax on their tea. The Pilgrims were spiritual pioneers with a grand and thrilling motive, but they had strayed away from the motive to follow the lure of the commercial spirit. They had lived *on* nature rather than *in* it. The *coureurs de bois* had been mere adventurers, looking for lives of titillated ease. The heroic Jesuits had been held in thrall by a small and foolish superstition. In each enterprise the idealism had somehow failed (pp. 222–23).

Disillusioned with the pioneer Americans, Thoreau turned to the Indian in his search. In his *Journal* for 1841 he wrote, "The charm of the Indian to me is that he stands free and unconstrained in Nature, is her inhabitant and not her guest, and wears her easily and gracefully" (J, I, 253). Thoreau felt "the Indian could teach the white man, who was pathetically involved in his self-created civilization, the necessity of a more congenial *rapport* with a natural environment" (Cook, *Passage to Walden*, p. 87). But eventually, as he grew older, he became disillusioned and disappointed because "the Indian had made no attempt to cultivate the spiritual side of his being" (Willson, "The Influence of Early North American History and Legend," p. 280). "In the case of the savage," Thoreau says in his *Journal* (V, 410), "the accompaniment of simplicity is idleness with its attendant vices, but in the case of the philosopher, it is the highest employment and development."

Thoreau was led to admire the hunters and trappers of Concord, men such as Haines, Melvin, and Goodwin, who, because of their closeness to nature, were outcasts in the eyes of most Concordians. Twice he speaks of Haines's reminding him of the Indian (J, VI, 233; J, III, 290). And again he says: "The woodcutter and his practices and experiences are more to be attended to; his accidents, perhaps more than any other's, should mark the epochs in the winter day. Now that the Indian is gone, he stands nearest to nature" (J, III, 244). But again, as did the Indian, they had one serious failing: they lacked a spiritual, an aesthetic sense. Nowhere in the past or in the present could Thoreau find his ideal man. He could only hope that such a man would develop in the future. He concentrated therefore upon developing such a man. And consistent with his philosophy, he began with himself.

The search for beauty was one of the primary motivations in Thoreau's life. It is impossible to read at any length in any of his writings without becoming aware of that fact. Beauty, along with goodness and truth, was one of the members of the trinity he substituted for the orthodox Christian Trinity. It is surprising, therefore, to discover that he devotes little space to exposition of an aesthetic theory. Charles Reid Metzger, after attempting to study Thoreau's aesthetics, comes to the conclusion that "what

Thoreau had to say about art in general . . . is too fragmentary and too vague to be dignified by the title art theory" ("The Transcendental Esthetics in America," p. 237). "Thoreau sought to experience beauty rather than apprehend principles" (p. 252). Virtually the only time he made any extended attempt to formulate an aesthetic theory occurred in the spring of 1852 after a reading of the works of William Gilpin on the picturesque. But even then his interest centered primarily on natural beauty rather than formal art. "He had the artist's eye for whatever beauty he found in nature, but of art as such he had almost no knowledge or appreciation" (Huffert, "Thoreau as a Teacher," p. 408). "What is a gallery in the house to a gallery in the streets!" Thoreau wrote. "I think that there is not a picture-gallery in the country which would be worth so much to us as is the western view under the elms of our main street" (J, XI, 220).

We can search in vain through Thoreau's writings for any extended comments on any of the great masterpieces of painting or sculpture. They were simply outside his ken. For Thoreau "the highest condition of art is artlessness" (J, I, 153) and he found more beauty in an ink blot than in a formal painting (J, I, 119). "The too exquisitely cultured" he avoided as he did the theater (J, IV, 154).

The plastic arts appealed to him a little more, and he was impressed when he discovered an Indian stone pestle fashioned into the likeness of a bird. It convinced him that the Indian had "so far begun to leave behind him war, and even hunting, and to redeem himself from the savage state" (J, V, 526). But even sculpture, to meet his approval, had to be representative rather than abstract, and the more it was akin to nature, the greater its appeal for him (J, I, 380).

Thoreau had a lifelong interest in music. But he was more interested in the music of nature than in the music of man: "One will lose no music by not attending oratorios and operas" (J, II, 379). "I get my new experiences still, not at the opera listening to the Swedish Nightingale [Jenny Lind], but at Beck Stow's Swamp listening to the native wood thrush" (J, IX, 43).

It was for architecture that Thoreau reserved his greatest interest, and his aesthetic approach was primarily functional. In this he anticipated such modern creative geniuses as Frank Lloyd

Wright and Louis Sullivan. Wright wrote me (February 28, 1952), "The history of American Architecture would be incomplete without Thoreau's wise observations on the subject."

Thoreau says in *Walden* (p. 52):

What of architectural beauty I now see, I know has gradually grown from within outward, out of the necessities and character of the indweller, who is the only builder. . . . The most interesting dwellings in this country, as the painter knows, are the most unpretending, humble log huts and cottages of the poor commonly; it is the life of the inhabitants whose shells they are, and not any peculiarity in their surfaces merely, which makes them *picturesque.*

As he strove for simplicity and economy in his life, he strove for simplicity and economy in his art. He was not alone in this, for Emerson, Horatio Greenough, and Walt Whitman, approaching the problem from different angles, each arrived at the same concept at approximately the same time. But Thoreau was perhaps the most practical and the most concrete of the four. Yet I do not wish to imply that Thoreau's approach to architecture was purely from the standpoint of economy. He was able to appreciate the beauty of the functional approach. The functional building, he thought, blended into its background. He even suggested that "the architect take a hint from the pyramidal or conical form of the muskrat's house. . . . Something of this form and color, like a large haycock in the meadow, would be in harmony with the scenery" (J, IV, 423). The early American houses were "earth-loving"; they needed "no coping of bricks to catch the eye, no alto or basso relievo" (J, III, 34). In contrast, the Victorian house of Thoreau's own period, with its gingerbread ornamentation and sugar-coating, was offensive to his eye.

Thoreau's interest in the field of education has been generally ignored; yet it was a subject that concerned him most of his life. The principles he put into practice in his own school were a distinct foreshadowing of modern progressive education. "Nature study, local history, physical education, and nature appreciation were integrated to an extent not yet achieved on a wide scale in our own day" (Huffert, p. 413). A good part of the school day was spent out of doors, in hiking, rowing, swimming, and observing natural history and local history in the field. Thoreau advocated the introduction of nature studies into the elementary schools fifty years before it was in general use (pp. 376–77). "Learning by doing" is John Dewey's phrase, but Thoreau put the concept into practice years before Dewey.

In disciplinary methods Thoreau was equally progressive. He resigned his position in the Concord public schools rather than use physical force. To Orestes Brownson he wrote (December 30, 1837), "I have ever been disposed to regard the cowhide as a nonconductor." And when he established his own school, he used understanding and an appeal to the moral sense of the child as his principal disciplinary devices.

The basis for his whole educational theory was that the child was innately good and that it was the purpose of the school to foster and stimulate the child's inner development toward perfection. As I have pointed out earlier, Thoreau was convinced that paradise could be achieved on this earth through the full development of man's potentialities, and all his educational philosophy was aimed in that direction.

Thoreau was consistently critical of the collegiate education of his day. He once remarked to Emerson that Harvard taught all the branches of learning but got to none of the roots. Too much time was spent in studying theory, too little in actual practice: "To my astonishment I was informed on leaving college that I had studied navigation!" he says in *Walden* (p. 57); "—why, if I had taken one turn down the harbor I should have known more about it." He rejoiced when, some years after his graduation, Harvard established a school of science (W, VI, 138). But on the other hand, he did not deny the value of a liberal education: "The learning of trades and professions which is designed to enable men to earn their living, or to fit them for a particular station in life—is *servile*" (J, XIII, 15).

He was critical of college faculties. There were "professors of philosophy, but not philosophers" (W, II, 16). They were not interested in searching for truth, but lived in the shadow of their established institutions and spent their time defending the *status quo*. True educators, he believed, should broaden their students' horizons; they should at least teach the students "where the arsenal is, in case they should ever want to use any of its weapons" (J, XIII, 67). All the while he was at Harvard, he wrote his class secretary later, "My spirit yearned for the sympathy of my old and almost forgotten friend Nature."

A further contribution by Thoreau was his interest in adult education, expressed primarily through the lyceum movement of his day. He was an active member of the Concord Lyceum from its founding in 1829 until his death, lecturing before it nineteen times and serving several terms as its curator. In the mid-forties he was one of the leaders of the successful movement to permit controversial subjects such as abolitionism to be discussed from the lyceum platform. And in *Walden* he urged his fellow towns-men to devote more funds to the lyceum even at the expense of omitting one bridge over a river (pp. 121–22).

From an early point in his career, probably as early as 1840, Thoreau considered himself a professional writer, and throughout his career he was vitally interested in the craft of writing. One could make a fairly sizable collection of his comments on the subject. Yet, "it is doubtful that Thoreau was systematic or pur-poseful enough or even original enough to warrant being con-sidered among the first rank of American critical writers" (George Craig, "Literary Criticism in the Works of Henry David Thoreau," p. 5). "Thoreau's interest in technique was normally limited to a concern with his own technique. When he discusses other writers, his concern is more with emotional impact" (p. 141).

It is surprising that "within the twenty-six printed volumes by Thoreau and beyond them in unpublished manuscripts there are several hundred pages of literary criticism, yet one finds few pages, perhaps a total of ten, in which Thoreau concerns him-self with discussing the duties of a critic and the function of criticism" (Adams, "Henry Thoreau's Literary Theory and Criti-cism," p. 120). Thoreau said so little on the subject, Adams feels, because Wordsworth, Coleridge, Carlyle, and the other early romanticists had already so well formulated his ideas that he felt no need of re-expressing them.

Though there is not one new element in Thoreau's critical theory, there is not another theory like it in all particulars or even in outline. Thoreau laid emphases where they had not been laid before. He worked out some of his critical dicta to lengths that had not been attempted hitherto. He was always running some theory down to its ultimate end.

For instance, no other transcendentalist stated the "labor doctrine" so forcefully or persistently, though virtually all transcendentalists held it. . . . No one else spoke so affectionately, so personally of Nature as the ally of the poet, though a hundred critics before Thoreau's time had considered nature as a source of inspiration. . . . Health may long have been the subject of those who sought in some measure to account for genius, but few critics have so consistently demanded health as a basis for true poetry (pp. 166–67).

The recent growth of interest in the organic theory of literature has quite naturally focused attention on Thoreau as one of its outstanding proponents. Fred W. Lorch, in "Thoreau and the Organic Principle in Poetry," has made the most authoritative study of the subject, and in summary says:

In conceiving of poetry as something that grows like an organism in nature rather than as something that is "made," Thoreau reveals his discipleship to the organic theorists. He believed the source of the poet's intuition to be the divine and universal Intelligence, which expresses itself and comes to poetic fruition through the agency of the poet; and that genius, or the divine element in the poet, and talent, the human element, are both essential in poetic expression. Thoreau failed to differentiate clearly between the conception on the one hand that outer form is the imitation of inner form, and the conception on the other that form is organic, but despite this confusion, he customarily regarded form as an inherent quality of the intuition, which proceeds from within outward. Beauty is both *essentially* and *ethically* organic. Poetry is the fruit of the poet; it grows like an organism from the soul of the poet's character; and consequently, the nobility of a poem is a symbol of the nobility of the poet. The highest function of poetry is the improvement of man. The purest poetry manifests itself not primarily in a poem "written and done," but in the character of the poet; the finest poem is the life-poem. Thoreau's conception of the organic principle [thus] . . . suggests an approach to a better understanding of his efforts at self-improvement (pp. 48–49).

It is surprising that although Thoreau was always vitally concerned with form, he has been continually criticized for the formlessness of his works. "Thoreau's books are formless. . . . His emphasis was much on *matter* and very little on *manner,*" says Raymond Adams (p. 102). "In 'Walden' the sentences bear no more plastic relation to each other than do the stones of the cairn which now marks the site of Thoreau's hut," adds J. B. Atkinson in "Concerning Thoreau's Style." Perhaps it was Thoreau's own description of his method of composition that led them to these conclusions: "From all points of the compass, from the earth beneath and the heavens above, have come these inspirations and been entered duly in the order of their arrival in the journal. Thereafter, when the time arrived, they were winnowed into lectures, and again, in due time, from lectures into essays" (J, I, 413). "When I select one here and another there, and strive to join sundered thoughts, I make but a partial heap after all," he complains at another point (J, I, 199–200). But they reckoned without the extensive revision and amalgamation to which Thoreau subjected all his work. "Seldom have I known an author who made more drafts of what he might sometime print, or more persistently revised what he had once composed," wrote F. B. Sanborn (*The Life of Henry David Thoreau,* p. 55), who handled so many of his manuscripts. "I wish that I could buy at the shops some kind of india-rubber that would rub out at once all that in my writing which it now costs me so many perusals, so many months if not years, and so much reluctance, to erase," Thoreau complained (J, VI, 30). Recent research (see Shanley's study of *Walden* and Hovde's of *A Week,* in Chapter Two, for example) has confirmed the tremendous amount of revision to which Thoreau subjected his work. It has also demonstrated that the labor was worth while. It is the unanimous opinion of those critics who have examined his manuscripts in their various stages that Thoreau revised and reworked his papers with great skill.

Early critics tended to think of Thoreau as a master of the sentence. Lowell in 1865 said, "There are sentences of his as perfect as anything in the language." By 1906 Bradford Torrey saw that "the sentences might be complete in themselves, detachable, able to stand alone, but the paragraph never lacked a logical and even formal cohesion" (*Friends on the Shelf,* p. 126). In recent years critics have at last begun to realize the essential unity of his books as wholes. Most obvious was Thoreau's use of the unity of time. In *A Week* he used the seven days of the week for chapter divisions (although his journey had actually taken two weeks); in *Cape Cod* he unified three separate excursions into one narrative; and in *Walden* he adopted the device most successfully, combining the adventures of two years and two months into one year, and using the circle of the seasons to trace symbolically his spiritual growth. Indeed, *Walden* is a masterwork of integrated form, and Sherman Paul's brilliant discussion of its structure (see Chapter Two, above) should silence any further charges that Thoreau lacked the ability to unify his work.

"It is not in man to determine what his style shall be. He might as well determine what his thoughts shall be." Thus wrote Thoreau in his essay on Carlyle (W, IV, 330). But whether it was consciously or unconsciously created, Thoreau's style has long won admiration. "His literary style has not been excelled by any other essayist in our literature," says Adaline Conway in *The Essay in American Literature* (p. 68).

Perhaps the most notable characteristic of Thoreau's style is the concreteness of his diction. Abstractness, abstruseness, and often vapidness were altogether too frequently characteristics of his fellow Transcendentalists' styles—even that of Emerson. But these are charges that can rarely, if ever, be brought against Thoreau except in his early apprenticeship.

He loved homely, down-to-earth phrases such as "finger-cold," "a jag of wood," "apple-pie order," and "full of the devil." He loved "good old English words" (J, III, 41), words "that can be traced back to a Celtic original" (J, III, 232–33). Indeed, he was prone to go off on an etymological digression at the least provocation— or with none at all. He was delighted when his rural neighbors, especially George Minott, "the most poetical farmer in Concord," sent him to his dictionary with an Elizabethan word usage. It is not surprising therefore to discover that he had twenty-nine dictionaries and grammars in his library. On the other hand, although his vocabulary was large (note his use of such words as "sempiternal," "fuscous," "susurrus," "crepusculum," and "sesquipedalian"), he was not pedantic. He complained: "A writer who does not speak out of a full experience uses torpid words, wooden or lifeless words, such words as 'humanitary,' which have a paralysis in their tails" (J, IV, 225; see also J, X, 261). And he also complained: "When I read some of the rules for speaking and writing the English language correctly,—as that a sentence must never end with a particle,—and perceive how implicitly even the learned obey it, I think—

> Any fool can make a rule
> And every fool will mind it." (J, XIII, 125)

He thought that "the first requisite and rule [of grammar] is that expression shall be vital and natural" (J, XI, 386).

One of the few affectations in his use of words was his occasional tendency (although not nearly so pronounced as Emerson's) to use archaic words and forms, such as "fain," "methinks," "wot," "clomb," and "blowed." Another was his affinity for Indian words; he referred to the muskrat as the "musquash," and wished that Lakeville, Massachusetts, had been named "Assawampsett" or "Sanacus" (J, VIII, 395).

His style is highly figurative, filled with similes, metaphors, hyperbole, and synecdoche. I once checked a list of more than fifty different types of figures of speech against *Walden* and found virtually every one represented, most of them many times over. As one might expect, a large percentage of the figures are based on nature. "Natural objects and phenomena are the original symbols or types which express our thoughts and feelings," he believed (J, V, 135; see also J, XII, 389). "River and lake images are the most fundamental in Thoreau, and have implications not yet fully read. The river 'of our thoughts' is the dominant figure for the *Week*" (William Drake, "A Formal Study of Thoreau," p. 18). Although John Broderick and Sherman Paul (see Chapter Two) have made a good start at examining more closely the images of Thoreau's writing, much more work needs to be done.

The chief error of many of Thoreau's critics, from Lowell on down, is that they fail to detect his humor. They accept him literally despite his many warnings that he was an exaggerator who liked to "brag as lustily as chanticleer" (W, II, 94).

Harold Guthrie asserts that "a proper adjustment of our critical view of Thoreau's humor is not only important in itself, but . . . it is also essential to a just and complete view of the man and his works" ("The Humor of Thoreau," p. 1). "The dangers and demerits of a paradoxical style are sufficiently obvious; and no writer has ever been less careful than Thoreau to safeguard himself against misunderstandings on this score. He has consequently been much misunderstood, and will always be so, save where the reader brings to his task a certain amount of sympathy and kindred sense of humor" (Salt, *The Life of Henry D. Thoreau*, p. 263).

That Thoreau had a well-developed sense of humor is obvious on examination of both his writings and the memoirs of his friends such as Sanborn, Channing, and Edward Emerson. Indeed, he expounds his principles of humor quite explicitly in his essay on Thomas Carlyle. "His humor is an inseparable part of the man and his writings; . . . it is based on good nature and love of fun, and . . . his sole negative qualification for humor in general is that it should never be merely idle nor frankly degrading" (Guthrie, p. 51). "Thoreau's humor could be warmly human" (p. 48). And "a list of the things he considered laughable . . . reveals a normal, unsophisticated New Englander,—sane, genial, even fun-loving" (p. 47). Thus Lowell, in saying that Thoreau was without humor, clearly missed the point of most of his writing. And when Stevenson condemned Thoreau as a prig for expurgating humorous passages from his writings, he did not realize that Thoreau was merely trying to "reduce the egotistical, deliberately humorous passages" (p. 39).

"Thoreau believed that a general function, or service of humor, especially in all forms of 'transcendental' writings, is to provide a leaven that renders it digestible" (p. 90). One of Thoreau's aims was humorously to satirize the follies and vices of men (p. 92). "His moral censure and satirical disquisitions . . . are but the reverse side of his life-long search for truth" (p. 93).

"If Thoreau continually employs humor in his writings, and if that humor is often paradoxical, exaggerative, and metaphorical, then a literal reading of his works which takes no account of his humor, must inevitably result in frequent misapprehension of his meaning" (p. 106). Indeed, George Ripley, James Russell Lowell, Emerson, Alcott, Ellery Channing, and Stevenson all misinterpreted Thoreau because they thus misread his humor. Salt was the first to understand the true function of humor in Thoreau's writings.

Guthrie thus analyzes Thoreau's humor:

Thoreau generally laughs at, not the unconventional or bizarre in human behaviour, but the conventional. . . . Unthinking conformity to foolish tradition rouses Thoreau's sharpest laughter, and since some of his readers are incapable of sharing his point of view, they are more irritated than amused by his humor (p. 17).

[Thoreau] disavowed the practice of humor as an end in itself (p. 109). His real calling is to expose and discountenance all forms of human folly and vice, for it is Thoreau's conviction that "if we only see clearly enough how mean our lives are, they will be splendid enough." His favorite weapon for the extirpation of such meanness is a genial humor of exaggeration, paradox, and metaphor; but occasionally, when the meanness appears to him outrageous, his moral indignation finds vent in bitter irony and sardonic word-play which are closer to invective than raillery (p. 109). His goal is to free as many minds as possible by humorously exposing the meanness and desperation of conventional modes of thought and behaviour (p. 115a).

Certainly a reading of [*Walden*] which mistakes Thoreau's humorous overstatement and genial satire for splenetic and uncompromising assertion must result in the impression that Thoreau counseled his readers to renounce society completely (p. 117). [But] Thoreau's true position, clearly, is not a renunciation of society but a carefully qualified acceptance of such social institutions and practices as do not degrade men nor dissipate their energies (pp. 122–23). Thoreau's social and economic views, when examined in the light of humorous satire, appear actually quite moderate (p. 129). For those who understand it, his satirical attacks on men and institutions arouse, not resentment and counterattack, but laughter and a return to our senses (p. 151).

As Raymond Adams has pointed out, the mock-heroic is one of Thoreau's standard humorous devices. Not only does he use it in such well-known passages as the battle of the ants in *Walden*, but it is also the basic pattern of the whole of *A Week*. Use of this technique permitted him to approach in prose the close-up photography of present-day naturalists. Later nature writers seized upon his use of the mock-heroic and incorporated it into their writings so that he brought about "a literature of nature such as had not existed before" ("Thoreau's Mock-Heroics and the American Natural History Writers," p. 97).

It is surprising that Thoreau's abilities for characterization have not been more widely recognized. Note, for example, his "Dutch sailor with a singular bullfrog or trilobite expression of the eyes, whose eyes were like frog ponds in the broad platter of his cheeks and gleamed like a pool covered with frog-spittle" (J, II, 79). Or Mrs. Field, "with the never absent mop in one hand, and yet no effects of it visible anywhere" (W, II, 227). Or the "regular countrywoman with half an acre of face" (J, VII, 476). A novelist friend of mine once told me after noting several such descriptions that she mourned the fact that Thoreau never tried his hand at writing fiction.

But fiction to Thoreau was for entertainment. And he was writing not to entertain but to enlighten. He deliberately avoided the striking, the sensational.

I omit the unusual—the hurricanes and earthquakes—and describe the common. . . . You may have the extraordinary for your province, if you will let me have the ordinary. Give me the obscure life, the cottage of the poor and humble, the workdays of the world, the barren fields, the smallest share of all things but poetic perception (J, II, 428–29). I know that no subject is too trivial for me. . . . The theme is nothing, the life is everything. All that interests the reader is the depth and intensity of the life excited. . . . Give me simple, cheap, and homely themes (J, IX, 121).

That Thoreau had that "poetic perception" goes almost without saying. "Great art consists in the imaginative heightening of the immediate," says R. W. B. Lewis. And therein lies Thoreau's greatest strength. He makes us see all that which lies around us, but which, until he pointed it out, we never saw before.

One final word must be spoken on Thoreau's ideas. Thoreau was a critic of society, but primarily a positive rather than a negative critic. "There are many statements in the writings of Thoreau, which taken together, seem to indicate that he was a thorough-going pessimist and a hater of mankind. . . . But these statements . . . are merely the . . . statements of the . . . idealist who loved men too well to see them tossing aside their opportunities for moral and intellectual growth and the good life" (Lawrence Willson, "The Influence of Early North American History and Legend," p. 153). "It was not his carelessness of man's good but the precise opposite, his passion for it, that made him denounce so bitterly the society into which he was born and to assume the part of the gadfly stinging it into virtue" (Norman Foerster, *Nature in American Literature,* p. 137). "Probably he himself would have been distressed to think that he might be remembered chiefly as a satirist or a critic; as a man who had managed to convey only his dissatisfaction with the world and not the happiness which he believed to have been his" (Krutch, p. 276).

Basically Thoreau's life was a happy one. A few weeks before he died he wrote a letter to Myron Benton (March 21, 1862) saying, "I have not many months to live. . . . I may add that I am enjoying existence as much as ever, and regret nothing." Of all the many and varied titles Thoreau has been given, perhaps none is more felicitous than Hildegarde Hawthorne's "Concord's Happy Rebel."

SOURCES FOR CHAPTER FOUR

The two most detailed studies of Thoreau's ideas are Joseph Wood Krutch, *Henry David Thoreau* (New York, 1948) and Reginald L. Cook, *Passage to Walden* (Boston, 1949). Henry Seidel Canby, "Henry David Thoreau," in *Classic Americans* (New York, 1931, pp. 184–225), is a thoughtful brief analysis. Louis B. Salomon, "The Practical Thoreau" (*CE*, XVII, 1956, 229–32), refutes eight of the commonest misinterpretations of Thoreau's ideas with specific quotations from his writings. However, in reply see Wade Thompson, "The Impractical Thoreau" (*CE*, XIX, 1957, 67–70). One of the few studies to deal with the gradual development and change of Thoreau's ideas is William Drake, "A Formal Study of Thoreau" (Iowa University, M.A., 1948). It would be a great service to Thoreau scholars to have this work in print and to have its implications studied further.

Mary Edith Cochnower, "Thoreau and Stoicism" (Iowa University, Ph.D., 1938), is the only detailed study of the stoic element in Thoreau's life and philosophy.

An early but still provocative study of the Transcendentalist basis of Thoreau's thought is Daniel Gregory Mason, "The Idealistic Basis of Thoreau's Genius" (*Harvard Monthly*, XXV, 1897, 82–93). For an analysis of Thoreau's use of sound as the agency of Transcendental correspondence in achieving the mystical experience, see Sherman Paul, "The Wise Silence" (*NEQ*, XXII, 1949, 511–27).

For Thoreau's influence on the development of the natural history essay, see Philip Marshall Hicks, *The Development of the Natural History Essay in American Literature* (Philadelphia, 1924); Richard E. Haymaker, "The Out-of-Door Essay" in his

From Pampas to Hedgerows and Downs: A Study of W. H. Hudson (New York, 1954, pp. 45–84); and Reginald Cook, "Nature's Eye-Witness" in his *Passage to Walden*. See also Henry Chester Tracy, *American Naturists* (New York, 1930), Alec Lucas, "Thoreau, Field Naturalist" (*UTQ*, XXIII, 1954, 227–32), and Robert Henry Welker, "Literary Birdman: Henry David Thoreau" in *Birds & Men* (Cambridge, Mass., 1955, pp. 91–115), which traces Thoreau's changing attitude toward ornithology. See also Hans Huth, *Nature and the American* (Berkeley, Calif., 1957).

For disparaging comments on Thoreau's ability as a naturalist, see Francis Allen, *Thoreau's Bird-Lore* (Boston, 1925), Fannie Hardy Eckstorm, "Thoreau's 'Maine Woods'" (*Atlantic Monthly*, CII, 1908, 242–50; *TCC*); W. L. McAtee, "Adaptationist Naïveté" (*Scientific Monthly*, XLVIII, 1939, 253–55); and John Burroughs, "Another Word on Thoreau" in *The Last Harvest* (Boston, 1922, pp. 103–71).

For Thoreau's work with Agassiz, see *Familiar Letters* (W, VI, 125–32); with Harris, see Joseph Wade, "Friendship of Two Old-Time Naturalists" (*Scientific Monthly*, XXIII, 1926, 152–60). Edward S. Deevey's study of Thoreau's limnology will be found in "A Re-examination of Thoreau's 'Walden'" (*Quarterly Review of Biology*, XVII, 1942, 1–11). Leo Stoller, "A Note on Thoreau's Place in the History of Phenology" (*Isis*, XLVII, 1956, 172–81), cites Leopold's comment and refutes it. Thoreau's importance to the nature study movement is evaluated in Anna Botsford Comstock, "Henry David Thoreau" (*Nature and Science Education Review*, II, 1930, 49–55).

For further studies of Thoreau's science, see Raymond Adams, "Thoreau's Science" (*Scientific Monthly*, LX, 1945, 379–82), perhaps the best discussion to date of Thoreau's gradually changing attitude toward science; Lee Marten Nash, "Ecology in the Writings of Henry David Thoreau" (University of Washington, M.A., 1951); Ludlow Griscom, *Birds of Concord* (Cambridge, Mass., 1949); Joseph Wade, "Some Insects of Thoreau's Writings" (*Journal of the New York Entomological Society*, XXXV, 1927, 1–21), a thorough summary and evaluation of his comments on insects; Kathryn Whitford, "Thoreau and the Woodlots of Concord" (*NEQ*, XXIII, 1950, 291–306), the best evaluation of Thoreau's findings in his "Succession of Forest Trees"; Philip and Kathryn

Whitford, "Thoreau: Pioneer Ecologist and Conservationist" (*Scientific Monthly*, LXXIII, 1951, 291–96; *TCC*); H. S. Canby, "What He Lived For" in *Thoreau* (Boston, 1939, pp. 322–42); Charles Reid Metzger, "The Transcendental Esthetics in America" (University of Washington, Ph.D., 1954, pp. 202–12), which discusses Thoreau as a taxonomist and ecologist; and Reginald Cook, *Passage to Walden* (Boston, 1949, pp. 173–204), which discusses Thoreau's attitude toward science and nature, as does William H. Kirchner, "Henry David Thoreau as a Social Critic" (University of Minnesota, Ph.D., 1938, pp. 155–77). Reginald Heber Howe, "Thoreau, the Lichenist" (*Guide to Nature*, May, 1912, 17–20), anthologizes Thoreau's comments on lichens. See also Charles Metzger, "Thoreau on Science" (*Annals of Science*, XII, 1956, 206–11).

The major discussion of Thoreau's theology is John Sylvester Smith, "The Philosophical Naturism of Henry David Thoreau" (Drew University, Ph.D., 1948). Briefer studies include Harry Elmore Hurd, "The Religion of Henry David Thoreau" (*Christian Leader*, August 25 and September 1, 1928) and R. Lester Mondale, "Henry David Thoreau and the Naturalizing of Religion" (*Unity*, CXXXVII, 1951, 14–17). Reginald Cook discusses Thoreau's mysticism in *Passage to Walden* (pp. 122–43). Raymond Adams summarizes Thoreau's attitude toward an afterlife in "Thoreau and Immortality" (*SP*, XXVI, 1929, 58–66), using a number of unpublished Thoreau manuscripts. I have written a brief note on Thoreau's reactions to the Quakers in "Thoreau Attends Quaker Meeting" (*Friends Intelligencer*, Fifth Month 6, 1944). His attitude toward the Roman Catholics is discussed in Lawrence Willson, "Thoreau and Roman Catholicism" (*CathHR*, XLII, 1956, 157–72). For a discussion of Thoreau as a free-thinker, see "An Ideal for Freethinkers" (*Truth Seeker*, June 24, 1893). For an interpretation of him as a Theosophist, see "Theosophist Unaware" (*Theosophy*, 1944, 290–95, 330–34). See also R. W. B. Lewis, *American Adam* (Chicago, 1955).

For Thoreau and the reform movements of his day, see William H. Kirchner, "Henry David Thoreau as a Social Critic" (University of Minnesota, Ph.D., 1938). The most detailed study of his relationship with the abolitionists is Wendell Glick, "Thoreau and Radical Abolitionism" (Northwestern University, Ph.D.,

1950). See also Nick Aaron Ford, "Henry David Thoreau, Abolitionist" (*NEQ*, XIX, 1946, 359–71); Walter Harding, "Thoreau and the Negro" (*Negro History Bulletin*, October, 1946); and Howard R. Floan, *The South in Northern Eyes, 1831 to 1861* (Austin, Tex., 1958, pp. 62–70).

On Thoreau's attitude toward government, see the Kirchner dissertation cited above; Eunice M. Schuster, "Native American Anarchism" (*Smith College Studies in History*, XVII, 1931, 46–51); John C. Broderick, "Thoreau's Proposals for Legislation" (*AQ*, VII, 1955, 285–90) and Broderick, "Thoreau's Principle of Simplicity" (University of North Carolina, Ph.D., 1953). See also Charles Madison, "Henry David Thoreau, Transcendental Individualist" in *Critics and Crusaders* (New York, 1947, pp. 174–93); Rudolf Rocker, *Pioneers of American Freedom* (Los Angeles, 1949, 24–31); Charles H. Nichols, "Thoreau on the Citizen and His Government" (*Pylon*, XIII, 1952, 19–24); and Paul H. Oehser, "Pioneers in Conservation" (*Nature Magazine*, XXXVIII, 1945, 188–90).

Thoreau's economic theory is discussed in detail in the Kirchner dissertation cited above; but see also Francis B. Dedmond, "Economic Protest in Thoreau's Journals" (*SN*, XXVI, 1954, 65–76); James Dabbs, "Thoreau, the Adventurer as Economist" (*YR*, XXXVI, 1947, 667–72); and Leo Stoller, "Thoreau's Doctrine of Simplicity" (*NEQ*, XXIX, 1956, 443–61).

For Thoreau's attitude toward civilization and primitivism, see the Broderick dissertation listed above and also John Christie, "Thoreau, Traveler" (Duke University, Ph.D., 1955); Reginald Cook, "The Machine Age and Man" in *Passage to Walden* (Boston, 1949, 99–121); H. S. Canby, "Thoreau and the Machine Age" (*YR*, XX, 1931, 517–31); G. Ferris Cronkhite, "The Transcendental Railroad" (*NEQ*, XXIV, 1951, 306–28); Georges Poulet, *Studies in Human Time*, translated from the French by Elliott Coleman (Baltimore, 1956, pp. 334–37); Kenneth Robinson, "Thoreau and the Wild Appetite" (*TSB* XII); and Mary Culhane, "Thoreau, Melville, Poe, and the Romantic Quest" (University of Minnesota, Ph.D., 1945).

For Thoreau's ideas on solitude, see particularly Robert Paul Cobb, "Society Versus Solitude: Studies in Emerson, Thoreau, Hawthorne, and Whitman" (University of Michigan, Ph.D., 1955);

but see also many of the articles listed in the paragraph above, particularly the Broderick dissertation.

For Thoreau's interest in the pioneer and the Indian, see Lawrence Willson, "The Influence of Early North American History and Legend on the Writings of Henry David Thoreau" (Yale University, Ph.D., 1944); Jason Almus Russell, "Thoreau, the Interpreter of the Real Indian" (*QQ*, XXXV, 1927, 37–48); Arthur Volkman, "Excerpts from Works on Henry David Thoreau" (*Archaeological Society of Delaware Papers*, V, 1943, 1–11), an anthology of Thoreau's comments on the Indian; and studies listed in the Sources for Chapter Three on Thoreau's sources in Indian literature. Thoreau's Indian collections are described in *Reports of the Peabody Museum of American Archaeology and Ethnology* (I, 1876, 6–7). See also Lawrence Willson, "From Thoreau's Indian Manuscripts" (*ESQ*, XI, 1958, 52–55). An important study of Thoreau's Indian notebooks is Lawrence Willson, "Thoreau and the Natural Diet" (*SAQ*, LVII, 1958, 86–103).

The most complete exposition of Thoreau's theory of aesthetics is Charles Reid Metzger, "The Transcendental Esthetics in America" (University of Washington, Ph.D., 1954); but see also the Kirchner dissertation listed above, particularly pp. 177 ff. For an explanation of Thoreau's apparent misinterpretation of Horatio Greenough's aesthetic theories, see William J. Griffin, "Thoreau's Reactions to Horatio Greenough" (*NEQ*, XXX, 1957, 508–12).

The most authoritative discussion of Thoreau's educational theories is Anton M. Huffert, "Thoreau as a Teacher, Lecturer, and Educational Thinker" (New York University, Ph.D., 1951). See also Raymond Adams, "Thoreau, Pioneer in Adult Education" (*Institute Magazine*, III, 1930, 6 ff.); Harry Elmore Hurd, "Henry David Thoreau—A Pioneer in the Field of Education" (*Education*, XLIX, 1929, 372–76); John Dewey, "On Thoreau" (*TSB* 30); the Kirchner dissertation, particularly "The Educational World" (pp. 8–38); and Walter Harding, "Thoreau and the Concord Lyceum" (*TSB* 30).

Harry H. Crosby, "Henry David Thoreau and the Art of Writing" (University of Iowa, M.A., 1947), although very generalized in its approach, lists in the footnotes many of Thoreau's comments on writing. A good brief selection of Thoreau's comments is gathered together in Harrison Hayford and Howard Vincent, *Reader and Writer* (Boston, 1954, 176–78). Edwin Way Teale of

Baldwin, N. Y., has made a much fuller compilation, but it is not yet published.

There are two lengthy studies of Thoreau's literary theory: George D. Craig, "Literary Criticism in the Works of Henry David Thoreau" (University of Utah, Ph.D., 1951), and Raymond Adams, "Henry Thoreau's Literary Theory and Criticism" (University of North Carolina, Ph.D., 1928). The latter is the pioneer American dissertation on Thoreau, and, although unpublished, has had a wide influence on all subsequent studies of Thoreau.

The most authoritative study of Thoreau's use of the organic theory is Fred W. Lorch, "Thoreau and the Organic Principle in Poetry" (University of Iowa, Ph.D., 1936), published almost in its entirety in *PMLA* (LIII, 1938, 286–302). There is also a very provocative discussion in F. O. Matthiessen, *American Renaissance* (New York, 1941, *passim*). One should also consult Carl Bode's edition of Thoreau's *Collected Poems* (Chicago, 1943, p. 338).

On Thoreau's style, see J. Brooks Atkinson, "Concerning Thoreau's Style" (*Freeman*, VI, 1922, 8–10); Adaline Conway, *The Essay in American Literature* (New York, 1914, pp. 68–78); F. O. Matthiessen, *American Renaissance* (pp. 92–99); Sherman Paul's introduction to his edition of *Walden* (Boston, 1957); and Walter Harding, "Henry David Thoreau: Philologist" (*WS*, XIX, 1944, 7).

A good discussion of Thoreau's use of humor is Harold N. Guthrie, "The Humor of Thoreau" (University of Iowa, Ph.D., 1953); but see also George Beardsley, "Thoreau as a Humorist" (*Dial*, XXVIII, 1900, 241–43), and James Paul Brawner, "Thoreau as Wit and Humorist" (*SAQ*, XLIV, 1945, 170–76). By far the best discussion of Thoreau's humor is J. Golden Taylor, "Neighbor Thoreau's Critical Humor" (*Utah State University Monograph Series*, VI, 1958), which unfortunately appeared too late to be discussed in this chapter. Raymond Adams discusses Thoreau's use of the mock-heroic in "Thoreau's Mock-Heroics and the American Natural History Writers" (*SP*, LII, 1955, 86–97). A recent and exceptionally good article, although it is by no means exhaustive, is C. Grant Loomis, "Henry David Thoreau as Folklorist" (*WF*, XVI, 1957, 90–106). It should arouse further interest and research in this virtually untouched area of Thoreau's interest.

CHAPTER FIVE

Thoreau's Fame

One of the most striking phenomena of American literary history has been the gradual growth of Thoreau's reputation. From one who in his own lifetime was dismissed generally as a minor figure and an imitator of Emerson, he has risen to the rank of one of our five or six greatest writers. The growth has been very gradual and not without its setbacks, but it can easily be traced through the comments of the critics over the years.

Thoreau had to suffer none of the tribulations of the literary lion. Few admirers made pilgrimages to see him. He received only an occasional request for an autograph or a photograph. Few editors asked him to write for them. His services as a lecturer were not in great demand. Indeed, his greatest problem was getting his work into print, getting his writing noticed.

Aside from a brief article printed anonymously in the Concord newspaper, Thoreau first broke into print in the pages of the *Dial,* but only at the strong behest of Emerson and over the protest of the editor, Margaret Fuller. Commentators on the *Dial* rarely bothered to single out his writings as exceptional. When the *Dial* foundered, it was chiefly through the good offices of his friend Horace Greeley that he succeeded in placing any further magazine articles—and even then he found it difficult to collect any pay for his work.

Ironically, the first recognition Thoreau won was in James Russell Lowell, *A Fable for Critics* (1848), wherein Lowell chastised "———" for not letting "Neighbor Emerson's orchards alone" because "——— has picked up all the windfalls before." It is almost an academic question which of the blanks refers to Thoreau and which to his friend Ellery Channing, for Lowell is charging both with too much imitation of Emerson.

When Thoreau had completed *A Week,* despite Emerson's efforts he could find no publisher willing to underwrite it, and he was forced to pay the Boston publisher, Munroe, to bring it out. It received few reviews. "Nearly every page is instinct with genuine Poetry except those wherein verse is haltingly attempted. . . . There is a misplaced Pantheistic attack on the Christian Faith," complained his friend George Ripley. James Russell Lowell declared: "The great charm of Mr. Thoreau's book seems to be, that its being a book at all is a happy fortuity. The door of the portfolio-cage has been left open, and the thoughts have flown out of themselves." *Godey's Lady's Book,* for some unknown reason, attributed it to John Greenleaf Whittier. The *Pictorial National Library* dismissed it in three sentences. On October 28, 1853, Munroe notified Thoreau that of the edition of 1,000 copies, 75 had been given away and only 219 sold. The publishers were returning the remaining 706 copies to clear their shelves.

Although *Walden* was announced as "will soon be published" in the back pages of *A Week,* the first book's dismal failure frightened off all publishers. Finally, in 1854 the rising firm of Ticknor & Fields was persuaded to bring it out in an edition of two thousand copies. It received comparatively wider and more favorable notice. Horace Greeley quoted lengthy selections, with words of praise, in an advance notice in the *New York Tribune.* The *Providence Journal* gave it two sentences, deciding that it was "not remarkably stirring." The *Southern Literary Messenger* "commended" it to its readers in four sentences; the *National Magazine* thought it "cooling and refreshing"; and *Graham's Magazine* thought it "eccentric." *Putnam's Monthly* gave it its first lengthy review (six pages), on the whole favorable, but nonetheless complaining that "although he paints his shanty-life in rose-colored tints, we do not believe he liked it, else why not stick to it?" The *North American Review* bothered to say little more than that it was "more curious than useful." The *National Anti-Slavery Standard* gave it one of the most understanding reviews it was ever to receive, saying in part: "If men were to follow in Mr. Thoreau's steps, by being more obedient to their loftiest instincts, there would, indeed, be a falling off in the splendor of our houses, in the richness of our furniture and dress, in the luxury of our tables, but how poor are these things in comparison with the new grandeur and beauty which would appear in the souls of men." Edwin Morton, a Harvard undergradute, wrote a combined review of Thoreau's two books in the *Harvard Magazine,* deciding that *A Week* "is an artistic and beautiful performance,—more so, I think than 'Walden.' " The *Knickerbocker* dismissed Thoreau and P. T. Barnum as "town and rural humbugs," but added: "If ever a book required an antidote, it is the auto-biography of Barnum, and we know of no other so well calculated to furnish this antidote as the book of Thoreau's."

Thoreau received a few other notices in print during his lifetime. C. C. Felton, his Greek professor at Harvard, mentioned his translation of "Prometheus Unbound" briefly in the *North American Review.* Fredrika Bremer, the Finnish novelist, devoted two sentences to him in her two-volume account of her visit to the United States, but mistakenly named him "F——." George William Curtis little more than mentions him in his essay on Emerson in *Homes of American Authors.* Thoreau also received occasional notice of his lectures in the newspapers. It is thought by some that Hawthorne attempted to depict Thoreau as Donatello in his *Marble Faun* and that Melville satirized him in *The Confidence Man* and several of his short stories. But it was Bronson Alcott's essay "The Forester," published just a few weeks before Thoreau's death, that gave him his most sympathetic evaluation— "I had never thought of knowing a man so thoroughly of the country as this friend of mine, and so purely a son of Nature"— although, ironically, Alcott nowhere in it mentioned Thoreau by name.

Little encouragement came to Thoreau from his fellow townsmen. For the most part they looked upon him as a crank and did not hesitate to tell him so to his face. Far more memorable to them than his life at Walden or his writings was the fact that he once let a campfire get out of control and burn down a wood lot. They were willing to purchase his services as a surveyor. "I am frequently invited to survey farms in a rude manner, a very [*sic*] and insignificant labor, though I manage to get more out of it than my employers; but I am never invited by the community to do anything quite worth the while to do," he complained in his *Journal* (IV, 252). They were willing to listen to his lectures before the Concord Lyceum—since he did not charge for his services. They admitted the pencils he manufactured were the best in America, although they could not understand why he did not devote himself to the business and make himself a fortune. In his last years they began to recognize him as a local authority on natural history and consulted him when they ran across any strange or unusual phenomenon. Just before Thoreau's death, Bronson Alcott, who was then superintendent of the Concord schools, persuaded the town authorities to ask Thoreau to compile an "Atlas of Concord" for use in the public schools, but his death prevented its completion.

Ironically, the first turning point in the growth of Thoreau's fame coincided approximately with his death in 1862. For one so comparatively little known, Thoreau received many eulogies. Obituaries appeared in the *Boston Daily Advertiser* for May 8 (written by Emerson, but not to be confused with his funeral oration), the *Concord Monitor* for May 10 and 17, the *Boston Transcript* for May 17, the *Christian Register* for May 17, the *Harvard Magazine* for May, the *Liberator* for May 23, the *Saturday Evening Post*, the *New York Tribune*, *Harper's Monthly* for July, the *Atlantic Monthly* for August (Emerson's funeral address), the *Annual of Scientific Discovery for 1863*, the *Proceedings of the Boston Society of Natural History* for 1862, and the *Necrology of Alumni of Harvard College* (Boston, 1864). Of all these, Emerson's funeral address was unquestionably the most influential in forming Thoreau's posthumous reputation. Although it was written with the highest motives, it emphasized Thoreau's negative rather than positive characteristics—"He was a protestant *à outrance*, and few lives contained so many renunciations"—and in the long run did more harm than good.

Just before his death Thoreau devoted his time to revising many of his lectures for publication. Four of these appeared in the *Atlantic Monthly* for 1862, two in 1863, and two in 1864. *Walden*, out of print since 1859, went into its second printing (280 copies) in 1862, its third printing in 1863 (again 280 copies), and continued to be reissued almost annually from then on. The stillborn first edition of *A Week* was reissued by Ticknor & Fields in 1862 and reprinted in a revised edition in 1867.

In 1863 his sister Sophia collected many of his essays in a volume entitled *Excursions*. In 1864, with Ellery Channing, she edited *The Maine Woods*. In 1865 they edited *Cape Cod,* and that same year Emerson edited the *Letters to Various Persons*. In 1866 *A Yankee in Canada with Anti-Slavery and Reform Papers* was issued. Thus in the four years after Thoreau's death, five new volumes of his works were published.

It has often been assumed that the publication of these five volumes attracted little notice. However, John C. Broderick, in digging through the periodical files of the period, has recently uncovered thirty-six reviews and critical notices. It is true that most of the critics considered Thoreau only as a nature writer and often deplored the eccentricities of his character ("Good citizens are not manufactured after this type"—*The New York Times,* November 23, 1863); nonetheless "the extent to which notice was taken of Thoreau's publications and the familiarity with the man and his writings which the reviews exhibit are evidence of a certain standing in the literary community" (Broderick, "American Reviews of Thoreau's Posthumous Books," p. 136).

The most influential of these reviews was that by James Russell Lowell. Ostensibly it was a review of the *Letters,* but actually it was an essay on Thoreau and his works. Lowell's whole philosophy of life was such that it was impossible for him to understand or appreciate Thoreau. And apparently after their quarrel over the publication of "Chesuncook" in the *Atlantic Monthly* for July, 1858 (see above, p. 75), Lowell became embittered. He repeated his charge that Thoreau was "among the pistillate plants kindled to fruitage by the Emersonian pollen." He thought Thoreau "was not by nature an observer," that he "had not a healthy mind," and that he "had no humor." It is true that in his closing sentences Lowell said: "There are sentences of his as perfect as anything in the language," but the overwhelming effect of the essay is negative. Since Lowell was accepted as the leading critic of his day, his essay had tremendous influence; probably it postponed a true appreciation of Thoreau for a generation or more.

Two other important notices of this period were those by John

Weiss and W. R. Alger. Weiss, a leading Unitarian clergyman, had been a classmate of Thoreau's at Harvard. Although he speaks of an "ever-deepening regard" for Thoreau and pays thoughtful attention to his books, he devotes most of his space to an account of Thoreau's college days, producing a portrait of a stoic that fits the image established by Emerson. It was not until the 1940's that Adams and McGill uncovered a quite different picture of his Harvard days.

Alger, another Unitarian clergyman, was violent in his reactions. He thought Thoreau "was unhealthy and unjust in all his thoughts on society. . . . He evidently had the jaundice of desiring men to think as well of him as he thought of himself; and, when they would not, he ran into the woods. . . . Few persons have cherished a more preposterous idea of self than Thoreau."

Raymond Adams has unearthed another essay of this period scribbled in a copy of *Walden* and unpublished until Adams' discovery. Written by an Irish lawyer from New York, Aug. O'Neil, it says in part: "His excellent knowledge of English seems to us to conceal a great deal of ignorance on other subjects. We think that he can scarcely be aware of the drift of some of his own remarks. His culture seems quite complete in some points and not even commenced upon others."

In the 1870's there was a noticeable decline of interest in Thoreau's works. Philip M. Hicks is probably correct in ascribing it to "the general decline of Idealism before the growing interest in science" (*Natural History Essay,* p. 115). The Thoreauvian philosophy was not in tune with the gilded age, or vice versa. Yet Mrs. L. A. Millington wrote an exuberant and uncritical eulogy of Thoreau's natural history essays in "Thoreau and Wilson Flagg." In that same year, 1875, John Greenleaf Whittier wrote to Thoreau's Quaker friend Daniel Ricketson, "What a rare genius he [Thoreau] was; to take up his books is like a stroll in the woods or a sail on the lake—the leaves rustle and the water ripples along his pages." And Thoreau received an odd sort of recognition when Alfred Barron published his *Footnotes or Walking as a Fine Art,* asserting that the spirit of Thoreau had aided him in its composition. One of the most scathing attacks on Transcendentalism in general and Thoreau in particular appeared in the *Catholic World* (edited by Thoreau's friend Father Isaac Hecker).

It admitted that Thoreau's nature writing was charming, but warned its readers to beware of the heresies and the utter nonsense of its economic theories. Four months later, in *Scribner's Monthly*, Emily Dickinson's friend J. G. Holland asserted: "Of one thing we may be reasonably sure, viz., that when the genuine geniuses of this period shall be appreciated at their full value . . . , their countrymen will have ceased discussing Poe and Thoreau and Walt Whitman." In 1880 Henry James commented in his biography of Hawthorne: "He [Thoreau] was imperfect, unfinished, inartistic; he was worse than provincial—he was parochial; it is only at his best that he is readable. But at his best he has an extreme natural charm" (p. 94).

Interest in Thoreau was revived once more with the publication by H. G. O. Blake of the first extended series of excerpts from the *Journal* in four volumes entitled *Early Spring in Massachusetts* (1881), *Summer* (1884), *Winter* (1887), and *Autumn* (1892). Blake tended to emphasize Thoreau's nature writings at the expense of his social criticism. It proved to be the right choice. The publication of these volumes coincided with the end of the American frontier and the great upsurge of interest in nature essays. Thoreau's writings found a popularity they had never enjoyed before. John Burroughs' various essays on Thoreau in this period undoubtedly also helped to spread his fame. But there were still a good many denunciations, best exemplified perhaps by the comments of Francis H. Underwood, Lowell's assistant on the *Atlantic Monthly* years before, when he described Thoreau as clownish, eccentric, exasperating, conceited, perverse, ludicrous, and harebrained. A writer in the New York *Commercial Advertiser* in 1888 took the middle ground when he claimed that Thoreau's ideas were "of no use to anybody nowadays," but that his pictures of forest, field, and stream have "enduring and great value." Joel Benton, writing on "The Poetry of Thoreau," was a decided exception, for not only did he unqualifiedly defend Thoreau but also thought him "a poet of striking qualities," an opinion that few others in any period have echoed.

In 1893 Houghton Mifflin, Thoreau's hereditary publishers, found the demand for his works sufficient to justify the issuing of the first collected edition, the ten-volume Riverside Edition, and in 1894 they added *Familiar Letters*, edited by F. B. Sanborn, greatly enlarging Emerson's earlier volume, although, if anything, sinking beneath it in editorial mistreatment. Representative criticism of this decade may be found in Edward A. Horton's essay on "Thoreau: Love of Nature": "No doubt he was excessive; he claimed too much value for a life spent alone. But a spirit like his clears away a great deal of fog, and enables us to see more accurately where we are." Joshua William Caldwell felt that "there seems to be no reason for concluding that Thoreau can maintain his present prominence among American writers, or that his place in literature, if permanent at all, will be a high one." Hiram Stanley, on the other hand, thought that Thoreau's place in "the eternal Pantheon of Art . . . though small [is] secure and permanent."

In the first decade of the new century we find Frederick M. Smith thinking Thoreau's chief attraction was his "iconoclasm." Paul Elmer More, considered him "the greatest by far of our writers on Nature." Hamilton W. Mabie thought Thoreau "lost the balance and went too far; but this was a small matter when the vast majority of men and women are rushing pellmell in the opposite direction." Alice Hubbard said: "Keep your ideals, is the hint Thoreau gives us. Live up to the highest promptings of your own intelligence." And Thomas Wentworth Higginson, in one of his last essays, was one of the first to recognize that Thoreau "never proclaimed the intrinsic superiority of the wilderness . . . ranking it only as 'a resource and a background.' "

In this decade Sanborn issued various unpublished Thoreau manuscripts that had come his way. But the major event of the decade was the publication by Houghton Mifflin in 1906 of the twenty-volume Walden or Manuscript Edition, including an almost complete transcription of the *Journal* in fourteen volumes, edited by Bradford Torrey and Francis H. Allen. The publication attracted wide notice, and for the first time readers were able to see that proportionately nature lore took up comparatively little space in the *Journal*. Thoreau as a philosopher and social critic began to come into his own.

In 1910 the copyright of *Walden* expired, and many publishers brought out inexpensive editions of the book aimed for use in public schools and colleges. But Houghton Mifflin maintained its superiority by issuing the only thoroughly annotated edition to appear to date. In the introduction Francis H. Allen said: "Underneath his contempt for the mere conventions of society Thoreau had a genuine love for his fellow men, and we shall miss the best part of *Walden* if we overlook these bits of real humanity, and if we fail to perceive the deep interest in mankind and the earnest desire to serve them which animates the whole book."

A few years later Robert Collyer, a Unitarian minister who had known Thoreau personally, said, "We need such men as Thoreau in every generation, full to the brim and running over with the dissidence of dissent." George H. Fitch continued in the same vein: "He was far more than a remarkable student and observer of nature; he was an original thinker who foretold many of the problems of our day." In 1917 the centennial of Thoreau's birth was observed with a commemorative meeting in Concord, the publication of several books on Thoreau, and widespread editorial comment in newspapers and magazines. In one of the best of these editorials the editors of *Seven Arts* asserted: "Thoreau is a perpetual reminder, the most vivid reminder our history affords us, that it is the toughness, the intransigence of the spiritual unit which alone gives edge to democracy."

In the 1920's there was a comparative lull in Thoreau activity, although the widespread introduction of American literature into college curriculums fostered some interest. Odell Shepard saw Thoreau as " a mystic and a mathematician, a seer and a surveyor, in one human skin," who "draws the mystery of the wilderness about our very doors" and "helps us to be content with what we have by making us see the glory of the near and familiar." On the other hand, Maud Emma Kingsley thought "Thoreau's philosophy . . . possible only to one who recognizes no social obligations. His criticism of civilization is destructive, not helpful." And John Burroughs, writing his final estimate of Thoreau, felt that "he presents that curious phenomenon of a man who is an extreme product of culture and civilization, and yet who so hungers and thirsts for the wild and the primitive that he is unfair to the forces and conditions out of which he came, and by which he is at all times nourished and upheld." But Lewis Mumford declared: "Thoreau in his life and letters shows what the pioneer movement might have come to if this great migration had sought culture rather than material conquest," and James O'Donnell

Bennett rated Thoreau "the bonniest, gravest, honestest spirit in our literature"; while Gorham B. Munson thought Thoreau "a sound 'working model' for higher education" because of his consistent love for experimentation in life. Henry Seidel Canby, in one of his early discussions of Thoreau, believed that "Thoreau will never be popularized, . . . [but] he will be still growing in many an intellect when New England is once again a deer forest."

It was in the depression years of the thirties that Thoreau really came into his own. A friend of mine once commented, "Thoreau is the only author I know of that I can read without a nickel in my pocket and not feel insulted." Certainly the simple life forced upon many people by financial necessity through those years turned many of them to reading Thoreau with a new insight, and for the first time Thoreau was treated generally as a social philosopher rather than just a nature writer. Perhaps typical of the comments of this decade is that by Max Lerner: "It was his tragedy to be forced by the crudities of an expanding capitalism into a revulsion against society and its institutions that has until recently obscured the real force of his social thought. But there is about that thought a spare and canny strength and a quality of being unfooled that will survive even such a tragedy." In 1937 Sinclair Lewis, watching the rise of the dictators in Europe, recommended *Walden* as "one of the three or four unquestionable classics of American literature" and suggested Thoreau's philosophy as an antidote for fascism. Charles Stewart wrote a rebuttal of Burroughs' criticisms of Thoreau's natural history, concluding that Burroughs misunderstood Thoreau's scientific intentions. Donald Culross Peattie, on the other hand, felt that the scientific progress of the past century had been so great that Thoreau's ideas were outdated and that only his nature writing is still worth reading, although that is "nearly perfect, and probably immortal."

When the depression was over, the interest in Thoreau did not fade, as many thought it might. Canby's biography was a best seller for many months in the winter of 1939–1940. In the late 1930's Raymond Adams, of the University of North Carolina, began occasional publication of a privately circulated "Thoreau Newsletter." And in 1941 a small group established the Thoreau Society, which since that time has held annual meetings in Concord and published a quarterly bulletin and occasional booklets to a membership of nearly five hundred scattered not only over the United States but in many foreign countries.

Approaching Thoreau as a thinker and social philosopher, Charles Child Walcutt, in one of the most forceful discussions of the applicability of Thoreau's ideas today, finds that they "have lost none of their validity with the passage of years." Gene Tunney, the intellectual prizefighter, confessed that he read Thoreau during his training period for his final heavyweight championship fight and found that "the spirit of Thoreau lends its luminous wisdom to man and nature wherever they meet." Edward Dahlberg said "No other American but [Randolph] Bourne has taken such a deep and accurate measure of the secular despotism of government as Thoreau," but we fail to heed his message because "we cannot perceive what we canonize." James Norman Hall, of *Mutiny on the Bounty* fame, in "A Belated Rebuttal" replied to Robert Louis Stevenson's essay: "No doubt there are people who still feel as Stevenson did about Thoreau; who dip into his books now and then, and lay them aside, puzzled to understand what others find in him. But I believe that there comes a time in nearly every man's life when, if he is so fortunate as to turn to Thoreau, he will suddenly know why this man has such a host of loyal and grateful friends."

In 1945 the centennial of Thoreau's going to Walden was celebrated both by many meetings and exhibitions and by essays and editorial comment. Raymond Adams said: "There is a direct relationship and a direct proportion between the submerging of the individual in the mechanics of life, the growing complexity of society, the frustrations of people by mass prejudice and custom and the emerging of Thoreau's book [*Walden*] into the American consciousness." Joel Hedgpeth said: "Thoreau saw more than nature itself, he saw what familiarity with it could mean in the spirit of man, and used his own life to demonstrate his conviction." The next year Stanley Edgar Hyman, in one of the few Freudian studies of Thoreau, wrote: "Thoreau was . . . a writer in the great stream of the American tradition, the mythic and non-realist writers." In 1946 Henry Miller, "the bad boy of American literature," edited a privately printed volume of *Three Essays by Henry David Thoreau,* prefacing it with a discerning essay on Thoreau in the atomic age, saying in part: "By living his own life in his own 'eccentric' way Thoreau demonstrated the futility and absurdity of the life of the (so-called) masses."

Meanwhile scholarly research on Thoreau increased tremendously. In the period from 1940 to 1950 there were 134 scholarly articles published on Thoreau, as against 44 in the previous decade. Only Melville and Whitman attracted the attention of more scholars. Whereas the first American Ph.D. dissertation devoted entirely to Thoreau appeared in 1929 (that by Raymond Adams), by 1940 there was an average of one dissertation a year on Thoreau. James Woodress' *Dissertations on American Literature,* (1957) lists a current total of 32 on Thoreau.

By the late 1940's the interest in Thoreau had grown to sufficient proportions to persuade Houghton Mifflin to reissue the fourteen-volume edition of the *Journal.* Joseph Wood Krutch, reviewing the new edition, explained Thoreau's increasing popularity: "There are . . . a great many more now than there once were who are willing to consider sympathetically his negative criticism, his insistence that the pursuit of wealth and the actual achievement of wealth have not produced the results hoped for."

In 1954 another centennial was celebrated—the publication of *Walden*—and again commemorative essays appeared in many leading periodicals. Said Lewis Leary: "If it seems almost a miracle . . . that 'Walden' has survived the lack of consistently intelligent response in the United States and what may appear today the alarmingly revolutionary response abroad, it seems, as has often been said, equally a miracle that a book so potentially incendiary is allowed today on public shelves where its doctrines can contaminate contemporaries to thinking as Thoreau thought." Michael Moloney wrote: "*Walden* is a humanist manifesto, the most pregnant which American humanism has yet produced. Man is Thoreau's primary concern, not God. However, he was still near enough to Christianity which he outwardly rejected to be quite certain that man without the Spirit is not man." And Robert Frost, interviewed by Reginald Lansing Cook, said, "In Thoreau's declaration of independence from the modern pace is where I find most justification for my own propensities." This survey can be appropriately closed with Philip Young's comment in *Folio* (XX, 1955, 18–22), that Thoreau is our greatest American prose stylist.

The path of Thoreau's fame can also be charted through the histories of American literature. During his own lifetime he was accorded recognition in only one: Evert and George Duyckinck, *Cyclopaedia of American Literature* (1855), in which *A Week* and *Walden* were described as "two of the most noticeable books in American literature on the score of a certain quaint study of natural history and scenery."

It was 1870 before he was noticed again, and then in Rufus Wilmot Griswold, *The Prose Writers of America,* where he was described as a "wayward genius." In 1872, however, John Hart, in *A Manual of American Literature,* said: "With Thoreau's wonderfully acute power of observation, and his fine taste and skill in word-painting, he might have made a first-class naturalist. His works are to the last degree original and quaint." In 1878 Charles F. Richardson continued the emphasis on Thoreau's nature writing by saying, *"Walden* is his best book; but in seven other volumes he carries the reader straight to Nature's heart." In 1879 Thomas Wentworth Higginson, in his *Short Studies of American Authors,* declared that *Walden* was "the only book yet written in America, to my thinking, that bears an annual perusal" and added that "the impression that Thoreau was but a minor Emerson will in time pass away."

In 1882 John Nichol, in *American Literature,* dismissed Thoreau as "little else than water added to the wine of Emerson and Lowell." In 1886 Charles F. Richardson, despite his earlier praise, said in *American Literature* that he considered Thoreau "inferior to Emerson in every trait of character and in every element of genius." Henry A. Beers, in *An Outline Sketch of American Letters* (1887), continued the condemnation by stating, "The most distinctive note in Thoreau is his inhumanity." Albert Smyth, in his *American Literature* (1889), said: "He was the most original character among his distinguished townspeople, and has as permanent a place in literature as any of them."

In 1891 Julian Hawthorne and Leonard Lemmon, in *American Literature,* wrote a lengthy and violent diatribe against Thoreau, denouncing him as "bilious," "defiant," "stealthy," "egotistical," and "disagreeable." They saw his writings as chiefly Emersonian, "thinly overspread with Thoreau." In 1893 Francis Underwood, in *The Builders of American Literature,* said, "What-

ever we may think of the eccentric man and his philosophy of living, we acknowledge a great debt to him for his fresh and delightful books." In 1894 Mildred Rutherford, in *American Authors*,
said, "He was a naturalist, and his life and work are of conse-
quence as having given an impulse in that direction." In that same
year Mildred Cabell Watkins dismissed him in one paragraph of
American Literature as "eccentric." However, in 1896, Brander
Matthews, in *An Introduction to the Study of American Literature*, concluded a lengthy and favorable evaluation of Thoreau:
"He was above all an artist in words, a ruler of the vocabulary, a
master phrase-maker." In that same year Fred Lewis Pattee, in
A History of American Literature, presented a primarily negative
picture of Thoreau, although he did admit that "no other writer
has done more for the independence of American thought."
Katharine Lee Bates, in *American Literature* (1897), discussed
Thoreau as a nature writer and said of him, "Not the best of his
disciples . . . can reach his upper notes." In that same year
F. V. N. Painter, in *Introduction to American Literature*, dismissed him in two sentences as "a recluse and observer of nature."
In 1898 Henry S. Pancoast, in *An Introduction to American Literature*, dismissed Thoreau as "Emerson's eccentric disciple." Although Donald G. Mitchell, in *American Lands and Letters* (1899),
devoted considerable space to Thoreau, he was on the whole disparaging and decided that Thoreau was not either a first-rate
essayist, poet, or scientist.

In 1900, in *A Literary History of America*, Barrett Wendell
admitted that Thoreau was "in his own way a literary artist of
unusual merit," although he thought him "eccentric" and "un-
practically individual," and classified him among "the lesser men
of Concord." In that same year Walter Bronson, in *A Short History of American Literature*, said, "On the whole, Thoreau must
be classed with the minor American authors." Alphonso G. New-
comer, in *American Literature* (1901), devoted a surprisingly large
amount of space to Thoreau and, on the whole, was sympathetic,
although he commented, "Not many of us will care to accept the
philosophy of *Walden*, so extreme is it," and finally came to the
conclusion: "The parts of Thoreau's work upon which his fame
rests most securely to-day are his nature studies." In 1902 William
C. Lawton, in *Introduction to the Study of American Literature*,

said: "He . . . has taken an honored place beside, yet apart from, Emerson himself, among the authors whom the world cannot now spare, and apparently will not soon suffer to be forgotten." In a generally skeptical account of Thoreau's life in *American Litera-ture in the Colonial and National Periods* (1902), Lorenzo Sears said: "A great part of his charm as a writer is the naïve simplicity with which he describes things as new that several other observers were already familiar with." In that same year William Cranston Lawton, in *Introduction to the Study of American Literature,* considered Thoreau's life at Walden "an interesting failure," but thought that he "is interesting chiefly for his originality, not for his loyalty to Emerson." In 1903 T. W. Higginson and H. W. Boynton, in *A Reader's History of American Literature,* said, "Time is rapidly melting away the dross from his writings, and exhibiting their gold." William P. Trent, in *A History of Ameri-can Literature* (1903), affirmed that "it is as a writer rather than as a thinker or observer that Thoreau deserves heartiest admira-tion." In 1908 John Macy, in what is often termed one of the most influential books in the field, *The Spirit of American Literature,* wrote, "Thoreau's vision shot beyond the horizon which bounded and still bounds the sight even of that part of the world which fancies itself liberal and emancipated." Abby Willis Howes, in *A Primer of American Literature* (1909), thought Thoreau "a man of true and rare genius."

In 1910 William Morton Payne, in *Leading American Essayists,* said of Thoreau: "When we look back toward his life from our present twentieth century point of vantage, it is easily seen that he was the principal figure among those who lived in the circle of Emerson's radiance and felt directly the inspiration of his ex-ample." In the next year Reuben P. Halleck, in *History of Ameri-can Literature,* said: "In spite of some Utopian philosophy and too much insistence on the self-sufficiency of the individual, *Walden* has proved a regenerative force in the lives of many readers who have not passed their plastic stage." In 1912 W. P. Trent and John Erskine wrote in *Great American Writers:* "If we should compare the influence of any one of Emerson's books with the influence of *Walden* upon thought in America and Europe, the result would show in Thoreau an astonishing power of fertilizing other minds." Said William Cairns, in *A History of*

American Literature (1912): "Though his eccentricities prevent him from ranking with the greatest American essayists, he has a unique charm for many readers, and his place in American literature seems secure." William J. Long, in *American Literature* (1913), suggested since "Thoreau's oddity has received perhaps too much attention, to the neglect of his better qualities," that "the beginner . . . make the acquaintance of the man himself rather than of his critics or biographers." In 1914 Adaline May Conway, in *The Essay in American Literature,* said, "As a stylist, we have no more admirable writer in our American literature." In 1915 Fred Lewis Pattee, in *A History of American Literature Since 1870,* reflected a change from his opinion of nearly twenty years before when he said: "His rehabilitation has come solely because of that element condemned by Lowell as a certain 'modern sentimentalism about Nature.' . . . It was because he brought to the study of Nature a new manner." In 1918 Bliss Perry, in *The American Spirit in Literature,* commented: "To the student of American thought Thoreau's prime value lies in the courage and consistency with which he endeavored to realize the gospel of Transcendentalism in his own inner life." In that same year, although Archibald MacMechan devoted a whole chapter to Thoreau in the *Cambridge History of American Literature,* he epitomized his attitude: "The truth is that Thoreau with all his genuine appreciation of the classics never learned their lessons of proportion, restraint, 'nothing too much.'" In 1919 Percy Boynton, in *A History of American Literature,* rounded off the decade with the comment: "As a citizen and as a critic of society, Thoreau lacked the sturdy Puritan conscience which is the bone and sinew of Emerson's character."

In 1926 Stanley T. Williams, in *The American Spirit in Letters,* for Yale University's "Chronicles of America" series, said, "Thoreau is the high-water mark of New England Transcendentalism." In the next year V. L. Parrington, in his epoch-making *Main Currents in American Thought,* discussing primarily Thoreau's economic theory, concluded, "One of the greatest names in American literature is the name of Henry Thoreau." Yet in that same year Lucy Hazard, in *The Frontier in American Literature,* wrote: "*Walden* is fascinating as the adventure of a solitary pioneer; it is fallacious as the guidebook for a general migration. An idyll of the golden age of transcendentalism, it is an ineffectual protest against the gilded age of industrialism." E. E. Leisy, in *American Literature* (1929), wrote: "His tonic simplification of life is giving him a fresh vogue, and it seems that the village crank who wrote with aboriginal vigor is at last coming into his own."

Russell Blankenship, in *American Literature as an Expression of the National Mind* (1931), devoted only one page to Thoreau as a nature writer, but ten pages to his social theory. He thought "Civil Disobedience" the "capstone of Thoreau's works" and stressed that his life, rather than being negative, "was one long-drawn affirmative." In that same year Gilbert Seldes, in John Macy, *American Writers on American Literature,* thought that Thoreau's "importance to us then is in the assertion that wisdom, nobility, the things of the spirit exist to gratify man and make him truly complete and happy." Yet that same year Constance Rourke, in *American Humor,* said: "He produced no philosophy, though he obviously intended to construct a philosophy. . . . He is read for the aphorism or the brief description." In 1932 Grant C. Knight, in *American Literature and Culture,* felt that "no American means more to our times than Thoreau." In the same year Ludwig Lewisohn, in *Expression in America,* after condemning Thoreau's comments on chastity and sensuality as too puritanical, decided that "Thoreau . . . must be saved in spite of his limitations." In 1933 Ralph Boas and Katherine Burton, in *Social Backgrounds of American Literature,* affirmed that *"Walden* is one of the few American classics which have achieved international fame." Carl Van Doren, in *What Is American Literature?* (1933), wrote: "In the long run he has become what he was from the first: a hero of the mind, not legendary or abstract but concrete and positive." And Stanley T. Williams, in *American Literature* (1933), said, "Proleptic, he expressed a mood of our civilization which today is vocal indeed." In 1936 Percy Boynton, in *Literature and American Life,* wrote that Thoreau was "a master of invective, passionately assailing the foes of human liberty," and Walter Fuller Taylor, in *A History of American Letters,* concluded that "historically, it is evident that Thoreau represents the extreme reach in America of (1) the romantic return to nature, and (2) romantic individualism." Bernard Smith, in *Forces in American Criticism* (1939), declared that Thoreau "was the first

American to urge the union of labor and art—an ideal which has become a catalytic influence in modern letters."

In 1940 G. Harrison Orians, in *A Short History of American Literature,* asserted that "though Thoreau did not make an impression on his age, he became one of the notable voices of the 'Golden Day.'" James Hart, in the *Oxford Companion to American Literature* (1941), said: "His observations of nature were distinguished not merely by his scientific knowledge, which was occasionally erroneous, but by his all-inclusive love of life." In *American Idealism* (1943) Floyd Stovall declared: "The greatest single contribution of Thoreau to American idealism was his uncompromising individualism, and the next greatest was his enthusiasm for nature." W. Tasker Witham, in the *Panorama of American Literature* (1947), decided that Thoreau was "the greatest of the Concord group next to Emerson." One of the best indications of the tremendous rise in Thoreau's prestige among literary critics is Townsend Scudder's essay in Spiller, Thorp, Johnson, and Canby, *Literary History of the United States* (1948), which concludes, "Thoreau has become one of America's great." Decidedly in contrast to that is Arthur Hobson Quinn's decision in *The Literature of the American People* (1951) that "Thoreau will probably remain one of those figures in our literature that represent an acquired taste, and a reputation based largely upon one book, *Walden.*" Far more typical of current opinion was the decision of the American Literature Group of the Modern Language Association to include Thoreau in its bibliographical survey of our outstanding authors, *Eight American Authors* (1957).

Thus once again we have seen that Thoreau was first dismissed as an eccentric and a minor disciple of Emerson, then accepted as a nature writer, and finally granted a place among the greatest of American authors both as a stylist and thinker.

Turning to England, we find a somewhat different pattern of fame. British critics were much quicker to recognize Thoreau's genius, although there were dissenters there too.

In 1849, when *A Week* was published in Boston, a few copies were sent to the firm of John Chapman in London for distribution. It received only two reviews. The *Athenaeum* termed it one of the "worst offshoots of Carlyle and Emerson." But the *West-*

minster Review commented: "Notwithstanding occasional attempts at fine writing, and some rather long-winded disquisitions
upon religion, literature, and other matters,—sometimes naturally
arising from the incidents of the voyage, sometimes lugged in apparently without rhyme or reason,—the book is an agreeable
book." Thoreau had complimentary copies sent to a few prominent Englishmen, and one, James Anthony Froude, wrote to him
in thanks, "In your book . . . I see hope for the coming world."

In 1854, when *Walden* was published, again a few copies were
sent to England. George Eliot gave it a brief but favorable notice
in the *Westminster Review* and six months later wrote her friend
Miss Sara Hennell, "I thought 'Walden' . . . a charming book,
from its freshness and sincerity, as well as for its bits of description." *Chambers's Journal* gave it an unfavorable notice almost
entirely cribbed from the American reviews in *Putnam's* and the
Knickerbocker, but added: "The natural sights and sounds of the
woods, as described by Mr. Thoreau, form much pleasanter reading than his vague and scarcely comprehensible social theories."

The anonymous article, "An American Rousseau," is an excellent example of the ability of the British to understand and
appreciate Thoreau long before his own countrymen did. Reviewing the first edition of *Excursions,* the critic analyzes the essays,
recognizing the scientific value of "The Succession of Forest
Trees" and pointing out that in such pieces as "Autumnal Tints"
Thoreau is not "seeing sermons in stones," but suggesting a "significant parallelism between the mind and heart of man and the
economy of nature."

Mabel Collins, in "Thoreau, Hermit and Thinker," thought
that "some of his works are better worth studying than the more
elaborate works of the popular professors of philosophy." But
Robert Louis Stevenson decided, "In one word, Thoreau was a
skulker." Gilbert P. Coleman, writing some years later, said: "Of
those opinions of Thoreau which have evidently been based on
insufficient information, the most incomplete, unsatisfactory, in-
adequate, though possibly the cleverest and most brilliant, is that
of Robert Louis Stevenson." A. H. Japp, the British biographer
of Thoreau, made haste to write Stevenson, suggesting that he
had misunderstood Thoreau's character. In a later preface to his
essay Stevenson retracted much that he had said, commenting:

"Here is an admirable instance of the 'point of view' forced throughout, and of too earnest reflection on imperfect facts. . . . I have scarce written ten sentences since I was introduced to him, but his influence might be somewhere detected by a close observer." But it was the earlier essay that won the wider hearing.

Although British publishers imported American editions of Thoreau's works for many years, in 1886 Walter Scott issued the first true English edition of *Walden* in the Camelot Classics. Other volumes followed rapidly, so that by 1900 there were at least twenty editions of Thoreau's books in print in the British Isles. Typical of comments of the period are Havelock Ellis' "Thoreau has heightened for us the wildness of Nature"; W. H. Hudson's "*Walden* . . . I should be inclined to regard as the one golden book in any century of best books"; and Will H. Dircks' "Thoreau's is a rare and remarkable spirit."

It was however the Fabians and early Labour party members who really popularized Thoreau in England. Robert Blatchford, whose *Merrie England,* with a sale of two million copies, was the first Labour party best seller, began his book with the injunction that if his readers first read *Walden,* they would more easily understand his book, and confessed that he slept with *Walden* under his pillow. Many local units of the Labour party were called Walden Clubs. Inexpensive paperbound editions of *Walden* and *Civil Disobedience* were distributed with the party's blessing. William Archer, the translator of Ibsen, lived from 1890 to 1895 near Ockham, Surrey, in a cottage that he called "Walden." Edward Carpenter confessed that *Walden* served "to make me uncomfortable for some years" and frequently quoted from it in *Towards Democracy. The Eagle and the Serpent,* a "little magazine" published in London from 1898 to 1902, was "dedicated to the philosophy of life enunciated by Nietzsche, Emerson, Stirner, Thoreau and Goethe." In Ireland William Butler Yeats, inspired by his father's reading of *Walden,* wrote one of his most beloved poems, "The Lake Isle of Innisfree." But Arthur Rickett thought that Thoreau's reputation was being harmed by the overzealous attempts of his followers to defend him from any and all charges of wrongdoing. And Arthur Christopher Benson, in *From a College Window,* thought Thoreau an egotist who espoused the simple life only because he was too indolent to do otherwise.

The centenary of Thoreau's birth was celebrated in London in 1917 at a public meeting at which W. H. Hudson proclaimed that "when the bicentenary comes around . . . he will be regarded as . . . one without master or mate . . . and who was in the foremost ranks of the prophets." The London *Bookman* devoted a whole issue to Thoreau, including a long reminiscent essay by Emerson's son Edward.

In the 1920's H. W. Nevinson thought *Walden* "the most beautiful product that ever sprang from American soil," and later H. M. Tomlinson confessed: "I suppose Thoreau has done as much as any other writer to give my mind a cast. . . . There have been reviewers who have hinted at origins for my books, but not one of them has ever noticed that I must have brooded long on Walden Pond." Yet Llewellyn Powys dismissed Thoreau as "neither a profound thinker nor a great writer."

More recent comments on Thoreau include Somerset Maugham's remark: "The interest of Walden must depend on the taste of the reader. For my part, I read it without boredom, but without exhilaration." Cartwright Timms thought Thoreau has a pertinent message for us "in this age, when so many people are content to live their lives at second-hand"; Charles Morgan, the novelist, thought Thoreau "a man completely undaunted by the pressure of collectivism, in the highest sense an Uncommon Man, whose teaching is even more closely applicable to our age than it was to his"; Hubert Woodford said, "The philosophy of Thoreau may be regarded as a corrective and a tonic for much of the artificiality of average human life"; and Holbrook Jackson declared: "He becomes what many men entangled in the world would like to be, but which, lacking even his negative courage, they can never be."

Unfortunately, there has never been a thoroughgoing attempt to study Thoreau's influence and fame outside the English-speaking nations. Nonetheless, his influence has been widespread, for his works have been translated into virtually every major modern language, and he is perhaps as widely read abroad today as any nineteenth-century American essayist.

Perhaps the outstanding fact in any consideration of Thoreau's influence abroad is that it is primarily a twentieth-century phenomenon. This is outstandingly true in Latin America. José Marti, the late nineteenth-century Cuban radical, was familiar with Thoreau's writings and mentioned him occasionally in his essays, but he stirred up no widespread interest in Thoreau among his countrymen. *Walden* was first translated into Spanish by Julio Molina y Vedia in Buenos Aires in 1945. A superior translation by Justo Garate appeared in Buenos Aires in 1949 and was sufficiently popular to require a second, revised edition before the year was out. Previously a selection from Thoreau's *Journal* and essays, translated by Horacio E. Roque, had appeared in Buenos Aires in 1937. And a translation by Ernesto Montenegro of "Civil Disobedience" was published in Santiago, Chile, in 1949. A Portuguese translation by E. C. Caldas of *Walden* was published in Rio de Janeiro in 1953. Canby's biography (translated by Pablo Simon) was published in Buenos Aires in 1944, as was Luis Echavarri's translation of Theodore Dreiser's *Living Thoughts of Thoreau*. A brief tribute *Thoreau: El Quijote de Walden,* by V. Munoz, was published in Montevideo, Uruguay, in 1958. So far as I know, no editions of Thoreau's works have appeared in either Spain or Portugal, and there have been no book-length critical studies or biographies in either language.

Walden was translated into French by L. Fabulet in Paris in 1922. It has remained in print continually since that date and is now in its seventh printing. Regis Michaud translated a volume of selections from Thoreau in Paris in 1930. Leon Bazalgette published a fictionalized biography in Paris in 1924. And in 1929 Andrée Bruel published in Paris her doctoral dissertation "Emerson et Thoreau," one of the most detailed studies we have of the relationship of the two men.

There are other indications of an interest in Thoreau in France. On September 15, 1887, Th. Bentzon published an article on "Le Naturalisme aux Etats-Unis" in the *Revue des Deux Mondes,* stating that if *Walden* were to be translated into French, it would be sufficient "à établir en France la réputation de Thoreau comme écrivain et comme penseur." In 1904 Marcel Proust wrote to the Comtesse de Noailles: "Lisez . . . les pages admirables de *Walden.* Il me semble qu'on les lise en soi-même tant elles sortent du fond de notre expérience intime." And André Gide has written: "I remember the day when Fabulet met me in the Place de la Madeleine and told me about his discovery [of *Walden*]. 'An extraordinary book,' he said, 'and one that nobody in France has heard about.' It happened that I had a copy of 'Walden' in my pocket."

Thoreau has received marked attention in Germany. *Walden* was first translated into German by Emma Emmerich in 1897. It has since been translated by Wilhelm Nobbe in 1905, Frz. Reuss in 1914, F. Meyer in 1922, Siegfried Lang in 1945, Augusta V. Bronner in 1947 (a condensed version), Anneliese Dangel in 1949, and by Fritz Krokel in 1950 (another condensed version). H. G. O. Blake's selections from the *Journal,* entitled *Winter,* were translated by Emma Emmerich in 1900.

In 1895 A. Prinzinger published a pamphlet biography, *Henry D. Thoreau, Ein Amerikanischer Naturschilderer.* And in 1899 Karl Knortz, Whitman's friend and translator, published another pamphlet biography, *Ein Amerikanischer Diogenes.* There have been numerous critical essays on Thoreau published in various German periodicals and books, and a surprising number of doctoral dissertations in German universities. The latter include Klaus Becker, *"Der Stil in den Essays von Henry David Thoreau"* (Marburg, 1953); Helga Innerhofer, *"Henry David Thoreau, seine Stellung zu seiner Zeit, zu Mensch und Natur"* (Innsbruck, 1951); Leopold Irsiegler, *"Naturbeobachtung und Naturgefühl bei Henry David Thoreau"* (Vienna, 1951); Karl J. Zwanzig, *"Thoreau als Kritiker der Gesellschaft"* (Berlin, 1956); and the earliest of all dissertations on Thoreau, Helen Snyder, *Thoreau's Philosophy of Life, with Special Consideration of the Influence of Hindoo Philosophy* (Heidelberg, 1900[?]). There are numerous other dissertations on Thoreau recently announced as "in progress." Unfortunately, of all these named above, I have been able to obtain only the Snyder dissertation for use in this book.

Frederik van Eeden, a Dutch short-story writer and socialist, was chiefly responsible for the interest in Thoreau in Holland. In 1897 he set about establishing a utopian community at Bussum, near Amsterdam, which he named Walden in honor of Thoreau. In 1902 Miss Suze de Jongh van Damwoude translated *Walden* into Dutch, for which van Eeden wrote a foreword.

Interest in Thoreau in Denmark reached a high point during World War II, when leaders of the Danish resistance movement looked upon "Civil Disobedience" as a manual of arms. Soon after the war Martin Ashfield, one of the resisters, began a translation of *Walden*, but abandoned it when a translation by Ole Jacobsen appeared in 1949. A. Ejvind Larson, the publisher of this translation, wrote me (February 2, 1950) that the edition was a tremendous and totally unexpected success. When he commissioned it, he "hoped it would be possible to make the Danish public realize how great he [Thoreau] was." The first edition was exhausted in seventeen days and a new edition was demanded and printed immediately. In 1951 Ole Jacobsen translated a pamphlet edition of "Walking" and "A Winter Walk."

In 1947 Frans B. Bengtsson translated *Walden* into Swedish in an edition beautifully illustrated by Stig Asberg. In 1953 it was translated into Norwegian by Andreas Eriksen. A Finnish translation by Mikko Kilpi appeared in Helsinki in 1955.

In 1901 Count Leo Tolstoi, in "A Message to the American People," said:

If I had to address the American people, I should like to thank them for the great help I have received from their writers who flourished about the fifties. I would mention Garrison, Parker, Emerson, Ballou and Thoreau, not as the greatest, but as those who, I think, specially influenced me. . . . And I should like to ask the American people why they do not pay more attention to these voices (hardly to be replaced by those of financial and industrial millionaires, or successful generals and admirals), and continue the good work in which they made such hopeful progress.

Tolstoi includes many selections from Thoreau in his anthology *A Circle of Reading.* And Gandhi and Tolstoi found a common interest in Thoreau in their extended correspondence. An abridged translation of *Walden* was published in Moscow in 1900 and a complete translation, by P. A. Bulanizke, in Moscow in 1910. A brief collection of selections from Thoreau's writings, translated by I. Nikashidze, appeared in Moscow in 1903. So far as I know, there have been no translations since the revolution.

Walden was first translated into Czechoslovak in 1924. It was translated again in 1933 by Milos Seifert, and a third translation was made in 1950. But before this third edition could be published it was seized by the Russians, "pending ideological investigation into its contents," and so far as I can discover has never been released.

The Italian Guido Ferrando translated *Walden* in 1920; and it was reissued in 1928. In 1954 Biancamaria Tedeschini Lalli published a biographical study, *Henry David Thoreau*, apparently based chiefly on Canby's biography. A Greek translation of *Walden*, by J. Zacharakis, appeared in Athens in 1955.

There has been a long-sustained interest in Thoreau among the Jews. "Civil Disobedience" was translated into Yiddish in New York in 1907 and again in Los Angeles in 1950. There have been frequent articles on Thoreau in Yiddish newspapers around the world. It is my understanding that *Walden* is at the moment being translated into Hebrew in Israel.

The interest in Thoreau in Japan has been phenomenal. *Walden* has been published in English four times—in 1922, 1929, and twice in 1957. It has been translated into Japanese eleven times—in 1925, 1933 (twice), 1948, 1949, 1950, 1951 (three times), and 1953 (twice). There have also been editions of *A Week* (1951), selections from the *Journal* (1949), "Civil Disobedience" (1949), and three different volumes of selections from Thoreau's writings (1912, 1921, and 1949). In 1934 a biography of Thoreau by Akira Tomita was published.

To my knowledge, Thoreau has never been published in China. But Lin Yutang, in his *Importance of Living*, says: "Thoreau is the most Chinese of all American authors in his entire view of life. . . . I could translate passages of Thoreau into my own language and pass them off as original writing by a Chinese poet, without raising any suspicion." Brooks Atkinson told me that when he was a *New York Times* correspondent in China during World War II, his copy of *Walden* disappeared. He learned later that his houseboy had started reading it and was so entranced that he started to translate it into Chinese.

The most notable example of Thoreau's influence on the modern world was Mahatma Gandhi's use of "Civil Disobedience." Gandhi went to England as a young man to study law. Through his vegetarian principles he became acquainted with Henry Salt, the British editor and biographer of Thoreau, who was also a

vegetarian. Later, in 1906 or 1907, when Gandhi was fighting for
the rights of Indians in South Africa, a friend sent him a copy of
"Civil Disobedience." Gandhi told Webb Miller:

His [Thoreau's] ideas influenced me greatly. I adopted some of
them and recommended the study of Thoreau to all my friends
who were helping me in the cause of Indian independence. Why,
I actually took the name of my movement from Thoreau's essay,
"On the Duty of Civil Disobedience." . . . Until I read that
essay I never found a suitable English translation for my Indian
word *Satyagraha*. . . . There is no doubt that Thoreau's ideas
greatly influenced my movement in India (*I Found No Peace*, pp.
238–39).

Gandhi printed copious extracts from "Civil Disobedience" in
his South African newspaper *Indian Opinion* for October 26,
1907, and later reprinted these in pamphlet form for distribution
among his followers. Roger Baldwin, then the director of the
American Civil Liberties Union, met Gandhi in France in 1931,
on his way to the London Conference, and noticed that he carried
a copy of "Civil Disobedience" with him (*TSB* 11). And it has
often been noted that he always carried a copy with him during
his many imprisonments.

Nor was he unacquainted with Thoreau's other writings. In
1929 he wrote Henry Salt: "I felt the need of knowing more of
Thoreau, and I came across your Life of him, his 'Walden,' and
other shorter essays, all of which I read with great pleasure and
equal profit." Like so many other followers of Thoreau, he found
"Life Without Principle" another major document in the Thoreau canon and reprinted long portions of it in his *Indian Opinion*
for June 10 and July 22, 1911. It is difficult to imagine Gandhi
and the work he accomplished in India and Africa without the
influence of Thoreau. That interest in Thoreau in India has continued since Gandhi's death is reflected in the recent publication
in Delhi of an anonymous pamphlet biography entitled *Henry
David Thoreau: The Man Who Moulded the Mahatma's Mind*.
In the summer of 1956 the Indian government announced that it
was sponsoring the translation and publication of *Walden* in
fifteen of the major Indian languages. Thus Thoreau, who fed
upon the literature of the Orient, returned in kind to the Orient
full measure.

One cannot fairly discuss Thoreau's fame without at least mentioning the attraction he has had for the various types of radicals. Walt Whitman explained this appeal when he said: "One thing about Thoreau keeps him very near to me: I refer to his lawlessness—his dissent—his going his absolute own road let hell blaze all it chooses." Understandably, it has been the anarchists who have been most attracted. Kropotkin, Tolstoi, Emma Goldman, and Alexander Berkman have all professed their interest in Thoreau. Rare is the issue of an anarchist magazine in this country or abroad that does not somewhere in it cite him.

Allied, at least in philosophy, to the anarchists are the decentralists. And, says Benson Y. Landis, in "The Decentralist at Walden Pond": "Today the tiny school of decentralists, crying in the wilderness, points to the productive homestead as an essential cornerstone of its movement. The squatter at Walden in his miniature productive home uttered and demonstrated many of the essential doctrines of this group."

It is harder to understand the interest that the Communists have taken in Thoreau, for as C. R. B. Combellack has pointed out in "Two Critics of Society": "It is characteristic of them that Marx thought primarily of changing the environment, the system, and that Thoreau's concern was not with the environing social structure but with the individual. . . . The different ways they had of seeing individuals is fundamental. Where Marx saw classes of men, Thoreau saw men." R. N. Stromberg in "Thoreau and Marx: A Century After," avers that "he who reads 'Life without Principle,' unlike the reader of *The Communist Manifesto,* will emerge spiritually refreshed and with, perchance, a philosophy of life"; and Joseph Wood Krutch (p. 258) adds: "Had he [Thoreau] ever heard the theory that the state will ultimately wither away but that we must make it all powerful first, he would undoubtedly have replied as he did when he heard of the would-be poet who proposed to get rich in order that he might have leisure for poetry, 'He should have gone up to the garret at once.' " Yet Samuel Sillen, in "Thoreau in Our Time," claims that "Marxists see in the author of *Walden* a man deeply devoted to the welfare of humanity, deeply concerned about America's course," and Adam Lupin, writing in *The Worker* "On the 135th Anniversary of Henry Thoreau" (July 27, 1952), says: "His meaning for today is to be found in his realization that he, the most non-political of human beings, had to engage in political struggle [the John Brown incident] if he were not to betray himself and his love of life and nature." V. F. Calverton, in *The Liberation of American Literature,* holds a more tenable Marxist approach when he complains that Thoreau "was wrong in pursuing the life he did . . . because the doctrine he adopted was based upon a social error. Man is a social animal and cannot live in individual isolation"; so does Bernard Smith, when he believes that Thoreau was led "to an acceptance of propositions which later proved irrelevant to the problems and struggles that have disturbed his country."

It is far more understandable that the vegetarians have espoused Thoreau. John Davies, in "Thoreau and the Ethics of Food," says, "It encourages us, in the promulgation of this basic reform, to find Thoreau among the many stalwarts on our side," and adds, in "Centennial of Thoreau's 'Walden,' " that Thoreau in *Walden* gives the best reasons "that have ever been given" for refraining from animal food.

Even the nudists have laid claim to Thoreau. Lawrence Mac-Donald in "Henry Thoreau—Liberal, Unconventional, Nudist," says: "Living at the height of mid-Victorian puritanism and prudery at its worst, he [Thoreau] had the courage of his convictions to challenge the 'code of morals' which required him to hide his body from the sight of man, the sight of the sun, and even the sight of himself."

It is surprising that more use has not been made of Thoreau as a character in fiction. So far as I know, there has never been a novel based on his life (unless Bazalgette's biography is considered one), although he does appear as a minor or supporting character in a number of novels. Louisa May Alcott is thought to have used him as the basis for several of the characters in her novels. Anne Colver, in her *Listen for the Voices* (1939), gives the most vivid portrayal I have seen, and she has confessed to me that he almost ran away with her plot, he became so interesting to depict. Hildegarde Hawthorne (Nathaniel Hawthorne's granddaughter) introduced him briefly into several of her children's novels of Concord life, and he appears in a number of novelized biographies of John Brown and Walt Whitman.

Homer Croy, *Mr. Meek Marches On* (1941), is an attempt to depict what would happen if someone tried to apply the principles of "Civil Disobedience" today. B. F. Skinner, *Walden Two* (1948), portrays life in a modern utopia based on Thoreau's principles. Jack Iams, *Prophet by Experience* (1943), is a delightful spoof on a modern Thoreau living in a cave. J. William Lloyd, *The Natural Man* (1902), is a novelized paraphrase of *Walden*. Most unusual is Herbert Brean, *Hardly a Man Is Now Alive* (1950), a murder mystery involving an attempt to locate a novel written jointly by Thoreau and Emerson. And, finally, Jack London wrote a short story about a restaurant cook who, inspired by a quotation from Thoreau, became queen of an Indian tribe.

There has been an almost unceasing and quite overwhelming flood of poetic tributes to Thoreau over the past century. In 1943 I listed 137 in "A Bibliography of Thoreau in Poetry, Fiction and Drama." The number has probably doubled since then and is apparently unending. Unfortunately, most of it is mediocre, if not downright bad, poetry. The tributes are unquestionably sincerely made, but the expression is sentimental in the extreme. "O Walden Pond! thy classic shore," one begins. And many are worse than that. A few, such as Samuel Hoffenstein's "Grant me, O Lord, no meaner rhyme," are amusing parodies. Still fewer rise above the general level. Most notable of these is William Butler Yeats, "The Lake Isle of Innisfree," inspired by *Walden*. Among other outstanding ones are the free verse biography of Thoreau, *More Day to Dawn* (1941) by Harry Lee, and the two sonnet sequences, *Thoreau: Voice in the Edgeland* (1955) by Langley Carleton Keyes and *Farewell to Walden* (1939) by Florence Becker. Adin Ballou has been writing another sequence of sonnets, subtitled "after reading Thoreau," which have been appearing in various newspapers over the past fifteen or more years. It is his intention to gather them eventually into a volume. Mention should also be made of the "Memorial Verses" that Ellery Channing appended to his biography of Thoreau; the well-known "Thoreau's Flute," which Louisa May Alcott wrote for the *Atlantic Monthly;* and the several Thoreau poems by her father Bronson Alcott.

In 1854 the itinerant portrait painter Samuel Rowse did a crayon study of Thoreau that now hangs in the Concord Free Public Library. It is the earliest surviving authentic portrait and one of the few done from life. A few years after Thoreau's death Walton Ricketson, son of Thoreau's New Bedford friend, did a bust from memory and also a bas-relief medallion. In the twentieth century Thoreau has attracted the interest of a number of artists. Diego Rivera included a sketch of Thoreau peering out of prison windows in his controversial "Portrait of America" murals painted for the New Workers' School in New York City. Henry Varnum Poor, in his "Conservation of American Wild Life" murals for the Department of the Interior Building in Washington, includes an almost unrecognizable portrait of Thoreau surrounded by wild life. Barry Faulkner's 1950 series of murals for the Keene National Bank, Keene, New Hampshire, includes a panel of Thoreau on Monadnock. Robert Wild has done a miniature statue of Thoreau, and Jo Davidson modeled a projected life-size statue, hoping to raise funds for its erection in Concord, but the project was abandoned at his death. Thoreau has even been commemorated in stained glass in a memorial window in the chapel at Trinity College, Hartford, Connecticut.

The list of artists and photographers who have been inspired to illustrate Thoreau's works is altogether too long to include here. Among the best known are Eric Fitch Daglish, Henry Bugbee Kane, Thomas W. Nason, Rudolph Ruzicka, Edward Steichen, Edwin Way Teale, and N. C. Wyeth.

Thoreau has also attracted the attention of several composers. The most notable of these was Charles E. Ives, that most original of American musicians. Between 1909 and 1915 he composed his best-known work, the *Concord Sonata*. It is one of the most difficult pieces in piano literature, and only John Kirkpatrick has ventured to perform it in the concert hall. Lawrence Gilman of the *New York Herald Tribune* called it "the greatest music composed by an American." The sonata is made up of four movements, "Emerson," "Hawthorne," "The Alcotts," and "Thoreau." And for the final movement Ives comments, "If there shall be a program let it follow his thought on an autumn day of Indian summer at Walden." His *114 Songs* (1922) also contains a song entitled "Thoreau."

Daniel Gregory Mason in 1926 composed a "Chanticleer Overture," taking its title from the epigraph to *Walden*. Mason had a lifelong interest in Thoreau and once wrote a biography of him, which unfortunately was never published.

In the mid-1940's Edward T. Cone composed a brief *Excursions: Suite for a Capella Chorus,* with words from Thoreau.

Thoreau has taken a full century to achieve recognition. In American literature only Herman Melville has climbed more spectacularly the heights of literary fame from obscurity. In his own lifetime Thoreau was almost invariably dismissed as an eccentric and unimportant imitator of Emerson. Today he threatens to overshadow Emerson—if he has not already done so. Thoreau's reputation is waxing; Emerson's is barely holding its own and may indeed even be waning. We Americans are prone to compiling lists of the five, the ten, the twenty-five, the fifty, or the hundred greatest authors. And no such list in recent years fails to place Thoreau near the top.

There is still, however, one important qualification of his fame. He still lacks "official" recognition. He has not been elected to the Hall of Fame. He has appeared on no postage stamps. His alma mater, Harvard University, has named no chairs or halls in his honor. There is no statue of Thoreau gracing any city park. He is still *persona non grata* in certain circles for his political, social, and economic views. He can hardly yet be considered a "household author," and I doubt if he ever will be. Thoreau appeals to the individual, not the mass. But his place in American literature—and in world literature—is secure. As Ralph Waldo Emerson said in his funeral address for Thoreau, "Wherever there is knowledge, wherever there is virtue, wherever there is beauty, he will find a home."

SOURCES FOR CHAPTER FIVE

The foregoing is, I believe, the first extensive survey of the rise of Thoreau's fame. There have been two earlier brief summaries: Randall Stewart, "The Growth of Thoreau's Reputation" (*CE*, VII, 1946, 208–14), and Gilbert P. Coleman, "Thoreau and His Critics" (*Dial*, XL, 1906, 352–56). Samuel A. Jones gathered many of the early criticisms of Thoreau in his *Pertaining to Thoreau* (Detroit, 1901), which unfortunately appeared in a limited edition and is now even harder to find than many of the articles it reprints. I have gathered twenty-four of the more important critical articles in *Thoreau: A Century of Criticism* (Dallas, 1954). Some of the early criticisms have been reprinted in various issues of the *Thoreau Society Bulletin*. A good brief survey of the popularity of *Walden* over the years is Francis B. Dedmond, "100 Years of *Walden*" (*Concord Journal*, June 24, 1954). I have covered similar ground in "A Century of Walden" (*ColQ* III, 1954, 186–99). Walter Harding, *A Centennial Check-List of the Editions of Henry David Thoreau's Walden* (Charlottesville, Va., 1954), enumerates 132 different editions of *Walden* that appeared in its first hundred years.

Fuller bibliographical details for the various books and articles cited in the chapter follow: James Russell Lowell, *A Fable for Critics* (New York, 1848). See also E. J. Nichols, "Identification of Characters in Lowell's A Fable for Critics" (*AL*, IV, 1932, 191–94). Reviews of *A Week* appeared in the *New York Tribune* (by George Ripley, June 13, 1849, *PT*, *TCC*, *TSB* 27); the *Massachusetts Quarterly Review* (by James Russell Lowell, III, 1849, 40–51, *PT*, *TSB* 35); *Godey's Lady's Book* (XXXIX, 1849, 223, *TSB* 29); *Pictorial National Library* (III, 1849, 60–61, *TSB* 29).

Reviews of *Walden* appeared in the *New York Tribune,* July 29, 1854; the *Providence Journal,* August 11, 1854 (*TSB* 16); the *Southern Literary Messenger* (XX, 1854, 575, *TSB* 46); the *National Magazine* (V, 1854, 284–85, *TSB* 46); *Graham's Magazine* (XLV, 1854, 298–300, *TSB* 46); *Putnam's Monthly* (by Charles Frederick Briggs, IV, 1854, 443–48, *PT*); *North American Review* (LXXIX, 1854, 536); *National Anti-Slavery Standard,* December 16, 1854 (*TCC, TSB* 38); *Harvard Magazine* (by Edwin Morton, I, 1855, 87 ff., *PT*); *Knickerbocker* (XLV, 1855, 235 ff., *PT*).

Lifetime notices of Thoreau include C. C. Felton's review of Herbert's translation of Aeschylus in the *North American Review* (LXIX, 1849, 414, *TSB* 46); Fredrika Bremer, *The Homes of the New World* (New York, 1854, p. 167, *TSB* 54); George William Curtis, "Ralph Waldo Emerson," in *Homes of American Authors* (New York, 1852, p. 247) and Bronson Alcott, "The Forester" (*Atlantic Monthly,* IX, 1862, 443–45, *PT*). The question of whether Melville satirized Thoreau has been discussed in a number of places, among them Egbert Oliver, "A Second Look at 'Bartleby' " (*CE,* VI, 1945, 431–39); Oliver, "Melville's Picture of Emerson and Thoreau in 'The Confidence Man' " (*CE,* VIII, 1946, 61–72); and Oliver, " 'Cock-A-Doodle-Doo' and Transcendental Hocus-Pocus" (*NEQ,* XXI, 1948, 204–16). Alfred Kazin disagrees strongly with Oliver in "Ishmael in His Academic Heaven" (*New Yorker,* February 12, 1949, pp. 84–89). Further comments can be found in Elizabeth Foster's introduction to Melville's *Confidence Man* (New York, 1954) and Edward Rosenberry, *Melville and the Comic Spirit* (Cambridge, Mass., 1955, pp. 163, 168–70). Further evidence of Melville's reading of Thoreau is available in Frank Davidson, "Melville, Thoreau, and 'The Apple-Tree Table' " (*AL,* XXV, 1954, 479–88).

The reviews of Thoreau's posthumous books are evaluated in John C. Broderick, "American Reviews of Thoreau's Posthumous Books, 1863–1866" (*UTSE,* XXXIV, 1955, 125–39). Lowell's essay first appeared in the *North American Review* (CI, 1865, 597–608, *TCC*) and was later collected in *My Study Windows* (Boston, 1871). For discussions of Lowell's quarrel with Thoreau see Austin Warren, "Lowell on Thoreau" (*SP,* XXVII, 1930, 442–61) and Canby, *Thoreau* (pp. 374–76). John Weiss's review appeared in the *Christian Examiner* (LXXIX, 1865, 96–117, *PT*) and W. R. Alger's comments in *The Genius of Solitude* (Boston, 1866, pp. 329–38). The studies by Adams and McGill are covered in Chapter One. Aug. O'Neil's review was published by Raymond Adams in "An Irishman on Thoreau: A Stillborn Review of *Walden*" (*NEQ*, XIII, 1940, 697–99). Mrs. L. A. Millington, "Thoreau and Wilson Flagg," appeared in *Old and New* (I, 1875, 460–64). Whittier's letter to Ricketson is printed in Anna and Walton Ricketson, *Daniel Ricketson: Autobiographic and Miscellaneous* (New Bedford, Mass., 1910, p. 118). Alfred Barron, *Footnotes or Walking as a Fine Art* (Wallingford, Conn., 1875), is discussed in *TSB* 38. The anonymous "Thoreau and New England Transcendentalism" appeared in the *CathW* (XXVII, 1878, 289 ff.).

John Burroughs wrote on Thoreau in "Thoreau's Wildness" (*Critic*, 1, 1881, 74, *TCC*); "Henry D. Thoreau" (*Century*, 11, 1882, 368) and "Henry D. Thoreau" (*Chautauquan*, IX, 1889, 530). Most of these essays are reprinted in Burroughs' collected works.

Francis Underwood, "Henry David Thoreau," appeared in *Good Words* (XXIX, 1888, 445); Joel Benton, "The Poetry of Thoreau," in *Lippincott's Magazine* (XXXVII, 1885, 491). Edward Horton, "Thoreau: Love of Nature," appears in his collection of Sunday-school lessons entitled *Noble Lives and Noble Deeds* (Boston, 1893, pp. 106–8); Joshua William Caldwell, "Ten Volumes of Thoreau," in the *New Englander* (LV, 1891, 404); Hiram Stanley, "Thoreau as Prose Writer," in the *Dial* (XXI, 1896, 179–82); Frederick M. Smith, "Thoreau," in the *Critic* (XXXVII, 1900, 60–67); Paul Elmer More, "A Hermit's Notes on Thoreau," in the *Atlantic Monthly* (LXXXVII, 1901, 857–64, *TCC*); Hamilton Mabie, "Thoreau, a Prophet of Nature," in *Outlook* (LXXX, 1905, 278–82); Alice Hubbard, "Henry D. Thoreau," in *Life Lessons* (East Aurora, N. Y., 1909, pp. 123–48); Thomas Wentworth Higginson, "Henry David Thoreau," in *Carlyle's Laugh and Other Surprises* (Boston, 1909); Robert Collyer, "Henry David Thoreau," in *Clear Grit* (Boston, 1913); George Fitch, "Thoreau: The Pioneer Writer About Nature," in *Great Spiritual Writers of America* (San Francisco, 1916); the *Seven Arts* editorial is in II, 1917, 383–85 (*TCC*); Odell Shepard, "The Paradox of Thoreau," in *Scribner's Magazine* (LXVIII,

1920, 335–42); Maud Emma Kingsley, "Outline Study of Thoreau's Walden" in *Education* (XLI, 1921, 452–65); John Burroughs, "Another Word on Thoreau," in *The Last Harvest* (Boston, 1922, pp. 103–71); Lewis Mumford comments on Thoreau in *The Golden Day* (New York, 1926, p. 108); James O'Donnell Bennett, "Thoreau's 'Walden,'" is in *Much Loved Books: Best Sellers of the Ages* (New York, 1927, pp. 318–26); Gorham B. Munson, "A Dionysian in Concord," in *Outlook* (CXLIX, 1928, 690 ff); Henry Seidel Canby, "Thoreau," in *American Estimates* (New York, 1929, pp. 97–109); Max Lerner, "Henry David Thoreau," is in the *Encyclopaedia of Social Sciences* (XIV, 1934, 621–22); Sinclair Lewis, "One Man Revolution," in *Newsweek* (X, 1937, 33, *TCC*); Charles Stewart, "A Word for Thoreau," in *Atlantic Monthly* (CLVI, 1935, 110–16); Donald Culross Peattie, "Is Thoreau a Modern?" in *North American Review* (CCXLV, 1938, 159–69); Charles Child Walcutt, "Thoreau in the Twentieth Century," in *SAQ* (XXXIX, 1940, 168–84); Gene Tunney, "Me and Shakespeare," in the *Saturday Evening Post*, May 24, 1941; Edward Dahlberg, "Thoreau and Walden," in *Do These Bones Live?* (New York, 1941, pp. 8–18); James Norman Hall, "A Belated Rebuttal," in *Under a Thatched Roof* (Boston, 1942, pp. 105–16); Raymond Adams, "Thoreau at Walden," in *University of North Carolina Extension Bulletin* (XXIV, 1944, 9–24); Joel Hedgpeth, "A Hundred Years in the Woods," in *Land* (IV, 1945, 388–91); Stanley Edgar Hyman, "Henry Thoreau in Our Time," in *Atlantic Monthly* (CLXXVIII, 1946, 137–46); Joseph Wood Krutch, review of the *Journal* in *The New York Times*, May 20, 1951; Lewis Leary, "A Century of Walden," in *Nation* (CLXXIX, 1954, 114–15); Michael Moloney, "Walden: A Centenary," in *America* (XC, 1954, 683–85); and Robert Frost, "Thoreau's 'Walden,'" in *Listener* (LII, 1954, 319–20). Too recent to discuss in our text is Vincent Buranelli, "The Case Against Thoreau" (*Ethics*, LXVII, 1957, 257–68).

Two brief summaries of British criticism of Thoreau are James Playsted Wood, "English and American Criticism of Thoreau," in *NEQ* (VI, 1933, 733–46) and William Condry, "A Hundred Years of *Walden*," in *DM* (XXXI, 1955, 42–46). British reviews of *A Week* include those in the *Athenaeum* (October 27, 1849, p. 27, *TSB* 29) and the *Westminster Review* (LII, 1850, 309–10,

TSB 59). James Anthony Froude's letter is printed in S. A. Jones, *Some Unpublished Letters of Henry D. and Sophia E. Thoreau* (Jamaica, N. Y., 1899, pp. 11–13). English reviews of *Walden* appeared in the *Westminster Review* (by George Eliot [LXV, 1856, 302–3]) and *Chambers's Journal* (VIII, 1857, 330–32, *PT, TCC*). The anonymous "American Rousseau" appeared in *Saturday Review* (XVIII, 1864, 694–95); Mabel Collins, "Thoreau, Hermit and Thinker," in *Dublin University Magazine* (XC, 1877, 610–21); Robert Louis Stevenson, "Henry David Thoreau: His Character and Opinions," in *Cornhill Magazine* (XLI, 1880, 665–82, *TCC*) and his recantation in *Familiar Studies of Men and Books* (London, 1886); Gilbert Coleman's article is cited at the beginning of this chapter; Havelock Ellis comments at length on Thoreau in his essay on Whitman in *The New Spirit* (London, 1890, pp. 90–99, *TCC*); W. H. Hudson, in *Birds in a Village* (London, 1893, p. 190); Will H. Dircks, in his preface to *Essays and Other Writings of Henry David Thoreau* (London, 189[?]). British editions of Thoreau are discussed in Clarence Gohdes, *American Literature in Nineteenth-Century England* (New York, 1944, p. 46). The interest of British liberals in Thoreau is detailed in the Condry article cited above. For the influence of Thoreau on Yeats see Wendell Glick, "Yeats's Early Reading of *Walden*" (*BPLQ*, V, 1953, 164–66) and Robert Francis, "Of Walden and Innisfree," in *Christian Science Monitor*, November 6, 1952; see also, J. Lyndon Shanley, "Thoreau's Geese and Yeats's Swans" (*AL*, XXX, 1958, 361–64). Arthur Rickett, "Henry D. Thoreau," is in *The Vagabond in Literature* (London, 1906, pp. 89–114); Arthur Christopher Benson, in *From a College Window* (London, 1906, pp. 259–62); W. H. Hudson's comment is given in *TSB* 21; the June, 1917 number of the London *Bookman* (LII, 75–104) is devoted to Thoreau; H. W. Nevinson, "Nature's Priest and Rebel," is in *Essays in Freedom and Rebellion* (New Haven, Conn., 1921, pp. 108–14). H. M. Tomlinson, "Two Americans and a Whale," is in *HM* (CLII, 1926, 618–21, *TCC*); Llewellyn Powys, "Thoreau: A Disparagement," in *Bookman* (LXIX, 1929, 163–65, *TCC*); Somerset Maugham, "The Classic Books of America," in the *Saturday Evening Post*, January 6, 1940 (p. 64); Cartwright Timms, "The Philosophy of Henry David Thoreau," in *London Quarterly and Holburn Review* (CLXXI, 1947, 152–56); Charles Morgan,

"Walden and Beyond," in the London *Times,* November 9, 1947 (p. 3); Hubert Woodford, "Thoreau's 'Walden,' " in the *Inquirer,* November 22, 1947; and Holbrook Jackson, "Thoreau," in *Dreamers of Dreams* (London, 1949, pp. 211–52).

There is no comprehensive survey of Thoreau's influence and fame abroad. W. Stephen Thomas discusses Marti's interest in Thoreau in "Marti and Thoreau: Pioneers of Personal Freedom" (*Dos Pueblos,* IV, 1949, 1–3). Proust's comment is quoted by F. O. Matthiessen in *American Renaissance* (New York, 1941, p. 172). André Gide, "Imaginary Interview," appeared in the *New Republic,* February 7, 1944. Amusing reminiscences of assisting M. Fabulet with his French translation of *Walden* are given in Francis H. Allen, "The French Translation of *Walden*" (*TSB* 38). For the interest in Thoreau in Holland, see Walter Harding, "Thoreau in Holland" (*TSB* 14), which also includes a translation by C. W. Bieling of Van Eeden's foreword to the Dutch edition of *Walden.* Tolstoi, "A Message to the American People," appeared in the *North American Review* (CLXXII, 1901, 503). Tolstoi's interest in Thoreau is discussed in George Hendrick, "Thoreau and Gandhi" (University of Texas, Ph.D., 1954), and Clarence A. Manning has found many similarities in the philosophies of the two men in "Thoreau and Tolstoy" (*NEQ,* XVI, 1943, 234–43). A list of recent Russian commentaries on Thoreau can be found in *TSB* 63. Among the many articles on Thoreau in Yiddish are those by S. Tenenbaum in *La Libre Tribune* (Paris), September, 1951; in the *Jewish Voice* (Mexico City), March 16, 1946; and in his *Poets and Generations* (New York, 1955, pp. 55–65). I know of no study of Thoreau in Japanese, although, with the wealth of material at hand, it is obvious that such a study would be eminently worth while. Lin Yutang's remark can be found in *The Importance of Living* (New York, 1937). The authoritative study of Thoreau's influence on Gandhi is the George Hendrick dissertation mentioned above. It has been condensed in "The Influence of Thoreau's 'Civil Disobedience' on Gandhi's Satyagraha" (*NEQ,* XXIX, 1956, 462–71). "Gandhiana at TxU" (*LCUT,* V, 1954, 43–47) adds important bibliographical details. See also Webb Miller, *I Found No Peace* (New York, 1936); Robert B. Downs, "Individual Versus State," in *Books That Changed the World* (New York, 1956, pp. 65–75);

Pyarelal, "Thoreau, Tolstoy and Gandhiji" (*New Outlook*, X, 1957, 3–11); Walter Harding, "Gandhi and Thoreau" (*TSB* 23); and G. L. Mehta, "Thoreau and Gandhi" (*Congressional Record*, August 13, 1957).

There has been no really adequate coverage of the interest of the radicals in Thoreau. The Whitman quotation can be found in William Condry, "A Hundred Years of Walden" (*DM*, XXXI, 1955, 42; Benson Y. Landis' comments in "The Decentralist at Walden Pond" (*Christian Century*, LXII, 1945, 810–11); C. R. B. Combellack's, in "Two Critics of Society" (*PS*, III, 1949, 440–45); R. N. Stromberg's, in "Thoreau and Marx: A Century After" (*Social Studies*, XL, 1949, 53–56); Samuel Sillen's, in "Thoreau in Our Time" in *Looking Forward* (New York, 1954, pp. 153–64); V. F. Calverton's, in *The Liberation of American Literature* (New York, 1932, pp. 261–71); Bernard Smith's, in *Forces in American Criticism* (New York, 1939, pp. 92–93); John Davies', in "Thoreau and the Ethics of Food" (*Vegetarian Messenger*, XLIV, 1947, 40–41) and "Centennial of Thoreau's 'Walden' " (*Vegetarian News*, XXXIII, 1954, 40–41); and Lawrence MacDonald's, in "Henry Thoreau–Liberal, Unconventional, Nudist" (*Sunshine & Health*, January, 1943). Other articles on Thoreau's radicalism include Jo Ann Wheeler, "Reflections on an Early American Anarchist" (*Why?* July, 1943); George Woodcock, "Thoreau" (*War Commentary*, January, 1943); Hope Holway, "Henry Thoreau," in *Radicals of Yesterday* (Norman, Okla., 1941, pp. 24–31); Charles Madison, "Henry David Thoreau: Transcendental Individualist," in *Critics & Crusaders* (New York, 1947, pp. 174–93); Henry W. Nevinson, "Nature's Priest and Rebel," in *Essays in Freedom and Rebellion* (New Haven, Conn., 1921, pp. 108–14); Rudolf Rocker, "Ralph Waldo Emerson and Henry D. Thoreau," in *Pioneers of American Freedom* (Los Angeles, 1949, pp. 20–31); Eunice Schuster, *Native American Anarchism* (Northampton, Mass., 1932); Jack Schwartzman, "Henry David Thoreau," in *Rebels of Individualism* (New York, 1949, pp. 54–62); and the collected essays in *Thoreau: The Cosmic Yankee* (Los Angeles, 1946).

Walter Harding, "A Bibliography of Thoreau in Poetry, Fiction and Drama" (*BB*, XVIII, 1943, 15–18), lists many examples of Thoreau used in those fields, but needs to be brought up to date.

There is no authoritative bibliography of Thoreau iconography, although most of the paintings listed have been reproduced or described in the pages of *TSB*.

One should not attempt to listen to Ives's *Concord Sonata* without first reading his witty *Essays Before a Sonata* (New York, 1920). Henry and Sidney Cowell, *Charles Ives and His Music* (New York, 1955), has much to say on Ives's interest in Thoreau. The *Concord Sonata* itself has been published by the Arrow Press (New York, 1947) and its "Thoreau theme" reproduced in *TSB* 18. Mason's "Chanticleer Overture" is unpublished, but it has been performed by several major orchestras. Cone's "Excursions" was published in New York by the Independent Music Publishers (n.d.).

BIBLIOGRAPHIES

Students of Thoreau are fortunate in that there are available good bibliographies of both his works and the writings about him. Francis H. Allen, *Bibliography of Henry David Thoreau* (Boston, 1908), supersedes all earlier works. J. S. Wade, "A Contribution to a Bibliography from 1909 to 1936 of Henry David Thoreau" (*Journal of the New York Entomological Society*, XLVII, 1939, 163–203) and William White, *A Henry David Thoreau Bibliography 1908–1937* (Boston, 1939) duplicate each other in a large measure, but each contains material not in the other. They are both supplemented by Philip E. Burnham and Carvel Collins, "Contribution to a Bibliography of Thoreau, 1938–1945" (*BB*, XIX, 1946, 16–18, 37–40). Since 1941 there has been a running bibliography in each issue of the quarterly *Thoreau Society Bulletin*.

The best selective and annotated bibliography is that by Lewis Leary in Floyd Stovall, *Eight American Authors* (New York, 1956). A briefer selective bibliography by Thomas H. Johnson can be found in Robert E. Spiller *et al.*, *Literary History of the United States* (New York, 1948, III, 742–46). Bartholow V. Crawford's bibliography in *Thoreau: Representative Selections* (New York, 1934, lix–lxix) has excellent critical comments but is now out of date.

Raymond Adams, *The Thoreau Library of Raymond Adams* (Chapel Hill, N. C., 1936) and its *Supplement* (Chapel Hill, N. C., 1937), contain many ephemeral items not listed elsewhere. Specialized bibliographies include Walter Harding, "A Bibliography of Thoreau in Poetry, Fiction and Drama" (*BB*, XVIII, 1943, 15–18); Harding, *A Centennial Check-List of the Editions of Henry David*

Thoreau's Walden (Charlottesville, Va., 1954); and Harding, *Thoreau's Library* (Charlottesville, Va., 1957).

Catalogues of Thoreau manuscripts are listed among the Sources for Chapter Two.

An important source book for comments and criticisms on Thoreau in the late nineteenth century is Kenneth Cameron, *Emerson, Thoreau and Concord in Early Newspapers* (Hartford, Conn., 1958, *passim*).

INDEX